Project Management
in Hotel and Resort
Development

Project Management in Hotel and Resort Development

Margaret Huffadine

McGraw-Hill, Inc.

New York San Francisco Washington, D.C. Auckland Bogotá
Caracas Lisbon London Madrid Mexico City Milan
Montreal New Delhi San Juan Singapore
Sydney Tokyo Toronto

Library of Congress Cataloging-in-Publication Data

Huffadine, Margaret.
    Project management in hotel and resort development / Margaret
Huffadine.
        p.   cm.
    Includes bibliographical references.
    ISBN 0-07-030870-5
    1. Hotels—Planning. 2. Resorts—Planning.   3. Hotels Design
and construction.   4. Resorts—Design and construction.
I. Title
TX911.3.P46H84   1993   9315010
647.94'068—dc20   CIP

1 2 3 4 5 6 7 8 9 0   KP/KP   9 9 8 7 6 5 4 3

ISBN 0-07-030870

*The sponsoring editor for this book was Joel E. Stein, the designer was
Susan Maksuta, the editing supervisor was Kimberly A. Goff, and the
production supervisor was Suzanne W. Babeuf. It was set on a
MacIntosh system.*

Printed and bound by Kingsport Press.

 This book is printed on recycled, acid-free paper
containing a minimum of 50% recycled de-inked fiber.

To my daughters

Contents

Acknowledgments

My thanks and gratitude are due to the following people who have helped me during the production of this book, for without their kind support it surely could not have been written: my colleagues from Nihon Sekkei Inc., architects and engineers, of Shinjuku-ku, Tokyo, Japan, including Mr. A. Yamaki, Director of the International Division, Mr. N. Hirano, Mr. Josh Olsan, and Mr. T. Ito, Project Manager for Huis Ten Bosch Resort, Nagasaki, Japan, who have spent time for the initial selection and have provided many beautiful photographs of their hotel designs, together with control charts of projects they have managed; Mrs. Jane Donaldson, M. A. Oxon, of Sydney, Australia, who has given me so much kind encouragement, support, and assistance with editing; and Mrs. Catherine Katz, M. Comm., also of Sydney, for reading some of the chapters and giving me her kind suggestions and comments.

The Toyko Bay Hilton.   The ground floor canopy invites the guest to enter the hotel. Guest room windows form a repetitive pattern, while the vertical elevator and service shafts halt the visual flow along the curve of the facade. Nihon Sekkei, Inc., architects, engineers, and project managers. *(Photographer: Kawasumi Archi, Photograph Office.)*

Project Management
in Hotel and Resort
Development

The Tourist Industry and Project Management

Introduction

The objective of this book is to study the modern management and organizational systems that can best be used to control the design and development of large-scale building projects. Unlike production on the factory line, each building project is a unique process. The time, during which the creation of a design and documentation takes place and the construction is implemented and completed for a hotel project, is not only finite, but also of short duration (generally 2 or 3 years), if compared with the life cycle of a mass produced object in industry.

Requirements for the planning, construction, and service systems of most modern buildings are very complex; maintaining control of the process becomes a continuing issue for management, as the pressures to satisfy these diverse requirements are often in conflict.

Developing technology; raised expectations of higher living standards in advanced nations; worldwide communications; the spread of information about global political, social, and environmental issues; and high standards of education have combined to create an enormously complex and diverse scenario against which we initiate, develop, manage, and control projects worth millions of dollars. These circumstances, which have affected all business at the global level, are compounded in special industries, for example, by the international character of that industry.

The Tourist Industry

The international tourist industry is one of the richest and most widespread industries in the world, second only to that of oil. Nearly all countries participate in some way, for tourism is a very good income earner, and some depend very heavily on the industry for their economic livelihood.

The tourist product faces considerable competition in marketing. A heavy capital investment and initial outlay is necessary to meet international standards and expectations.

Unlike other export industries, the customer travels to the production area; this necessitates the provision of all kinds of extra facilities such as transport, accommodation, and supplies for the large numbers of people visiting the host country. The industry can bring rewards to a region or a nation only if adequate controls of cost, planning, and policy implementation are exercised.

A resort is perhaps one of the most complex projects of all in the construction industry, but also one of the most interesting and challenging. Expectations and standards for business conferences, entertainment, recreation, and relaxation from this industry have changed rapidly in the last decade. Managers are now receiving an increased demand for highly technical equipment for both business and recreation, as well as a high standard of room service and housekeeping facilities for their guests. As a result, the tourist industry forms a fascinating basis for discussion and development in any study of management systems and project management issues.

The need for control of the development phase of an international hotel project imposes criteria for system design on project management which may be compared in many ways with the complex task of producing a space probe. Both processes have a starting point, period of evolution, and completion date, and incorporate a great diversity of technological input.

As nations have prospered through industrialization, individuals can improve and expand the quality of their experiences and lifestyle. They select the type of free-time activity aided by the wealth of information and opportunity now available and can plan their recreational activities as never before.

The advanced industrial nations such as Japan, Germany, and the United States have emerged as prime consumers in the last decade. Economic conditions in these countries are enabling many different sections of society to travel, and the desire to escape from the pollution and congestion of urban working environments has also had a great impact on recent developmental trends in the tourist industry.[1]

These two factors have increased the desire and ability to escape from normal day-to-day events and stress in the workplace, for both recreational and business purposes, and have contributed to the pressures that compel people to take an annual vacation away from home. Frequently, in fact, stress actually appears to be exacerbated by the same expansion in technology which has given workers more free time away from their employment.[2]

It is remarkable that the number of business conferences held away from the home base increases even though other forms of rapid person-to-person communication are now readily available to every business.

Hotel guests want a change from routine and a variety in their choice of location. International travel satisfies this desire by placing the visitor among local residents with very different cultural backgrounds; however, the desire and therefore perceived need to support such action with sophisticated technology in quite remote situations is often in direct conflict with the necessity to conserve and protect these cultures. The effect on the total environment must be reconciled with the standards which have been established for accommodation and services during design and construction, or the primary reason for the location of the facility in the first instance will often be destroyed.

These days, guest requirements vary from the communication and information systems required by business travelers, to rest and relaxation and the escape from everyday activities of the holiday maker. Both groups expect the provision of highly technical equipment to satisfy these needs.

Local political, social, and environmental needs and issues contribute to the problems that must be accepted by the project designer and developer. We expect that a good interpretation of a highly technical, high-quality total system will have the flexibility to accommodate and support such requirements.

Project Management

In a study of project management in the construction industry, therefore, the development of a hotel or resort requires a very wide and comprehensive range of technology and services, more so than in many other building types.

First let us explore some of the diverse issues which have influenced the form that the industry now takes.

The study of the history of the hospitality industry is interesting because it portrays not only the origins but the types of services and facilities that traditionally have been offered to guests. These traditional customs continue, and the popularity of some famous resorts, which were established in the nineteenth century or earlier, endures. However, guest expectations have changed considerably with the increased availability of varied recreational facilities and the introduction of modern communication and other technologies.[2]

Since World War II, and particularly during the 1960s, there has been a phenomenal increase in tourism in and among Western nations, both domestically and internationally. Although it is difficult to say exactly where this impetus commenced, the eighteenth-to-nineteenth-century Industrial Revolution in Western countries laid the foundation for affluence which was reflected in the tourist boom of the 1960s to the 1980s.[3]

The following determinants, of great importance to the modern project manager's task, commenced during the nineteenth century. They combined to encourage the dramatic increase in travel through the 1960s and 1970s, when additional factors began to come into play.

The Rise of the Business Classes and the Spread of Wealth in the Nineteenth Century

The wealth generated by industry was acquired by the middle classes who began to supplant the traditional hereditary upper classes in prosperity.

Business travel. The business and professional classes, who began to travel for trade purposes, demanded good standards of accommodation in accordance with their new position of affluence.

Education and traditional customs. The newly acquired wealth enabled the middle and lower classes, as they became more educated and mobile during the nineteenth and early twentieth centuries, to follow customs that for centuries had been considered the perquisite of the upper classes. For example, citizens of nations with immigrant backgrounds, such as the United States and Australia, could afford to visit Europe; other travelers could visit cultural and historic sites to further their education.

Industrial welfare. The growing power of the trade unions and increasing government concern with social welfare led to legislation for the provision of rest days on weekends, followed by annual holidays with pay.

Transportation. The provision of adequate transportation is a necessary condition for the tourist industry. In the nineteenth century, the invention of the steam locomotive and the internal-combustion engine, combined with techniques for the improvement and extension of roads, increased population mobility rapidly. Transport facilities became cheaper and significantly better, making it easier for many people to consider traveling for the first time (Fig. 1.1).[3]

Modern management skills. Advances in the invention and development of all kinds of administrative, economic, and managerial techniques, and political agreement (such as passport and customs services, international banking, shipping, insurance, investment), allowed large numbers of travelers to be handled more efficiently, both internationally and domestically.

Tourism. As hotel accommodation improved, an associated con-

Figure 1.1 Central Airport, Berlin—Tempelhof, 2 P.M. flight to Halle, Munich, circa 1926. (Photograph by Archiv fur Kunst und Geschichte, Berlin.)

venience facility developed for the increasing volume of less affluent tourists who required help with the organizational problems of planning a journey. Guides planned the first package tours in cooperation with rail and shipping companies, with prearranged accommodation, protection of luggage, exchange of currency, and language facilities. These tours were for a limited number of participants at first, and included only those who were able to afford personal retainers to protect them from bandits. The tourist was already becoming something of a victim. Soon advances in administrative and economic techniques enabled the concept of mass tourism to develop, and more comprehensive facilities were planned accordingly.

The phenomenon of group tours began when Thomas Cook, the nineteenth-century English travel agent who originated the guided-tour concept, organized a rail excursion to a temperance meeting in northern England (Fig. 1.2). The return fare cost one shilling, and 570 people enjoyed the outing. Thomas Cook anticipated that an expansion of organizational facilities would meet a widespread demand and began to develop contacts in shipping, hotels, railways, and banks throughout Europe and the United States, while obtaining favorable rates for his tours.[3]

The development of transportation and management technologies

Figure 1.2   An early excursion between Darlington and Stockton, England, on September 27, 1825. (Photograph by Archiv fur Kunst und Geschichte, Berlin.)

are particularly important to the development of the hotel and resort industry, as they have produced an increase in tourist numbers and demand for a greater accommodation capacity. They have therefore influenced the form of building design.

The Development of Services for the Traveler

Improvement in facilities and services can be divided into three periods: prior to the railway age, pre-1840; the railway age itself, with trains and steamships; civil aviation and the automobile.

Prior to the railway age; 1840.   The Romans were the first to develop patterns of tourism somewhat similar to those found today. Assisted by the excellent system of roads built for military purposes, ordinary citizens began to tour, build holiday villas away from their homes, and visit places of historical interest.

In summer there was (and still is) a general exodus from Rome to the coast and countryside. Wealthy Romans built holiday villas in the mountains. Baiae, a full-scale resort, was developed a hundred miles from Rome on the Bay of Naples, and Camerina in Sicily was very popular.[4]

Like present-day resorts, the location was first "discovered" for recreational purposes by the wealthy elite who were quickly succeeded by followers and emulators. There was a real estate boom; villas, swimming pools, and fashionable and expensive gardens were built as the resort spread. It is not known whether fashionable restaurants also flourished. At any rate, before the decline of Baiae, the bikini was introduced as popular swimwear and an active trade had grown in souvenirs, so it seems quite likely that this ancient resort was astonishingly similar to its modern counterpart (Fig. 1.3).

Unfortunately, as Baiae grew, it developed into an extension of

Rome without the controls of the metropolis and became notorious for the number of criminal gangs operating there.[4]

Following the decline of Rome in Europe, up to the sixteenth century, hostels for travelers on pilgrimages and crusades were popular. These travelers were accommodated either in monasteries or in private inns. According to most accounts, these inns varied in quality and usually lacked basic comfort, although a well-cooked meal was often provided by the landlord's wife. Travelers who stayed overnight were expected to provide their own bed linen and tableware, and to reserve the whole establishment for themselves and their retainers. In practice, there were negotiations between first arrivals and latecomers who welcomed convivial evenings.[3]

Many travelers were also accommodated in private homes, as the rules of hospitality were very flexible. It was not necessary for a visitor to be a close friend or relative. This was an important reason for the late development of an efficient hotel network in Europe. A subsequent development arising from this form of accommodation was the *pension* or "bed and breakfast" type of family establishment.

The beginnings of modern tourism.   The beginnings of modern tourism today in English-speaking nations can be traced to Elizabethan England, with the emergence of the holiday away from home, encouraged by the Queen's own travels. This development commenced in about 1562 with the belief held by the medical profession that mineral water was beneficial to health. The spa in Bath in western England soon became the favorite location. At about the same time "watering places" in Europe also became popular as

Figure 1.3   A.D. 1992 or A.D. 2? The Villa Romana del Casale, Piazza Amerina, Sicily. Young sportswomen in a mosaic from a popular resort of Roman times show little change in taste in either leisure activities or beachwear styles. (Photograph by Scala Instituto Fotografico Editorale, Florence.)

resorts for the improvement of health and for recreation.[3]

Leisure and recreational activities in Japan seem to have had a history similar to that of Europe. As early as the tenth century, the nobility withdrew from court life to their country estates from time to time for relaxation. Later, during the eighteenth and nineteenth centuries, tours were taken to contemplate the beauties of nature, to paint, and to write poetry.[5]

Bathing in the beneficial waters of hot springs has long been a feature of life for the Japanese upper classes, and opportunity for this type of leisure activity spread with the breakdown of class structure in Japan, becoming particularly popular during the late nineteenth and early twentieth centuries (Fig. 1.4). Holiday travel, though, was until this century, almost entirely local.

In Europe entrepreneurs gradually realized that tourism benefited the local economy. Spas were established throughout Europe with or without the benefit of mineral springs, much to the annoyance of the medical profession.

The spread of the so-called spas encouraged wealthy people in Europe to become interested in art treasures and foreign culture. At this time Italy fascinated the English and the French, who regarded the country as a land of hyperelegant depravity.[7]

In the seventeenth century, travel was still for the very rich in Europe and England. It resembled life on a cruise, or in a small speciality resort, as the guests formed an exclusive, self-contained group.

Figure 1.4 Japanese Onsen. Onsen, the traditional resorts built near famous mineral hot springs, have for centuries, provided a popular leisure activity for the Japanese. Usually found in Japan's central mountain chain among magnificent scenery, the guest relaxes and enjoys the view, while the water temperature in some pools seems near to boiling.

The eighteenth century was the golden age for the "grand tour." While English architects and their patrons traveled to study classical architecture and art in Italy, ideas for the planning and development of spas and seaside resorts were no doubt noted for use in the design of the developing tourist industry.[2]

Slowly the practice of travel and tourism filtered down through the social scale, and by the late eighteenth century, watering places had become crowded, rather than exclusive holiday resorts. The pattern of growth shown to be typical throughout the centuries was exhibited again as the wealthy now started to patronize seaside fishing villages to avoid crowding. They came to realize that sea bathing had even more advantages than spa bathing.

Followers of this new sport bathed naked at first. It was not until the nineteenth century of puritan philosophies that enveloping bathing suits and bathing huts on wheels changed the appearance of popular beaches and resorts in England and Europe (see Fig. 1.5). The increasing volume of tourists also changed the style of resort centers. Fashions in beachwear have, of course, come almost full cycle, as we move toward the minimal on our contemporary beaches.

In nineteenth-century Europe, the cultural and philosophical development of romanticism has had notable repercussions in the tourist industry. Jean Jacques Rousseau, one of the most important figures in the movement, developed the cult of the "noble savage." This tended to confirm the preconceptions of the spectator-visitor of the preceding century, as well as defining and originating many of the reasons for modern travel and choice of location. Examples are the choice of a picturesque geographic location, the romance of foreign locations, history, and differing cultures.

The cult of the picturesque has a strong influence on our modern attitudes toward environmental conservation and the preservation of historic and architectural monuments.

Travelers during this period began to be taken as, and criticized for, being an international elite by the local population, whose intent was to safeguard, perpetuate, and emulate the interests of the upper classes. Even though this criticism has tended to diminish recently, the traveler's attitudes toward contact with foreigners and lower classes is still considered suspect by some. This has had a sequel in the present-day tendency to transport tourists in an environmental "bubble" of personal necessities and social habits from which the extraordinary conduct of others can be safely observed.[7]

Third-world countries experience these and associated problems in the establishment of a tourist industry.

Old interests continue in modern tourism. One example of tourist enticements which have continued in the industry from Roman times to the present is the human desire for regeneration, relaxation, escape, comfort, and glamour in one form or another, associated with affluence. This trend has continued through the years and has reflected, to a greater or lesser extent, the form of culture prevailing at the time.

The picturesque, if not already existing, has been manufactured from time to time by the construction of artificial ruins, for example of Greek temples and medieval castles (which are architectural

Figure 1.5   Bathing beauties. Leisure activities at the seaside, circa 1905. (Photograph by Archiv fur Kunst und Geschichte, Berlin.)

Figure 1.6   Nagasaki Holland Village Resort, Kyushu, Japan. Nihon Sekkei Inc., architects and engineers. (Copyright of Susumu Koshimizu.)

"Follies"), in the nineteenth century in the West. Other tourist attractions are educational-theme resorts based on local history. For example, two resorts in the Dutch style, complete with canals, designed by Nihon Sekkei Inc. near Nagasaki, on the island of Kyushu, are being built in Japan (Fig. 1.6).

Fantasy reproductions from American culture, such as Disneyland, flourish throughout the world. These attractions are often experienced only from the windows of a hotel or tour bus.[7]

Attitudes previously held by the French and British toward Italy were now held by the British toward France. France was typecast in the *Gentlemen's Guide* published in 1770 in England, as the "home of follies, vices, and of vain and superficial people" and therefore became extremely popular as an exciting foreign place to visit. The taste for international travel was commencing.[7]

Similar attitudes can be seen now, and represent liberation from the constraints and taboos of the tourist's home society, more often than not having sexual connotation. They are attitudes that can well have an adverse effect on the way the tourist group is viewed by the host country.

At the end of the 1970s the transition from national to international travel was still taking place for the industrialized nations, and during the 1980s, other nations such as the Japanese helped increase the volume of international tourism enormously.[8]

The World Tourism Organization.   The World Tourism Organization, established since the World War II, provides a tourist industry advisory service for national government operators. Statistics are published every year which show a steady increase worldwide in income received from the industry. Between 1984 and 1988, there was an increase in tourist receipts (in millions of dollars), by 76.8 percent, mostly to Europe. The Asia Pacific Region increased its share of the total receipts from 18 to 19 percent; on the other hand, the Americas' receipts declined. From 1987 to 1988, Australia's share of total world tourism increased by 26 percent, and the percentage continues to improve.[1]

Many of these new tourist trips originated in the newly affluent countries such as Japan and certain Southeast Asian nations. Japanese arrivals in Singapore increased in the same period by 11.29 percent, while visitors from the United States recorded an increase of only 1.56 percent (see Fig. 1.7).[1]

Influences

As we discover the historic reasons for traveling and the requirement of hospitality, we see that many of today's predilections originated and evolved quite early in history (Fig. 1.8).

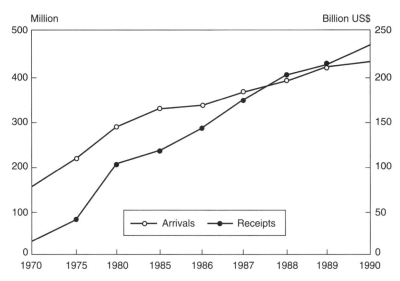

Development of international tourism worldwide 1970–1990

Source: World Tourism Organization (WTO)

(a)

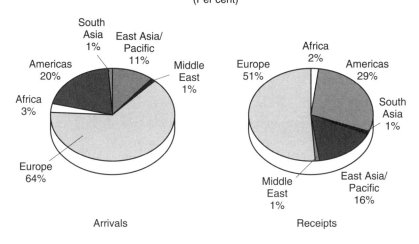

Share of each region in total international tourist arrivals and receipts worldwide - 1990

(Per cent)

Source: World Tourism Organization (WTO)

(b)

Figure 1.7 (*a*) Development of international tourism worldwide, 1970–1990. (*b*) Share of each region in total international tourist arrivals and receipts worldwide, 1990 (percent). (Source: World Tourism Organization (WTO).)

Many of the same problems that the project manager must recognize and control at the commencement of the project's development were exhibited even in Roman times. The recognition of these potentialities and problems serves as an important basis at the initial stages of development of a hotel when it is essential to recognize and anticipate all influences which may effect smooth production.

The Basic Forms of Tourist Facility, Past and Present

The basic historic forms of facility provide simple starting places and indicators for the commencement of the study and still present the source of some of the problems that are likely to occur.

The total background, including the location, social environment, and customer sources, should be thoroughly researched, and problems and risks that are likely to occur anticipated, so that appropriate planning can be undertaken in a comprehensive manner.[9]

It is interesting to note similarities between tourist facilities of previous centuries and present-day facilities and problems and solutions associated with previous tourist establishments that are relevant today. Historical problems and some examples of their modern variations and applications follow.

Transport

Roman roads built for military purposes allowed for the establishment

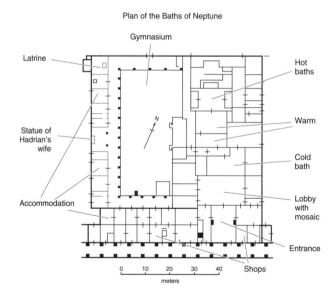

Figure 1.8   Plan, Roman Baths of Neptune, Ostia. This plan of a Roman resort, the Baths of Neptune at Ostia, includes spaces for activities that closely resemble those of a modern resort. Sporting events in the large gymnasium were a preliminary to hot and cold baths, separated by warming rooms on the east side of the building. Service areas are provided next to the baths. Shops and restaurants front the street on the south side; accommodation for other activities such as feasts and weddings is provided on the west. Stairs on the western side of the plan lead to serviced apartments on the upper floor.

of resort and other recreational facilities. Current considerations include whether the transport facilities are adequate for the proposed resort and whether an infrastructure of roads and airport must be built.

The Environment

In Rome, the environment became overused, overcrowded, and unsafe, causing the eventual decline of the resort area.

What steps will now be taken to conserve the environment, which attracted the development in the first instance?

Accommodation

We have seen that the Romans established resorts, initially for the upper classes, that soon became too popular in relation to their size and facility.

Can the proposed environment and location support an increasing volume of tourists? Alternatively, will the forecast number of tourists be able to ensure that the resort is profitable in the future?

Wealthy Romans built holiday villas for their families. Some of the current issues in resort planning are whether a mixed-use resort is indicated and what the needs of the intended market are?

Travelers in the period from ancient Rome to fifteenth-century Europe were mainly pilgrims. Facilities and quality of accommodations were very poor.

Do facilities and quality suit the expected traveler, whether millionaire or backpacker?

Supplies

The quality of roads and transportation limit the easy supply of resources.

Can the resort be supplied with quality goods and services? Is this possible both on a long-term basis and during construction?

Education and Information

In areas where accommodations were required, local people had no understanding of visitors, the type of facility, or the hospitality expected. Roads were unsafe, and travelers were suspect to villagers and often robbed on the highway.

Is the difference between living standards of the host nation and guests great? Can education assist in lessening hostility?

Infrastructure

Speciality resorts, similar to Bath spa in western England gradually became popular throughout Europe in the fifteenth century, and elegant establishments were built to accommodate the social activities of the wealthy. Although these resorts were also considered as health resorts, bathers often became ill from the pollution of mineral waters caused by sewage seeping into the baths. Indeed, there are still occasional reports of such infection dating from only 20 or 30 years ago.[3]

What necessary services are lacking? Is there a safe potable water supply? What infrastructure must be installed, and what civil engi-

Figure 1.9 Grand Hotels of the World: The Raffles Hotel, Singapore. Renovation of the Grill Room. Opened by the Sarkey Brothers in 1887, the Raffles Hotel had many famous guests. Among the most notable names were: Joseph Conrad, Noel Coward, Somerset Maugham, Charlie Chaplin, and Maurice Chevalier. (Photograph by kind permission of the Raffles Hotel Ltd., Singapore.)

neering works are necessary?

Speciality Tours: Romanticism

Europeans were encouraged to travel further by the growing interest in art and architectural treasures. As the rich took the "grand tour" to improve their education, which necessitated traveling widely, the fascination with differing cultures took hold. The interest was further encouraged by the cult of the primitive and picturesque. It became very fashionable to travel and encounter other cultures differing from one's own.

This underlies most of our modern reasons for traveling, and forms the incentive to preserve many historical buildings. For example, the historic old Raffles Hotel, in Singapore, has recently been renovated and returned to its original splendor (Fig. 1.9).

What has the surrounding environment and culture to offer?

Environmental Preservation

The present cognizance of the need to protect and conserve the environment arose from romanticism and interest in different climates and geography (Fig. 1.10).[9]

Is there a fragile natural environment to preserve?

Relationships between Guest and Host

The spread of wealth among members of the industrialized nations and the esoteric quality of the organized tour led to the attitude that travelers are an international elite, especially in poorer and less developed nations. The organization and protection given to tourists by the environmental bubble of the organized tour unfortunately creates problems of alienation within both host and tourist communities.[7]

Is this to be accepted, or can the resort be integrated into the local community with advantage?

Liberation

Tourists sometimes feel, through the contrast they experience between their own and different cultures, that they are temporarily liberated from the constraints of their own society. Behavior toward the host group often becomes a problem. Can plans be made to accommodate the desire for these experiences?

The Time-Share Resort

A very broad segment of the population in advanced countries, with two-income families, can now afford to take a vacation. The "baby boomers," born soon after World War II and now in their forties, are creating a demand for second homes for their family vacation, although the ownership of two homes may not be financially possible at first.[8]

To meet this demand another form of development has arisen. This is the "time share" resort formula. The concept is one of interval ownership, which may be for one or two weeks a year or for several months, when the family occupy their suite, condominium, or house which they have bought on a sharing basis. As the family grows, the period of ownership can be increased to whole ownership if desired. There are many time-share facilities in Honolulu, for example.

Figure 1.10 Ayers Rock Resort, Central Australia. Ayers Rock Resort, in central Australia, is built in a remote and fragile natural environment, and forms a small township. It has two hotels of different rating (five- and three-star), serviced apartments, camping grounds, a retail shopping center, and housing for staff and local residents. The acquisition of resources and supplies presented a major planning problem for project management during development, because all forms of infrastructure, materials, and resources had to be introduced into the area. (Photograph by kind permission of Ayers Rock Resort Nominees Pty. Ltd.)

The Mixed-Use and Speciality Resort

The mixed-use resort or speciality resort may include business and convention facilities, the traditional form of hotel, shops and boutiques, and recreational and entertainment facilities. The mixed-use format has experienced an explosion in popularity worldwide.

Other speciality examples are the casino, the theme resort, and the hotel-convention center. These have been the inspiration for the creation of other facilities that generally support the special theme, such as Disneyland, Tokyo Bay area, Japan; the nearby Tokyo Bay Hotel Tokyu designed by Nihon Sekkei (Fig. 1.11), continues this fantasy theme and has speciality shops selling memorabilia.

Golf resorts have been particularly encouraged by the demands of Japanese tourists who lack space for such facilities in their own country. They have been developed in many places with sufficient space in America, and the number of facilities is now rapidly expanding on Australia's Gold Coast.

The list of popular specialities increased in the late 1980s to include fishing, yachting marinas, trekking, and botanical interests, as well as forms of recreation that have always been popular, and are now gathering momentum and organized provision within the resort concept (see Fig. 1.12).

It is the project manager's responsibility to study all aspects of the background to the project at its commencement, so that future risk and problems can be anticipated. The more thoroughly this task is undertaken, the smoother will be the subsequent progress of the project process. Plans should be developed on the basis of detailed research and expert advice in order to facilitate the process of management and control and avoid many unexpected problems.

To achieve these objectives, it is helpful to study previous forms of resort development and the obstacles existing and solutions taken in

Figure 1.11   Tokyo Bay Hotel Tokyu, Atrium. Nihon Sekkei, architects and engineers. (Photograph by Kawasumi Architects, Photograph Office.)

Figure 1.12 New hotels in Southeast Asia: The Hyatt, Hong Kong. (Photograph by kind permission of the Hong Kong Tourist Association and Hyatt Hotels.)

the past. These provide a basic outline for inquiry; for the problems that were historically associated with the industry are still basic to present-day development. Furthermore, in this century, it can be shown that these forms have been considerably augmented and the modern market is still constantly ringing changes on the basic pattern.

It can be seen that these considerations have great influence on current plans for development. However, a solution that seems obvious for one problem often conflicts with the response to another; meanwhile, the demands for services continue to increase. The industry is in a constant state of variation as requirements shift and alter, according to social changes and the influence of fashion.

References

1. *World Tourism Organization, Publications,* Madrid. 1991.
2. Manual Baud Bovy and F. Lawson, *Tourism and Recreational Planning,* Architectural Press, London, 1977.
3. J. White, *A History of Tourism Leisure Art,* London, 1967.
4. J. V. P. Balsdon, *Life and Leisure in Ancient Rome,* McGraw-Hill, New York, 1969.
5. Ivan Morris, *The World of the Shining Prince; Court Life in Ancient Japan,* Penguin Books, London, 1964.
6. *Tourism in Japan 1986,* Japan National Tourist Organization, Tokyo, 1986.
7. R. L. Turner and J. Ash, *The Golden Hordes—International Tourism and the Pleasure Periphery,* St. Martin's Press, New York, 1976.
8. L. M. Dilsaver, *Effects of International Tourism, a Bibliography,* Council of Planning Libraries, 1977.
9. Clare A. Gunn, *Tourism Planning,* 2d ed., Taylor & Francis, New York, 1988.

Bibliography

American Hotel and Motel Association, *Lodging,* November 1989 and February 1990.

F. P. Bosselman, *In the Wake of the Tourist,* The Conservation Foundation, Washington, D.C.

Japan Travel News, February 1987, Japan Tourist Organization, Tokyo, 1987.

Lady Ochikubu, *Ochikubu Monagatari* (transl. Wilfred Whitehouse and Eizo Yanagisawa), Hokuseido Press, Tokyo, 1965.

Soseki Natsume, *Kokoro* (transl. Edwin McClellan), Charles E. Tuttle Co., Tokyo, 1987.

2

The Nature of Project Management

The Project Process: Definitions

The Client

The client has been traditionally viewed by project managers and other professionals engaged in development and construction of a project as the sponsor, investor, and decision maker. However, the definition of *client* should be extended to include the hotel management groups and all participants who are employed in the development and promotion of the facility, for they have an investment and strong financial motive to make the project successful.[1]

The definition can be expanded even further to include national governments and nations, who have learned in recent years that tourism is a major contributor to the national economy. The industry, for example, has become one of Australia's major foreign income earners in the last decade.

The expansion of the definition is important for the project manager, for the manager must plan and ensure that an efficient communication system exists which will link the participants, gain support, and encourage identification with the project.

The Sponsor

International hotel and resort investors have, in recent years, generally been international finance and investment companies, large international real estate companies (especially from Japan), international construction companies, one of the major hotel management chains, private investors, or an arranged joint venture between these entities.

Until a short while ago, there was adequate equity available, and 70 to 80 percent investment was an acceptable level from any one source. This varied from project to project, according to the credit rating of the sponsor and the ability of the professional team, contractor, and subcontractor to inspire confidence in the investor.

The World Bank has financed the establishment of first-class tourist facilities in developing countries, with the intention of promoting profitable opportunities for industry and employment. Among other financial institutions, the large international retail banks, for example, have issued loans for hotel and resort development purposes. The banks have subsequently made "club deals" with other investors in order to spread the investment and associated risk. Bankers, however, have never been long-term financiers and often seek to sell their holding at the completion of the construction phase. Japanese real estate firms and the six major Japanese construction companies who work internationally have also, in recent years, financed the development of resorts in joint venture with local companies in many areas around the Pacific Rim and in the United States.

Recently, however, the financial outlay has become so great for any one project that even the largest financial institutions have not had the capacity to lend or invest a major portion of the necessary finance. Many banks worldwide are in difficulty and their loans overextended.

Uncertainty, generated by recession conditions in the advanced nations, has also reduced the availability of large loans from all these sources; however, good returns on investment are now available, and the market is becoming fundamentally more sound. Most future lending and investment will be taken by syndicates composed of the several types of financial organizations mentioned, and new players are appearing. Insurance companies who were once disinterested in tourism as investment opportunity may commence to spread their funds to the industry.

These issues have combined to produce a business climate where far less speculation is acceptable, and the companies that are now emerging as major investors have very positively defined requirements for the identification, quantification, and elimination of areas of uncertainty. They demand the services of an experienced project manager to manage and control the areas of possible conflict and risk; experienced and proven contractors and market guaranteed refinancing.

The Project

A *project* may be defined as a successful undertaking with a finite term of production, which requires the combined and unconventional participation of more than one individual or organization. A project has a recognizable starting point, and defined goals and objectives which, when successfully obtained, signal the completion of the project.[2]

A project is a one-off production with an established commencement, life cycle, and termination. It has been described in a classic definition as: "a one-time unique goal with specific resource constraints."[3] This definition applies to the process of any single project and includes the promotion and establishment of facilities for the hospitality industry. The process itself, however, may be undertaken under conditions that vary considerably, especially in the international setting.

The Hotel Guest

The numbers and proportions of travelers of different nationalities has changed considerably during the years under discussion; Japanese travelers in particular, and other affluent groups from industrialized countries have added to the international tourist numbers. The national percentages are closely linked to national income.

Different nationalities bring different cultural expectations to the demand for provision of facilities, quality, and services. Although the expectations include similar standards of comfort, convenience, and luxury, the variation appears in the type of facilities and services.

The Project Manager

In accordance with investors requirements, increasing environmental problems, and the resulting need for the contribution of specialized and highly technical knowledge at the commencement of the project, it is becoming customary for a project manager with training in regional planning, architecture, engineering, or construction to be appointed very early.

A project manager from one of these professions has a broad general knowledge and experience of the construction industry which can be utilized to control and integrate all contributions from the diverse specialists with considerations of cost and future earning capacity. For example, the ability to anticipate the nature of the physical planning, construction requirements, and the sources of future problems and their effects is especially useful for solving the problems associated with the integration of a resort into a new rural area, or a city hotel, if zoning is restrictive and infrastructure is old or inadequate. Furthermore, the project manager will be able to recommend the appointment of specialist advisers at times that are appropriate to achieve cost-effectiveness and to support the program.

The chart in Fig. 2.1 represents the management structure for the Honolulu Convention Center and illustrates the type of structure used for the implementation of a very large project. The design is located in an area of 3,050,000 square feet (ft^2) in downtown Honolulu. It contains a hotel tower with 810 rooms, a condominium tower of 800 units, a retail shopping center of 109,730 ft^2, a convention center with

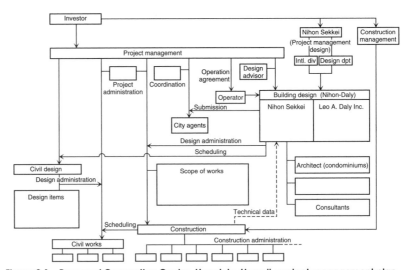

Figure 2.1 Proposed Convention Center, Honolulu, Hawaii, project management plan. The chart shows the interconnection between owner-investor and all participants in the development process. Nihon Sekkei control the design function and coordinate the owner's financial and administrative team, hotel operator, consultants, and construction management. Nihon Sekkei Inc., architects, engineers, and project managers.

a 120,000-ft^2 main exhibition hall, and other related facilities; and an office building. The development belongs to the "mixed use" type.

It can be seen from Fig. 2.1 that a separate financial team and a project management team drawn from Nihon Sekkei's group of architects, engineers, and project managers were appointed to the project. They report directly to the client and work in close cooperation with subcontracting firms of professionals and tradespeople. A model of the Honolulu Convention Center is shown in Fig. 2.2.

Figure 2.2 Model of the proposed Convention Center, Honolulu. Nihon Sekkei Inc., architects, engineers, and project managers. (Photograph: Suikosha.)

The Process of Development

All production processes achieve goals through interaction with the environment. In many industrial situations this interaction is relatively constant; for example, when there is an established market for a product, supply systems have been established, labor is fixed and stable, and a continuous process takes place (which may not change for many years).[4]

The Functional Management System

In the stable situation, a "vertical" system of management developed, which has been called the "functional system" (Fig. 2.3). This system has a strong hierarchy of authority, composed of only a few managers with real power at the top of the pyramid, supported by layers of junior management. Relatively few communication opportunities exist between those at the pinnacle of the cone and those at the base. Tasks do not change noticeably over long periods.[1,4]

Management of Short-Term, Finite Processes

A project such as a hotel is short-term and nonstandard, often referred to as "purpose-driven," with one achievable goal. Management skills and the structure of the development process need to be highly flexible to cope with nonstandard tasks. It is important to stress the *finite* characteristic of the one-off project, for many of the management problems inherent in the process stem from this quality. The functional management system has been shown to be inadequate for this purpose.[1]

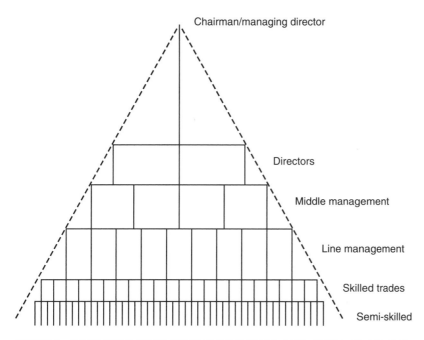

Figure 2.3   The functional system of management. The hierarchy of this system forms a tall cone. Vertical communication links are strong, although top management are often remote from the work force. Horizontal communication lines between workers at the same level in the hierarchy are usually weak.

Two definitions of the project process are useful in understanding the development of a project. The Project Management Institute of America defines the project process as "Any undertaking with a defined starting point and defined objectives by which completion is identified" (*PMBOK*, 1987).[2] NASA's [National Aeronautics and Space Administration (USA)] conception of project management (Chapman, 1973) is as follows: "In simplest terms, a project is a specific, time constrained task, the performance of which cuts across the traditional lines of structure and authority within an organization."[3]

Definitions of management skills that are appropriate for the finite process stress the attributes of flexibility and the ability to control all resources, human and material, while applying controls for the achievement of an objective. When applied to the project process, the manager's skill must be used to influence human behavior and actions, build a good "human relations" climate within the team, and motivate team members.[4]

According to Harrison (1985), planning launches the project and launch planning is the dominant function of management for the first 20 percent of the life cycle of a project. After the launch phase, planning and control merge to become an integrated management function. Harrison continues: "once a project is launched, *control is project management*."[6]

To meet the needs for management of a short-term, finite project, an alternative system of project management has evolved.

Matrix and Project Management Systems

These structures may be thought of as a "flat" cone. They allow easy and frequent communication between all participants and the project manager, who is at the center of the system (see Fig. 2.4).[4]

In order to provide highly trained technical staff for this short-term process, personnel must either be seconded from an existing organization (matrix system; see Fig. 2.5) or specially recruited for the life cycle of the project, with the advantage to the team of choice, when incorporating highly skilled technical staff on a temporary basis. They may be drawn from professions or trades who subcontract, and they are external to the main project management organization.

The matrix and project management systems are very flexible. Routes between professional contributors and decision makers are short. These "flat" management structures, with easy communication between team members, encourage creative recommendations and solutions from all members of the team during the production process.[4] Decision makers can be quickly informed of problems when they arise. In this way the "flat" system supports the use of quality assurance strategies, such as *total quality control* (TQC), first developed by Japanese industrialists.[1]

On the other hand, it has been found that job insecurity increases in the project management system toward the completion of the project, and motivation is difficult to maintain. Thus the finalization phase imposes extra difficulties related to the management of personnel for the project manager. Some companies appoint a special team on a temporary basis who are orientated toward the work involved in pro-

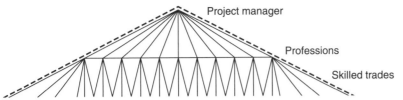

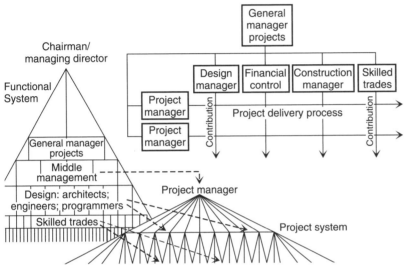

Figure 2.4 Structure of the project management system. This system, which demonstrates a much flatter hierarchical cone of management than the functional system, allows close communication connections to be maintained between the project manager and all members of the project team and a strong horizontal communication network to be established.

Figure 2.5 The matrix system of management. A typical example of matrix system management can be demonstrated by the large contractor-developer who produces by the design-construct method. The company usually undertake several projects simultaneously. Personnel are allocated on a temporary basis from the permanent staff for the life cycle of the project, as required.

ject completion. The project manager needs to ensure that the significance of each team member's contribution is recognized.[4]

In summary, organizational systems are thus divided into two categories:

The functional—mechanistic

The project—organic

A plan derived from the basic project management system must be evolved from which the project manager may plan his or her own tasks and the design of the many subsystems which contribute to the control of the special project process. The planning and design of these activities may be categorized as follows:

To organize and classify

To integrate

To correlate

To store and retrieve

To build on previous work

PMBOK[2]

In order to implement the project management system, several concepts have been utilized, and a structure of four sequential phases has been proposed by the Project Management Institute of America (*PMBOK*, 1987) (See Fig. 2.6). Typical activities contained in each phase are summarized here:

Phase 1: *concept* and initiation

Phase 2: planning and *development*

Phase 3: implementation and *execution*

Phase 4: commissioning and *finalization* (or termination)

The concept is very simple; however, it perhaps has the disadvantage, through oversimplification, of emphasizing the division rather than the integration and interface between phases. There is not, of course, a clear-cut division between activities in the phases, which overlap and flow into each other.

The *PMBOK* concept proposes the following activities be undertaken in each phase.[2]

Phase 1: concept. In this phase, activities lead up to and support the feasibility study, and Go/No-Go decisions are taken.

1. The concept is first appraised so that project objectives can be outlined.

2. An analysis of needs, opportunities, and constraints, based on market and environmental research, establishes project requirements.

3. The first members of the project team are appointed.

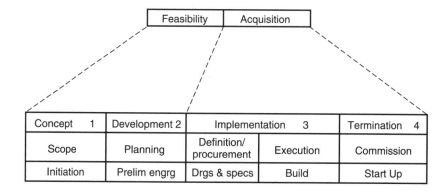

Figure 2.6   The *PMBOK* system of project management. This structure was designed by the Project Management institute (PMI) of America, for management of a short-term finite project. Project Management Body of Knowledge:. *1987.*)

4. Information is collected, and the scope of the concept is defined.

5. The design of a structure for the project process is developed and adapted to the project.

6. The planning process and analysis of the site and environment capabilities assist the development of the design criteria.

7. Proposals are made in sketch form.

8. The first budget estimate is made for approval.

9. Initial financial feasibility studies are undertaken.

10. Alternative solutions are generated and studied for feasibility, confirming or denying validity of the concept.

11. Government approvals are obtained.

12. Approvals are obtained for the concept.

The concept-initiation phase is difficult and complex, for at the introduction of the project, no background information has been collected to define the client's concept or the scope of work or to enable estimates of budget and program to be established.

Phase 2: development. The project team now typically includes architects, planners, engineers, accountants, and quantity surveyors, who begin the production of plans, programs, and construction schedules, based on the sketch proposals of Phase 1. The first definitions and sketch design proposals recognize the importance of site and environmental factors in the development of design criteria. The following activities take place during this phase:

1. Detailed needs, opportunities, and constraints, based on market and environmental research and client requirements are defined.

2. Professional consultants are appointed to the team.

3. Communication systems are established.

4. Good team relationships are promoted and any personnel-related issues resolved.

5. The concept is appraised so that project objectives can be defined in detail.

6. Programs and schedules are made.

7. Logistics are studied and the budget analysis is consolidated on the basis of open or invited bidding from contractors.

8. Alternatives continue to be generated and studied for work packages.

9. The structure and system for project management and control is refined.

10. The breakdown into work packages commences.

11. The continuing interpretation of customer requirements is related to the constraints brought into prominence by the develop

ment of design proposals. These may be from sources that are external or internal to the development processes.

12. Testing and feedback systems are designed for a continuous comparison and evaluation of progress during the process of construction.

13. During this phase the concept is translated from sketch form into full documentation, and as work progresses, potential problem areas are clarified and analyzed and strategies are established to avoid, ameliorate, or solve them.

14. Plans are made for early commissioning activities.

15. Each activity is tested against the established objectives, and client approvals are obtained.

As can be seen, the first two phases determine the design of the basic system on which management and control functions will be built to suit the specific project. Activities that are interconnected ar planned into the schedule. In each phase the activities are carried through and converge with activities of the following phase. The satisfactory completion of tasks in the phase interface are therefore critical and form an appropriate time for testing and approval.

Phase 3: execution. At the beginning of this phase a reappraisal again takes place for program efficiency and capability and for correspondence between outcome and goals. It is of primary importance for the success of the process to maintain flexibility.

Phase 3 is the phase of contract administration. If attention has been given to creating details of design, schedules, programs, alternatives, and contingencies that are realizable, the process proceeds smoothly and the project manager's major task becomes that of control. Typical activities follow:

1. Resources, suppliers, and their programs are identified; costs are confirmed; and orders are placed.

2. The organization is established for the construction of the pro ject, on the basis of these verifications.

3. The relationship between work packages and scheduling is confirmed.

4. The controls, physical work packages, and processes are put into practice.

5. Planning and communication systems which have been estab lished for the control of production, procurement scheduling, ongoing testing and approvals systems, supplier appraisals, cost controls, and contractual arrangements are now in use.

6. Feedback from regular reports is checked against the program of established criteria and objectives, and this data cycles back to assist the project management team to control and monitor the project process.

7. Appraisals are made, and approvals are obtained for progress payments.

Throughout the first three phases, the project manager and her or his team will direct, monitor, coordinate, and continue to be alert to unexpected problems. If good communications have been established and efficient monitoring carried out, solutions to problems that occur can immediately be put into operation on the basis of reliable and current information which has been assembled earlier in Phase 1.

Phase 4: finalization.   During Phases 3 and 4, the project manager must prepare and implement training procedures for hotel management and in-house staff as part of the commissioning program. These procedures train staff in the use of technological equipment and explain design features and the plans which complement hotel functions and operational facilities. The importance of efficient commissioning to the client, project manager, and all concerned is such that it may make or break the success of the project.

Commissioning tasks, which are carried on a progressive basis, merge for total handover during this phase. Activities include accounting and approval of variations and final payments, the release of retention sums, close-out tasks, settlement of costs related to shortfalls, staff reductions, finalization of contracts, and the commencement of warranty periods. The activities require many negotiated decisions and the resolution of difficulties and problems. Extra effort is needed to maintain the team impetus at this time.

Phase 4, the closing-out phase, like Phase 1, is a time of increased activity for the project manager. Typical activities follow:

1. Final accounting procedures commence.

2. Outstanding subcontractor commitments are identified.

3. A final inspection of the quality of the work and the checking of supplies against specifications is made.

4. The finished project is handed over to in-house management

5. Final approvals are obtained.

6. The project team is now to be disbanded.

The Project Delivery System[7]

The Project Delivery System has been developed to support project management by the Public Works of Canada (Fig. 2.7). It links together the standard elements required by the Canadian Public Works for planning and implementation of capital works projects. It has a general application to the development and construction management of large projects and concentrates on tasks to be carried out during the project life cycle. The system is orientated toward government projects, including engineering and infrastructure construction; it is, however, very comprehensive and can be recommended as a basic system for adaptation to hotel and resort development.

The six phases of the Project Delivery System display greater definition of tasks than the *PMBOK* system:

1. Planning

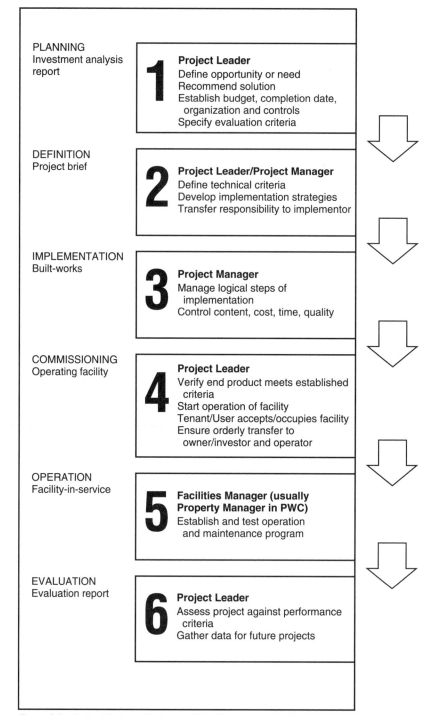

PLANNING
Investment analysis
report

1 **Project Leader**
Define opportunity or need
Recommend solution
Establish budget, completion date,
  organization and controls
Specify evaluation criteria

DEFINITION
Project brief

2 **Project Leader/Project Manager**
Define technical criteria
Develop implementation strategies
Transfer responsibility to implementor

IMPLEMENTATION
Built-works

3 **Project Manager**
Manage logical steps of
  implementation
Control content, cost, time, quality

COMMISSIONING
Operating facility

4 **Project Leader**
Verify end product meets established
  criteria
Start operation of facility
Tenant/User accepts/occupies facility
Ensure orderly transfer to
  owner/investor and operator

OPERATION
Facility-in-service

5 **Facilities Manager (usually
Property Manager in PWC)**
Establish and test operation
  and maintenance program

EVALUATION
Evaluation report

6 **Project Leader**
Assess project against performance
  criteria
Gather data for future projects

Figure 2.7   Project Delivery System: Public Works, Canada. The Project Delivery System is used to define the phases in the life cycle of a typical short-term development project. An analysis and identification of project needs and opportunities takes place in Phase 1, Planning; and the process proceeds through the phases of definition, implementation, commissioning, and operation. The system provides both a comprehensive view of the whole process and a basis for planning strategies for the integration of all project activities. Key players are the project leader, who represents the owner and is responsible for development and management of the project; the project manager, who represents the team who implement the process, and is often an architect or engineer in charge of design development; and the facilities manager, who represents the operator. (Project Delivery System, *1989.*)

2. Definition

3. Implementation

4. Commissioning

5. Operation

6. Evaluation

The identification of the key players of project leader, project manager, and facilities manager reflect the interests of the Canadian Public Works; however, tasks of management and control which must be undertaken are fundamentally the same in all project work.

Tasks in each phase of the Project Delivery System are developed and defined very comprehensively, and for planning purposes the apparent sharp division which exists between the phased activities in the *PMBOK* system is minimized. For further discussion of these systems, see Chapter 4. (See also Fig. 2.8.)

Summary: factors relating to both systems. Some important activities that take place during the first phases of both systems, affect the character and success of the project process and the quality of management and control of the project. These are typically the detailed definition of the client's concept, market feasibility and approvals, the establishment of efficient communications, discovery of areas of uncertainty and risk, establishment of alternatives and contingency plans, the planning and early establishment of a basic management structure, and environmental impact—achieving harmony with local social and cultural customs.

Feasibility studies and project planning. Project planning is predicting demand and anticipating future risk. Before the design and development work progresses too far, a comprehensive feasibility study must be undertaken to analyze all factors that may threaten the successful development of the process. The study contains estimates of budget, market, environment, construction, programs, and schedules from which risk factors and margins of risk become apparent.

The studies are carried out with the assistance of computer programs designed to suit various aspects of risk assessment, planning, and scheduling. They are very efficient tools with which to combine and process such a diversity of data. Nevertheless, the results, which are only as reliable as the quality and detail of the information fed into the computer, must be based on surveys of all the factors that contribute to the total financial and physical environment of the resort prior to development.

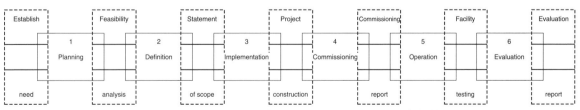

Figure 2.8 The interface between phases. The six phases of the Project Delivery System illustrated in this diagram produce essential integration and interconnections. (Project Delivery System, *1989*.)

Developers have often found difficulty in justifying the costs and time of an adequate in-depth investigation, but a lack of attention to detail at the commencement of the project has been the major cause for the failure of many ventures in the past.

Go/no-go decisions.   If the concept is acceptable in principle and given a provisional "go ahead," the project team will be implemented to prepare the basis for the development process of the project and control systems. The proposals are augmented by sketch designs of the whole concept and design of an appropriate program for control. The team will later be expanded again to implement a full statement of scope and produce documentation for the process of production. Meanwhile, the findings are presented to investors and other interested parties for comment and decision making.

At concept phase, the series of go/no-go decisions (Fig. 2.9) which evaluate the capability of the project to produce a return on investment and satisfy market demand are constantly under review.[4]

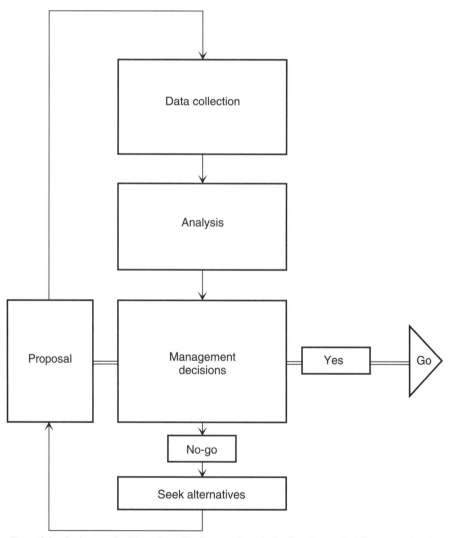

Figure 2.9   Go/no-go decisions. Investigations and analysis allow the project to proceed, or to be abandoned, on the basis of informed decision making.

Designing a Program of Action to Suit the Project Process

The development of a hotel or resort concept is always surrounded by uncertainty as to its future success and profitability. Sufficient information concerning all the issues that influence the particular proposal must be obtained to enable the clients and the project management team to make sound judgments. Nevertheless, within the concept of uncertainty, throughout the world there are some common elements to be found at the inception of a hotel project, whether it is to be constructed in a city, existing resort area, or a new and undeveloped location.

The statement of scope: project brief. The statement of scope is designed to define the client's concept and the requirements and resources which will be needed for development. It includes the design intent and schedules and programs for the construction work. It forms a basis for later management, monitoring, and control procedures.

The quality of the definition of the project concept is of fundamental importance for the successful completion of the life cycle of the project. This definition, which is in the form of a detailed written or drawn instruction, is a total description of the concept and process. The brief is made to describe each category of task, and as this is developed, the appropriate management technologies and design strategies for the management and control of the process are identified.

The basic structure of the phases which we have been discussing are used to assist the creation of a management program. This must contain all the components of the delivery process combined into a functioning whole. However, the orientation of management and control strategies is always influenced by the design criteria of the specific development project.

Because of the many conflicting issues that occur concurrently during the process, control will be threatened unless good strategies are adopted early.

Definition of goals and objectives. Specific goals and objectives are revealed as the project team proceeds to clarify the client's concept. As this work takes place, realistic earliest and latest dates for completion can be established, and the resources and processes that will be needed to construct the project are assessed from detailed designs and specifications, programs, and schedules.

The project management of any large building development is essentially a coordinative process that unifies output of many individual contributors, such as investors, developers, lawyers, architects, engineers, contractors, planners, accountants, quantity surveyors, and the future hotel management team who will help to develop the concept to a level of technology that can be used as a basis for a decision to proceed with or reject the proposal.

The first outline leads on to a comprehensively documented description, which continues to be redefined during Phases 1 and 2; indeed, many modifications will be needed throughout the ongoing project process. The management strategy must be supported by flexibility and a well-planned and effective communications system.

The activities which are involved in the definition of the scope of the proposal can be accounted for by both internal and external team functions. We can use project management principles to coordinate, manage, and control the interconnected processes of both types of function.

Internal team functions.   The internal functions can be usefully categorized into contractual and organizational functions. These include marketing and promotion, financial control, integration with regional conditions, the organization of supply systems, and communications.

Contractual Functions.   These include calling of bids, advising the sponsor on the appointment of professionals and subcontractor firms, and supervising the progress of contract formation.

Organizational Functions.   These include team building, the establishment of communication systems, design, and quality control; supervising construction programs, schedules, and monitoring; and coordinating with in-house management.[4]

External functions.   External functions may be classified under communication with persons outside the project team who are, for example, the sponsor and client, hotel operator, subcontractors, and government and local representatives. The external relationship to the project team organization is usually, but not always, contrived through legal arrangements, depending on local laws and customs in the host nation.

Project Management and the Hotel Industry

This book sets out to study the main principles of project management, and identify the strategies which can be used to facilitate and improve the process of development of a hotel, for it can be shown that the use of project management principles will improve the overall efficiency and quality of the product, enhance the development process, effect cost savings advantageously, and increase the level of customer satisfaction.

Historical Influences

In Chap. 1, we discussed tourist attractions and customs, and responses of the hospitality industry in various centuries. A study shows that several important needs and principles have been demonstrated by history and continue to inspire our modern industry. The requirements of hospitality which supported these customs appear to have remained essentially the same. The development of these customs has, however, been augmented almost beyond recognition by the technological advances of our society, and the level of expertise in the hospitality industry has expanded and matured to match these trends.

Let us consider some of the issues which have emerged in the industry during the last 10 years. The sponsor deduces that there is an opportunity for a certain type of development in the region. This inference may be derived (as we can see from surveys of historical

Figure 2.10 The Nusa Dua Beach Hotel, Bali: exterior and lobby. The Nusa Dua Hotel, patronized by presidents and princes, was the first five-star luxury resort to be built at Nusa, Bali. Balinese art forms are used to give cultural identity. The overall design of the resort has been inspired by the plan of a typical Balinese palace, and incorporates a Balinese temple within the complex. PT Aerowisata, Hotel Management. (Photograph by kind permission of Garuda Airlines, Indonesia.)

trends) from wealthy groups who showed interest in the area; or it may arise in answer to a strong market demand for some speciality such as a combination of recreational facilities and convention center.

Many national governments have now initiated programs of comprehensive planning for their tourist industry. They are in a favorable position to channel resources and guide development to locations where costs of infrastructure are at an acceptable level and a measure of environmental control can be exercised. Planning is important to secure the future of the region as well as the success of the resort.[8]

Bali: an example of rapid development. An example of rapid tourist development since the 1970s is that of Bali, Indonesia (Fig. 2.10). Bali's culture and tropical environment remained a travel prerogative of the wealthy or informed before that date, but has recently experienced an explosive growth. Bali now enjoys the benefits of money and employment brought by international tourists to the island. Unfortunately, through lack of planning and control, development has created many environmental problems for the existing social and cultural composition of the island. Pollution has increased, and all forms of infrastructure services are overtaxed, including transportion.

The Government of Indonesia was forced to suspend development on the island until a comprehensive assessment and plan for tourism could be made and controls for growth and the repair of environmental damage put in place. Indonesia initiated this program at the same time as a "Visit Indonesia Year" scheme was launched with the aim of revitalizing the tourist industry by attracting tourists to other parts of the beautiful island chain and elevating the industry to the position of second income earner. Indonesia's oil industry remains the first.[9]

The tourist industry has also become a prime international currency

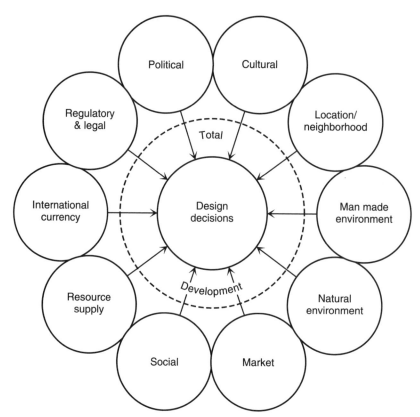

Figure 2.11   The influence of external factors. External factors have a major influence on the final outcome of the project.

earner and income for many small nations in the Pacific area, with the advantage of being relatively close to major tourist sources such as Japan, South East Asia, and the United States.

Early influences.   The type of difficulty, the costs of development, and the associated risks are variable according to location. For example, if new land is being put to use, infrastructure will almost certainly be needed and new environmental and often political considerations specific to the location will arise and must be reconciled. Difficulties are often exacerbated by import regulations and the need to plan and maintain a schedule for timely delivery of materials to suit the construction program. On the other hand, the success of inner-city development must also be considered in relation to existing and likely future competition from hotels of an equal standard and future popularity among the tourist population.

Factors that contribute to these issues, such as market potential, supply of human and material resources, legal and political considerations, and government approvals, in turn influence architectural and engineering design and design for coordination with the environment, and are blended to make a comprehensive statement of procedural intent, the "scope statement."

The results of international surveys and statistical inference are used to analyze market potential by in-house feasibility studies. Legal and economic factors must be made to comply with local laws and codes to the advantage of both national and local governments and the developer's goals. The following economic factors are typically considered; the means of securing the investment so that a financial return is assured and the utilization of local natural and human resources for construction and development purposes.

The external environment also exercises other influences, specifically, the conservation of the natural environment and surrounding land uses, which have attracted the development in the first place, and the utilization of the natural resources of the area to complement the characteristics of the hotel. (See Fig. 2.11.)

Material and physical influences. A standard and quality of product must be maintained to match the known and anticipated market requirements, and provide services to meet the expectations of guests. The product should also integrate and enhance living standards in the surrounding community so that good relationships are maintained, which will contribute toward an efficient, easy-to-run and maintainable entity.

All these issues are both interdependent and complementary and can be seen, especially in the case of environment and materials, to both affect and utilize local resources.

The management and control of diverse issues and resources is difficult and challenging especially in less developed nations. The project manager must possess many skills, not the least of which will be the skill to acknowledge and achieve compromise.

In planning a resort, the project manager must consider factors such as characteristics of the existing environment (Fig. 2.12).

The Environmental Impact Statement

An environmental impact statement is usually required for both the client and the project team's information and to comply with local city or state regulations, administrative codes, and ordinances. The impact statement enables an assessment of local conditions to be made, so that provisions for the construction phase, and the resort's future operating needs, can be forecast.

The submission contains a written proposal with a description of the building's potential effect on surrounding environmental conditions (at the time of construction and in the future), including the consideration of other development proposals. A full and complete description of project intent is compiled and analyzed by the team's professional technologists. Examples are the impact on rural flora and fauna, which may need protection and sometimes rehabilitation; or inner-city shadow diagrams which are usually required by city authorities.

This submission will include a written description, area maps, site plans, and sketch designs of the building concept, which is submitted to the authority for formal approval of zoning and development intent. The authority may request that the development be modified, for example, by restrictions of height, vehicular access, sewerage disposal, aspect, and orientation, because of calculated adverse impact on neighboring property. The submission is displayed and

Table of contents
1. Introduction
   a. Nature of proposal
   b. Agency data
   c. Authors and principal consultants
   d. Required permits (licenses)
   e. Location of background data
   f. Cost of copy
   g. Date of issue and deadline for comments
Contents
2. Distribution list
3. Summary
   a. The proposal
   b. Objectives of the proposal
   c. The natural environment
   d. The human environment
   e. Alternatives to the proposal
4. Description of the proposal
   a. Name of proposal and sponsors
   b. Location of proposal
   c. File number and other agencies
   d. Phasing of construction
   e. Major physical and engineering aspects of the proposal
   f. Comprehensive plan and zoning regulations
   (All the following categories include existing conditions, impacts of proposal, mitigation measures, and unavoidable adverse impacts.)
5 Index of elements of the environment
6. The natural environment

a. Earth	f. Light and glare
b. Air	g. Land use
c. Water	h. Natural resources
d. Flora and fauna	i. Risk of explosion or hazardous
e. Noise	emissions

7. The human environment

a. Population	f. Utilities
b. Housing	g. Human health
c. Transport and circulation	h. Aesthetics
d. Public services	i. Economic factors
e. Energy	j. Regional, city, and neighborhood goals, objectives, and policies

8. Analysis of alternative actions
   a. Introduction
   b. Analysis of alternatives
9. Relationship between local short-term uses of the environment, and maintenance and enhancement of long-term productivity and irreversible or irretrievable commitments of resources.
10. Summary of mitigating measures
11. Summary of unavoidable adverse impacts
Appendixes
Plates
Photographs

Figure 2.12 Contents of an environmental impact statement. The document was made for a downtown hotel in Washington State, U.S.A. The list of contents illustrates the information necessary for this type of analysis.

offered for public comment for a fixed period, usually about six weeks.

An environmental impact statement for the proposed development of a downtown hotel in Washington State, USA, follows. The list of contents illustrates the information necessary for this type of analysis.

Future project decisions, therefore, are influenced by the official reaction to this statement, and it becomes important to obtain an indicative response as soon as possible. Modification and further negotiations usually follow the preliminary submission, provided the project outcome appears financially viable to the client.

Requirements between states and nations vary in detail, but are surprisingly similar in content. Rejection by the authority of any of these issues may negate the concept's apparent financial validity.

A basic list of information which is usually included in an environmental impact statement follows.

- General information required:

    The owner, sponsor, or investor's name

    Permit requirements

    Principal contributors: professionals, managers, etc.

    Proposed program and phasing of construction

- The site:

    Site, file numbers, and ownership details

    Proposals for site use

    Location map

    The natural environment

    The human environment

    The built environment

    Surrounding road systems and traffic patterns

- The building:

    Number of hotel rooms

    Public spaces and facilities

    Proposed landscaping

    Alternatives

The financial feasibilities are influenced by the provision or lack of provision of infrastructure of all kinds; for example, access to an airport, roads, and water supply may be restricted or lacking. The need to provide infrastructure may be the deciding factor against proceeding, unless funds for development of a national tourist industry are immediately available from either the national government or international sources, such as the World Bank. Although national government plans may be in place to develop such facilities in the future, immediate costs may prohibit any civil work to be undertaken for a lengthy period.[8]

Figure 2.13 Environmental interaction matrix.

		Land use	Land form	Visual quality	Drainage pattern	Surface water	Groundwater	Soils/land stability	Vegetation	Fauna	Air quality	Noise and vibration	Resident population	Employment	Housing	Local/regional economy	Historic/archaeological sites	Road/transport system	Utilities provision (e.g. water, sewer, wastes)
OPERATION	Land clearing																		
	Earthworks																		
	Drainage construction																		
	Location of buildings or works																		
	Building construction																		
	Raw material inputs																		
	Equipment operation																		
	Labour requirements																		
	Proponent's expenditure patterns																		
	Traffic movements																		
	Potential emergencies (including hazards)																		
	Landscaping																		
CONSTRUCTION	Location of buildings or works																		
	Raw material inputs																		
	Equipment operation																		
	Storage/stockpiling																		
	Water demand																		
	Waste disposal																		
	Demand for services																		
	Labour requirements																		
	Proponent's expenditure patterns																		
	Production outputs																		
	Traffic movements																		
	Transport requirements																		
	Potential emergencies (including hazards)																		
	Landscaping																		

Figure 2.13 Environmental interaction matrix. The impact of a construction program for a proposed resort development is assessed against the characteristics of the existing environment

If, additionally, the area is relatively unknown, an expensive world-wide promotional program must be initiated.

Actions to Be Taken at This Time

- Project manager:

  Establish relationship with sponsor and clients

  Negotiate own conditions of contract

  Become familiar with client requirements

  Become familiar with environment and local conditions

Become familiar with local government regulations

Become familiar with professional companies and availability of skilled personnel

Assist sponsor to call for bids from professional companies, such as architects and engineers

Establish the hotel management group favored by the sponsor for this project, and their particular characteristics

Commence discussions with all professionals involved

Establish team and build team relationships

Supervise collection of information and files and references

Supervise progress of environmental impact statement

- Planners:

Negotiate contract conditions

Obtain information relevant to environmental, infrastructure issues, and environmental impact statement

Commence environmental impact statement

- Architects and engineers:

Negotiate contract conditions

Obtain all information relevant to the site and sketch designs for building development

Assist planners with environmental impact statement

References

1. *Master of Project Management course notes,* University of Technology Sydney, Sydney, Australia, 1990.

2. *Project Management Body of Knowledge (PMBOK),* Project Management Institute of America, Drexel Hill, Pennsylvania, 1987.

3. D. Lock, *Project Management,* Gower Press, London, 1969.

4. H. Kerzner, *Project Management, A Systems Approach to Planning, Scheduling & Controlling,* 3d ed., Van Nostrand Reinhold, New York, 1989.

5. R. L. Chapman, *Project Management in NASA; the System and Men,* Scientific and Technical Information Office, National Aeronautics and Space Administration. U.S. Government Printing Office, Washington, D.C., 1973.

6. F. L. Harrison, Advanced Project Management, 2d ed., Gower Publishing, Harrison, England, 1985.

7. *Project Delivery System,* Canadian Public Works Department, Ottawa, Canada, 1989.

8. Clare A. Gunn, *Tourism Planning,* 2d ed., Taylor & Francis, New York, 1988.

9. *AFR Survey; Indonesia,* Australian Financial Review, Sydney, NSW (New South Wales), May 28, 1991.

3

Uncertainty and Risk

Hotels and resorts last for a long time, and the development process always contains elements of future uncertainty; therefore, every investor and developer takes some risk when launching a project.

One of the most important aspects of the project manager's function in the development of a project is to assist in the recognition, monitoring, and supervision of these areas of risk throughout the project's life cycle.

Definitions of Uncertainty and Risk

Uncertainty and risk are defined by Marshall (1988) as follows.

Uncertainty

"Uncertainty refers to a state of knowledge about the variable inputs to an economic analysis." If the analyst is unsure of the value of the information used as a basis for the study, there is uncertainty.

Risk may refer either to risk exposure or risk attitude.

Risk Exposure

"Risk exposure refers to the probability that an investment will be made in a project which will have a less favorable economic outcome than desired or expected" (Marshall, 1988).

Risk Attitudes

Marshall (1988) describes three types of risk attitude; briefly these are:

Risk-adverse: Decision makers prefer to have a secure but low return on investment.

Risk-neutral: Decision makers act on a basis of reasonable expectation of monetary return.

Risk-taking: A risky venture is preferred, with the chance of a higher return than the sure cash payment of the risk-adverse category.[1]

Decision makers accept some deviation from the project goals and objectives, according to these categories and the degree of risk on a "best for us" basis. Their decisions are made within margins deemed acceptable, according to the project's basic requirements. The more conservative a decision maker's approach, the more likely the project will be cost-effective.

Uncertainty in Hotel and Resort Development

The uncertainty of the market and other factors in hotel and resort development creates risks to investment capital. For example, many important aspects of a hotel's future operational capacity are uncertain, such as future revenue levels, the working life span of the project, increasing operators' costs, quality maintenance, and tourism trends. Each of these factors may affect economic viability.

In the recent past, investors and developers assumed that a project would be successful if the location was good. This assumption paid off in periods of maximum demand and minimum supply. It has been proved invalid, however, in many international locations because an oversupply of accommodation was developed in the area, and the demand for accommodation was not supported by local activities, such as business, a convention facility, or a sufficient number and quality of tourist attractions.

We will discuss some of the factors which should be considered during the feasibility analysis and measures that can be taken to minimize or avoid exposure to general sources of risk encountered in the industry.

Analysis of Investment Potential

Analyses of investment potential are usually based on a "best estimate" financial evaluation. The success of the forecasts which are based on this evaluation vary directly with the quality of the back-

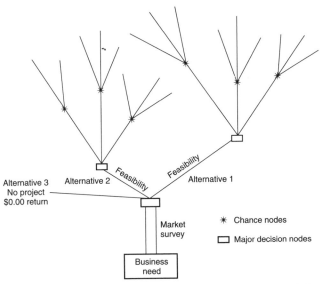

Alternative 3
No project
$0.00 return

Alternative 2

Feasibility

Feasibility

Alternative 1

Market
survey

✳ Chance nodes

▭ Major decision nodes

Business
need

Figure 3.1 The decision tree for investment in hotel development. The business need to earn a return on investment initiates a preliminary market survey to locate a viable proposition for the development of a new hotel or resort. A major decision node occurs after this initial market survey, and an alternative is selected according to the amount of financial outlay required and perceived potential percentage for return on investment. Difficulties imposed by the total environment and logistics are taken into account during the detailed financial feasibility study, and once an alternative is selected and approved, chance occurrences necessitate the selection of further alternatives and decision making during the delivery process. (Marshall, 1988.)

ground information which is incorporated into the study, and with the caliber of the mathematical test used for evaluation.[2]

The investor will wish to compare returns on the proposed investment with returns from alternative opportunities. (See Fig. 3.1.)

Costs are estimated by adding all anticipated payments, such as consultant services, obtaining government approvals, all construction works necessary to establish and complete the project, fit-out and furnishings, marketing and promotion, interest payment on loans during construction and before opening, and holding costs.

The use of investment money costs the investor the amount of interest lost during the unproductive development and construction period. The resultant interest payments are an additional capital cost to the project. Developers, therefore, evaluate real estate investment returns over a long period and amortize the initial losses against future returns.

Market Analysis

The factors that determine the focus of the preliminary analysis are in accordance with the type of facility that appears to be best suited to the location. This may be a resort, a city hotel, a convention hotel, or a mixed-use establishment.

In order to recognize and exert some measure of control over the areas of risk, a comprehensive market analysis is undertaken on the basis of information gathered from local and international sources. A variety of building types are considered for cost-effectiveness. (See Fig. 3.2.)

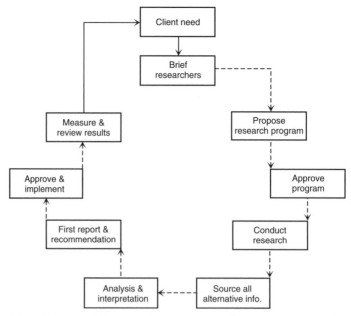

Figure 3.2 The market research process. The market research process is initiated to serve the business needs of the investor–developer-client. The research process is circular and continues until a financially acceptable project is discovered. The client should always be kept informed of progress, and a two-way flow of data between client and project manager must take place, for surprise information can lengthen research time unnecessarily.

Evaluation: Producing the Right Solution

An accurate evaluation of the market is an issue of major importance to the financial success of the venture. "Matching the project to the market" means producing the right solution at the right time and forecasting as accurately as possible future market demand.

The survey for the evaluation needs to be comprehensive, so that creative alternatives can be documented for the whole range of strategies, including those for the systematic control of risk. The proposal and project process should not fail for lack of a solution to one negative issue.

As evaluation progresses, the assembly of a database from the results of local market and environmental research allows the evaluation to have greater definition. The decision to proceed with the venture depends on informed forecasts which, in turn, depend on the quality of research into current and future economic and market opportunities.

To complete the evaluation, a financial feasibility study is based on market and marketing factors, forecasts of future occupancy levels and demand, forecasts of future revenues, and information incorporating risk factors which may arise from the design, development, and construction phases.

Miniproject. The investment analysis and feasibility studies form a miniproject within the total project life cycle. This is best carried out by a project management team composed of financial and other professional consultants from the building industry. It is to the client's advantage if the project manager, and members of this first group, continue on to form the team who manage and control the process of development.

Our calculations and comparisons would be simple if unexpected events and factors did not disrupt the development and construction process, for these increase the costs of the project, and therefore diminish future returns. However, by using proper research techniques and mathematical principles that have been developed to take account of uncertainty, a forecast can be made which will allow decision makers to evaluate the likely capital expenditure on a hotel or resort project and the probability of future benefits, revenues, savings, and costs.

The importance of alternatives and contingency planning. The creation of alternatives and contingency plans is very important to the success of the project and cannot be overstressed.

The proposal for alternatives should reach into all areas of the development process, for a delay from one "minor" cause may affect the whole of the construction program. The availability of such alternatives may also make the difference to the decisions made for or against proceeding with the project. The financial feasibility analysis helps decision makers forecast the future success of the project, by assessing the exposure to risk in the long term. A period of from 5 to 10 years is usually taken for the study.

The early establishment of development alternatives, an efficient system for planning and control of the process, and a sound evaluation of the risks involved have been virtually ignored in the industry. It is commonly believed that a speedy commencement after the acceptance of the financial feasibility of the study will save holding costs and costs of construction and anticipate problems. Although costs appear to be saved initially, these are soon lost through lack of preparation and planning. Delays, poor-quality construction, and miscalculation of demand are familiar results. Furthermore, the physical outcome may damage rather than enhance the surrounding environment on which it depends for success.

Project Development Phase

During the conceptual phase of the project, it is uncertain whether the final outcome will closely meet the original goals and objectives, or if the project will be developed in an amended form. Studies of risk aim to close the gap between the initial goals and the form of the eventual outcome.

Risk varies with the size of the project, the total scope, and each element. Consequently, we create a system relevant to the hotel industry which will allow us to forecast areas where uncertainty and the chance of risk may occur.

If risk has not been recognized or understood, and contingency plans have not been made, the required capital outlay will increase and become much greater than anticipated at commencement.

Comparison of Investment Opportunity

Usually, comparisons are made between the opportunity costs of several investments. It is important, therefore, to evaluate the degree of risk inherent in each proposal. Probability distributions take into account the exposure to risk in the calculation, and provide the investor or developer with a range of values on which to base decisions.[1]

The total return on an investment is composed of interest rate and profit and includes initial yield, income growth, and capital growth.

The most important considerations for any development project are future cash flows, returns, and the potential to increase the capital value. Ratios are often used to assist with the evaluation of these issues. (See Fig. 3.3.)

Techniques of Economic Analysis

There are, in general, four standard techniques used for evaluating uncertainty and risk in construction and development projects: (1) life-cycle cost (LCC), (2) net savings or net benefits, (3) benefit-to-cost ratio (BCR), and (4) adjusted internal rate of return (AIRR). Each accounts to some degree for uncertainty (although some do not take account of risk), and all usually base the analysis on the first 5 to 10 years of the hotel's business activity after completion.[1]

Life-cycle cost.   The purpose of the LCC analysis is to predict the cash flow to be expected from the project in future years, and compare this with the amount of capital outlay which must be invested to achieve such values and returns. The predictions include those returns to be expected from both business income and long-term appreciation of capital.

Net savings or net benefits.   The studies that underlie this analysis are prepared in the form of spreadsheets, which, thanks to modern computer technology, can hold many variables stable while the effects of a modification to one variable are evaluated. Several alternative development costs are prepared with detailed cash flows, so that profitable options can be discovered which arise directly from alternatives within the product or process. Naturally, as many variations to the concept proposal as are deemed necessary can be prepared for consideration in the form of sheets of calculated comparisons. However, remember that these comparisons are only as good as the information fed to the computer![1]

Benefit-to-cost and savings-to-investment ratios.   The benefit-to-cost ratio is also known as the *capitalization rate*. This ratio, simply expressed as "Cap rate" = income / value of building, is commonly used to analyze the long-term potential of income-producing properties, and the uncertainty connected with continued and sustainable revenues and future expectations.[1]

The ratio compares forecast revenues, which are derived from current market factors, against establishment costs and indicates both whether, and over what period of time, the project will be cost-effective. Typical factors which are taken into account for the analysis are

Quality and maintenance of accommodation and buildings services

The location of the project in relation to nearby buildings and businesses

Structure and leases of nearby buildings

Leases

RESULTS	Current prices	Price at completion	Year — Jul-92	Year 2 — Jul-93	Year 3 — Jul-94	Year 4 — Jul-95	Year 5 — Jul-96	Year 6 — Jul-97	Year 7 — Jul-98	Year 8 — Jul-99	Year 9 — Jul-2000	Year 10 — Jul-2001	Year 11 — Jul-2002
- Cash outlay ($M)													
• Land	163.7	163.7											
• Construction													
. Pre-construction													
. Contract	150.5	178.2											
. Variations	7.5	8.9											
. Prolongation	6.8	8.0											
. Sub-Total	164.8	195.1											
• Fees	19.8	23.4											
• Legal, etc	11.0	11.0											
• Authority contribs	5.0	5.0											
• Preopening expenses	5.0	5.0											
• Working capital	2.0	2.0											
• Prop contingency	7.5	8.9											
• Developers fee	9.23	10.93											
TOTAL CASH OUTLAY	387.9	425.0											
- Non cash outlay ($M)													
• Interest	54.6	57.9											
- Total outlay ($M)	442.5	482.9											
- Gross income ($M p.a.)													
. Rooms	31.42	39.66	39.66	49.85	59.44	67.39	71.43	75.71	80.26	85.07	90.18	95.59	101.32
. Food & beverages	20.28	25.60	25.60	28.21	32.16	37.74	40.00	42.40	44.94	47.64	50.50	53.53	56.74
. Telephones	1.46	1.86	1.86	2.11	2.51	2.85	3.02	3.20	3.39	3.59	3.81	4.04	4.28
. Minor departments	0.70	0.89	0.89	1.00	1.19	1.35	1.43	1.52	1.61	1.71	1.81	1.92	2.03
. Retail rental	2.28	2.80	2.80	2.97	3.15	3.33	3.53	3.75	3.97	4.21	4.46	4.73	5.01
. Car park rental	0.80	0.95	0.95	1.01	1.07	1.14	1.20	1.28	1.35	1.43	1.52	1.61	1.71
TOTAL GROSS INCOME	56.94	71.77	71.77	85.14	99.52	113.79	120.62	127.86	135.53	143.66	152.28	161.41	171.10
- Costs ($M p.a.)	38.13	47.99	47.99	53.39	60.41	67.75	71.81	76.12	80.69	85.53	90.66	96.10	101.87
- OPERATING PROFIT ($M)	18.81	23.78	23.78	31.75	39.11	46.04	48.81	51.73	54.84	58.13	61.62	65.31	69.23
Management fee	0.50	0.50	0.50	0.50	0.50	0.50	0.50	6.44	6.82	7.23	7.67	8.13	8.61
- NETT PROFIT	18.31	23.28	23.28	31.25	38.61	45.54	48.31	45.30	48.01	50.90	53.95	57.19	60.62
- Valuation		594.06 (based on year 3 income)										1065.10	
- IRR													
• Cash flow		-482.93	23.28	31.25	38.61	45.54	48.31	45.30	48.01	50.90	53.95	1122.29	
• IRR	14.5%												
- Costs/Square Metre (based on total outlay)	• Site area $132,781	• Gross area $7,392 (NOTE: Includes car parking area)											
- Developers margin	$111.1 or 23%												

Figure 3.3 Forecast of outlay for the development of a downtown hotel, Sydney, Australia. A summary of outlay costs includes the purchase price of land, construction costs, legal fees, authority approvals, contingencies and other expenses (1989 prices).

Estimated potential income from earnings minus expected expenses

The income lost from the inability to earn interest on capital investment elsewhere

The benefit-to-cost ratio is used to compare the project under study with other similar projects.

The formula of the benefit-to-cost ratio (BCR) is expressed as

$$\mathrm{BCR} = \overset{N}{\underset{t}{\mathrm{E}}} = 1 \; (B_t - C_t)/(1 + i)^t]/C_0$$

where B = benefits including resale values

C = present value of installation costs and replacement costs[1]

The savings-to-investment ratio gives similar results.

Adjusted internal rate of return. In this author's experience, the adjusted internal rate of return (AIRR) is the method most often used for financial analysis in the hotel industry. The method can be made sufficiently sensitive to produce a reliable analysis which takes into account an adjustment for future variations in interest rates received on reinvestments, a factor which is often forgotten.

The data, which uses results from the BCR analysis, estimates the eventual returns on investment, minus losses and deductions. The data is built into the analysis, and "compounded." That is to say, the interest that the principal has potential to earn over the long term is calculated as compound interest. In order to make a valid comparison it is necessary to convert future monetary values to a common base. These are "discounted" to make them comparable with current prices; for example, the benefits from compound rates of interest used in the calculations, development costs, and end returns from business activities are brought to an equal monetary value, at specified reinvestment rates, for the period under study. The "discount rate" and "compound rate" so obtained reflect the time value of money to the investor, called the "opportunity cost."[1]

The following equation is used to calculate the AIRR (Marshall, 1988):

$$\mathrm{AIRR} = -1 + (1 + r) \, (\mathrm{BCR})^{1/N}$$

where r = the rate of return on reinvestments of cash savings

BCR = benefit-to-cost ratio

N = period of study in years

r = constant

$r = i$

Inflationary factors will also distort the results and are generally included in the calculation as an average figure.[1]

Mathematical Techniques for Processing, Correction, and Evaluation of Data

Several mathematical techniques may be used during an economic analysis, each giving a slightly different orientation. Some use probability techniques; some do not, but instead give a simplified assessment which ignores the investor's attitudes (conservative or risk taking) toward risk exposure.

Techniques which do not use probability. There are four basic techniques:

1. Conservative benefit-and-cost estimating

2. Breakeven analysis

3. Sensitivity analysis

4. Risk-adjusted discount rate (RADR)[1]

Conservative benefit-and-cost estimating. This is a simple way of estimating a project's future worth. A conservative input value is used for areas of uncertainty and risk. The technique is acceptable if there is no penalty for rejecting a project. However, should there be a penalty, such as lost opportunity in the case of bidding for a construction project, the conservative bias will work against acceptance of a project which is in fact economically feasible.

Breakeven analysis. The breakeven point is the value at which construction costs equal forecast benefits.

The advantage of the breakeven point technique is that it can be computed quickly with limited information and thus is useful for a first simple evaluation of a proposal. For example, if a variable (critical to the success of the project) is seen to negatively influence achievement, maximum and minimum values can be defined which allow decision makers to evaluate the acceptable limit and propose alternatives. However, the technique does not give feedback on variable uncertainty.

Sensitivity analysis. Sensitivity analysis techniques are often used or combined with other methods for the analysis of a new development opportunity in the hotel and construction industry. For example, levels of room occupancy can be varied, and minimum required levels of occupancy for the period under study can be established. The sensitivity analysis will draw attention to areas of difficulty and uncertainty.

Risk-adjusted discount rate (RADR). This technique aims to raise the likelihood of receiving a net benefit or return from a project which has many high-risk areas of uncertainty. The net benefits or returns are calculated at a higher discount factor than for projects with more certainty of outcome.

Techniques that use probability.[1] Techniques which include probability to describe values and measures of project worth are more sensitive than techniques which do not include probability analysis. Reliability is gained because the techniques give an estimation of the maximum and minimum acceptable variance from the expected value within which the project will still be profitable. They therefore serve as a more reliable basis for decision making.

Some techniques are typically (1) input estimation using expected values, (2) mean variance criterion and coefficient of variation, (3) decision analysis, (4) simulation, and (5) mathematical analytical technique.

Sources of Risk in Hotel and Resort Development

Finance for development has traditionally taken one of two forms:

1. Debt without equity, subdivided into:

   Construction loans

   Commercial paper based on a guaranteed letter of credit

   Minipermanent; the building to be sold at the completion of construction

   Bullet loan—a long-term loan.[2]

2. Joint venture, or debt with equity:

   A 100 percent loan

   Participatory loan; this is almost identical to the lender having control over decisions.

The sources of risk arising from uncertainty factors can be divided into three general categories: (a) business and investment, (b) development and construction, and (c) foreign exchange.

Business and Investment

An analysis of business and investment is based on information obtained from market surveys of tourism potential for the area and current market activity and prices for resources in the building industry. Both sources of information may be influenced by fluctuations in foreign exchange rates.

Decisions made during the market analysis will determine the future form of the project and the project's financial feasibility and future financial success. For example, the following questions are generally examined:

Is there a market for this type of development?

Will it meet current and future market demand?

When will it give return on investment?

Is the project development viable in this physical location?

If the project proceeds, of what standard and type must it be?

Risk during Construction

Uncertainty factors within the design and construction process also affect the degree of risk to investment. Areas of uncertainty where problems occur typically include delays in construction, increases in prices, labor relations, availability of materials, delays in delivery, and maintenance of quality.

Additionally, the following issues arise in the international setting: availability of local skills, delays in the delivery of materials and furnishings, unforeseen environmental problems, reactions of local groups to the development, and cultural factors. These factors cause unexpected setbacks and often require changes to plans and procedures. They may seriously affect development costs if contingency plans have not been made in advance.

The first evaluation of areas of uncertainty and risk during construction is based on experience and comparison with similar projects being built at the time. Risks which are likely to occur during construction are, of course, more easily recognized once the process of planning, design, detailing, and programming get under way and tasks are divided into "work breakdown units."

The determination of areas of uncertainty in construction are difficult to establish but are an important source of data for the feasibility analyses. Recognition of, management of, and systems for the control of risk that may occur during the construction period are discussed more fully in a later chapter.

Foreign Exchange[3]

Investors, developers, and contractors of international real estate encounter risks associated with foreign exchange rate movements, whenever their interests expand to overseas projects.

The majority of major losses are incurred when international contracts are based in a national currency differing from the developer's own currency, which may be Japanese yen, American dollars, or other currencies that maintain a high value against local rates.

Relative exchange rates are important to domestic developers as well as those involved in international operations. When exchange rates are in favor of the international developer, international operators' organizations will grow at a faster rate and permit access to a wider range of capital markets and financial sources. They will then easily outperform the domestic developer.

All businesses with international competitors who are subject to international comparison should be aware of the relativity of foreign exchange in order to maintain their competitive position. For developers embarking on an offshore project, certain foreign exchange risks require specific attention; typically these are balance sheet risk and earnings translation risk.

Balance sheet risk. A balance sheet risk can arise in a number of ways during the funding of an offshore project. For example, if a loan is needed to fund a project and is in the form of an asset, an investment in the project, or a liability and is acquired in a currency denomination other than the developer's, fluctuations in the value of that currency can impact on the developer's financial profile. This may be in the form of realized or unrealized losses, according to different accounting treatments in different jurisdictions.

The process of development of an international hotel or resort may take up to five years or even more. During this period developers will be exposed to balance sheet risk, unless risk management action is taken.

Earnings translation risk. An earnings translation risk arises as a result of the impact of foreign exchange movements on earnings from the project, as opposed to balance-sheet items. If such earnings are denominated in the national currency of the project location, fluctuations in the relative values of international currency will increase or decrease the earnings from the project. Unless earnings are readily predictable, it is difficult to hedge for earnings translation risk.[3]

Hedging in the Financial Markets

An investor may use various procedures to protect an investment against adverse exchange variations in local currencies. Typically, the methods are

1. Hedging of risk in the financial markets through the use of foreign exchange contracts, options, or other financial products

2. Factoring, or the sale of right to receive payment in the future

3. Establishment of overseas financial subsidiaries, without recourse to the parent company

4. Subscriptions to overseas investment insurance

5. Formation of a nonrecourse joint-venture company (JVC)[3]

Hedging techniques. Hedging in the financial markets has become very sophisticated over the years and is the subject of a large amount of literature. Most major developers have teams of specialists devoted to the management of foreign exchange, interest rates, and in some cases commodities such as oil and coal, where these commodities are important to the success of the project.[3]

At a certain cost, almost any risk exposure can be hedged in the international financial markets using foreign exchange contracts, options, caps, floors, swaps, future rate agreements, commodity futures, and so on.[3]

Factoring. In this method, the right to collect the debt from future receivables is sold and the proceeds are converted to the developer's own currency to eliminate future risk. Under English law, future property cannot be sold, only the right to receive or collect.[3]

The establishment of overseas subsidiaries. When a large international development company intends to conduct business locally, a subsidiary company can be formed. The developer can provide the subsidiary with an independent capital base. Funding of projects can be undertaken by the subsidiary company. Dividends are paid to the parent company if the project is successful.

Income from any local business is received by the subsidiary company, and this income is assessed by local taxation authorities. If the international company wishes to repatriate funds at a future date, there may be dividend withholding tax, even though taxation agreements exist between countries, as is the case, for example, between Australia and Japan. Company law and taxation requirements are complex and vary between different countries.

Subscriptions to overseas investment insurance. Government export agencies often provide this form of agreement.[3]

Joint-venture companies (JVCs). JVCs are often formed both to hedge against loss through exchange fluctuations and to assist the international company with local business culture and requirements. They can be formed with the proportion of each partner's financial interest as desired, except where local government regulations require a minimum local investment, as is, for example, the case in Indonesia.

Indonesia and some other countries also require that international companies form a partnership with a local firm before business can be transacted locally.

Cycles of Development Activity

Development activity is shown to have distinct cycles over a period of time. These are typically (1) maximum demand and minimum supply, (2) reducing demand and increasing supply, (3) maximum supply and minimum demand, and (4) reducing supply and increasing demand.

When the typical time period for initiation, construction, and completion of a hotel or resort—generally from two to three years—has elapsed, an alternate cycle of market supply and demand will have commenced. Projects which have been initiated in a time of maximum demand and minimum supply will be forced to open during an alternate, perhaps much less favorable and more competitive cycle of maximum supply and minimum demand. The returns earned under the new conditions will be at considerable variance to the original forecast, and the project may show little return on investment for a much longer period than anticipated.[4]

Although developers on the whole may appreciate the need for market analysis, it is surprising that there is still a tendency to misjudge the appropriate time to initiate a hotel project. Many new hotels open at a time of maximum supply, with risk of low occupancy levels at commencement and for a few years afterward. The most appropriate time, therefore, to consider and initiate a project for successful commencement in a city or region is probably during periods of maximum supply and low demand.[4]

Evaluating Market Demand and Potential

The objective of market evaluation is to establish market demand and define appropriate goals and objectives that can be realized within the budget, taking account of future growth. The evaluation needs contributions from many different experts and varied sources. The issues are, however, interrelated.

A project manager, who will later plan and control work carried out by the project team for design and construction, will be closely involved with duties that include the assembly and coordination of information to support the financial evaluation. The project manager must anticipate areas of risk and uncertainty and obtain the necessary information that will be required for evaluation.

A communications system and database must be established at this time to coordinate the work of all contributors to the process, and support the next phase of planning, detailed design, and construction of the project.

Financial Feasibility Analysis

The feasibility study is a two-step process of research and evaluation, based on market demand, and forecasting financial risk and returns:

1. Research—preparing a cash flow estimate from current market findings, construction costs, forecasts of future income, and esti mates of development costs

2. Evaluation—evaluating research findings and alternatives

The first step, which involves the market analysis, aims to determine the likely market response to the proposed project. The level of demand is influenced by the existing circumstances in the total area and region. There are, of course, elements common to all proposals regardless of whether the project is to be constructed in a city or a previously developed resort area, or built in an undeveloped location for speciality or multiple use.

The following questions should be asked:

1. Is there sufficient market demand?

2. What type of physical product would be in line with future mar ket demand?

3. Would this type of development be within the budget?

4. Is this location suitable for the proposed development?

5. Is this the right time to commence development of this project?

There are many other issues to consider which contribute to the analysis; these include market competition, local attractions, characteristics of site and location, current and future accommodation demand, hotel management requirements, and political issues.

The feasibility analysis may be undertaken by the financial section of the client and/or investor's organization, by outside financial consultants, or by hotel management consultants.

The professionals who will be needed for the study, are typically the financial and legal team, urban and regional planners, architects and engineers, and hotel management experts. Other professional advice may be brought in as needed in accordance with the specific nature of the site and environment.

A "feasibility study" for a downtown hotel development project, using these techniques, is illustrated by the spreadsheet shown in Fig. 3.4. Occupancy levels have been varied over a 10-year period. Other variables such as construction costs are calculated and combined with market studies.

For feasibility study purposes, for example, sketch designs for three-, four-, or five-star hotels may be developed. The estimate will include the number of rooms and public areas, running costs, and maintenance costs which are taken at current market prices and adjusted against the internal rate of return (IRR). These sketch designs serve as a basis for an estimation of the capital outlay that will be required to achieve each alternative.

Costs must be adjusted for the difficulties of development and construction which vary from city to undeveloped area. If new ground is

DATA

- Site area:		3,637 sq.m.	Rate		$45,000 /sq.m.	Cost:	$163.67 million (todays prices)

- Development:	Area Type	Gross sq.m.	Nett sq.m.	FSR sq.m.	Constn cost ($/sq.m.gross)	Construction Cost ($millions)
. Basement	O	14,520			1,115	16.19
. Podium	O	12,970			2,455	31.84
. Tower	O	37,840			1,815	68.68
. Tunnel and bridge	-					5.75
. ---	-					0.00
. ---	-					0.00
. ---	-					0.00
. ---	-					0.00
. FF & E			560 rooms		50,000	28.00
TOTALS		65.330	0	0	0.00 $ million	150.46

- Timing:	Project start:	Jul-89	- Const'n duration:	36 months gross
	Finish (inc. delays):	Jul-92	- To start demol'n:	6 months
	Base date:	Jul-88	- To start const'n:	12 months

- Interest: 6.0% per annum

- Fees: 12.0% of construction cost including project management

- Pre-construction costs: 0.00 $ millions

- Authority contributions: 5.00 $ millions

- Escalation rate: 0.00% for land
7.00% for construction

- Legal costs,stamp duty etc 11.00 $ millions

- Variations percentage: 5.00% of contract value

- Proprietors contingency: 5.00% of contract value

- Delays: 25% of elapsed time   - Prolongation costs   0.020% of contract value

- Preopening expenses: 5.00 $ millions

- Working capital: 2.00 $ millions

- Developer's fee: 5.00% of design and construction cost

- Capitalisation rate: 6.50% for year 3 (used to calculate value on completion)
6.50% for final year

- Management fee: 0.5 $ millions fixed for first 5 years
2.00% of income plus   7.50% of gross operating profit

Figure 3.4   Financial feasibility study for a downtown hotel, Sydney, Australia (1989). This financial feasibility study combines data assembled to summarize the total development outlay, and to analyze the gross income and expenditure over 11 years. Occupancy rates are usually assumed to be low for the first three years. The internal rate of return (IRR) for this period is 14 percent.

being put to use, and the location is as yet unknown, new infrastructure services will almost certainly be needed among other expenditures, and the uncertainty, which is connected with the installation of these facilities introduces new factors of risk.

In summary, planning, architectural, engineering, and builders' input for the feasibility study will be needed for environmental data, sketch site plans, sketch plans for hotel layout, estimates of construction costs and materials, and future hotel management requirements.

Setting up a Database

Detailed information which is needed for decision making during the business feasibility study serves as a basis for both budget preparation and design and planning activities. A database must be established.

The computerized database system will have open access to all who will contribute to the project and will contain as wide a range of detailed information as possible. During the phases of development and construction discussed in Chaps. 2 and 4, the database is used for the purpose of defining the scope of the project and as a basic information source for the design team, planners, and programmers.

Actions to Be Taken at This Time

- Project manager:

    Become familiar with the investor's and sponsor's needs and requirements

    Establish a communication link between the sponsor and between all contributors to the project and feasibility analysis

    Establish a database

    Ensure that all local government regulations and environmental detail are available

    Plan, manage, and supervise the acquisition of all other information

    Advise and supervise contracts for the appointment of consultants

    Arrange to commence the analysis of information

    Supervise the production of appropriate planning, architectural, and engineering sketch proposals

- Planners:

    Research environmental issues

    Research infrastructure requirements and related issues

    Prepare an environmental impact statement if needed for financial feasibility and government approvals

- Architects and engineers—for the purposes of financial analysis, and government approvals:

    Prepare initial sketch plans for site layout

    Prepare initial sketch designs including alternatives

    Assist with the first estimates of construction costs

References

1. Harold E. Marshall, *Techniques for Treating Uncertainty and Risk in the Economic Evaluation of Buildings,* U.S. Department of Commerce, National Institute of Standards and Technology; NIST Special Publication 757, 1988.

2. Graham Peirson and R. Bird, *Business Finance,* 4th ed., McGraw-Hill, Sydney, 1989.

3. R. J. Katz, Comm. LL. B., *Discussions Concerning Exchange and Hedging Techniques,* T.N.T. Pty. Ltd., Sydney, 1991.

4. Alan Featherby, *Discussions,* Radisson Hotel Group, Australia, 1991.

Development: 1

The first project management systems were designed for particular purposes; for example, the requirements for management of the NASA space programs. They have since been broadened to offer a structured foundation for many different types of short-term projects in the construction industry.

The Design of a Management and Control System for a Project

Two Basic Systems

Two systems, proposed by the Project Management Institute of America and Canadian Public Works, were adapted for the construction industry. These have already been discussed in outline in Chap. 2.

The Project Delivery System is divided into six stages or phases (see Chap. 2). To recapitulate, these are

Phase 1: planning

Phase 2: definition

Phase 3: implementation

Phase 4: commissioning

Phase 5: operation

Phase 6: evaluation[1]

A system suitable for management of hotel or resort development may be based on either of these two systems. For example, the development of the concept of the project occurs in Phase 1: planning and is developed in detail in Phase 2: definition. However, the program must be adapted to relate to the particular circumstances and characteristics of the project under development. (See Fig. 4.1.)

Proposals have been made by other experts to augment these two basic systems. Some have additional advantages that help to identify various skills and expertise required in setting up a project team and the need for a training program for team participants.

Start-Up Procedures

Selecting an Organizational Model

The selection and adaptation is made easier as the financial feasibility analysis is carried out, because sufficient data is being assembled for the analysis to define the project's influences and constraints. This information can now be utilized concurrently, to assist the choice and implementation of a basic structure and commence the design of strategies for management and control. The data is used to determine the details of the system, and to program the tasks involved in pro-

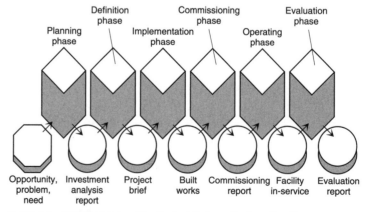

Figure 4.1   The six phases of the Project Delivery System. The diagram, issued by the Public Works, Canada, illustrates the activities that occur both within their six-phase system, and those that occur in the interface between the phases. The linking activities of the interfaces are of major importance for the maintenance of continuity and stable control of the process. (Project Delivery System, 1989.)

duction with the conditions and constraints of each specific project built into the definition of the design criteria.

The tasks associated with the design of the project can be divided into four stages: (1) researching the influences affecting the project, (2) coordinating and reviewing these influences, (3) reaching agreement on the decision-making hierarchy, and (4) implementing the approved management system model.

Influences

Many influences and constraints are specific to each unique project and must be incorporated into the management strategy and made to contribute to its final format. These are typically

Client and hotel management group influences

Budget and structure of proposed financing

Market demand

Time frame for realization of the project

Availability of resources, especially with regard to geographic location

Likelihood of major design changes

Availability of technology

Project access, infrastructure, and environmental influences

Availability of skilled work force[2]

Client influences. Recently the structure and type of organizations that may be included under the heading "client" have become very complex, and are now likely to be some combination of developers, construction companies, financiers, hotel management chains, and end users: national governments, local residents.

Consultants and contractors who are to contribute professional and trade expertise to the process should also be considered as clients or customers as they have a financial commitment in the provision of labor. The design of the project process will be influenced by the quality of their contribution and their special capabilities.

It is essential to consider the hotel management group who are appointed, as a client and involve their representatives in early decision making. These groups have their own in-house management practices, marketing and design, and philosophies and intentions, and the group's philosophy and expertise must fundamentally influence the total concept of the project.

Financial influences. Investment finance and the inspiration for hotel or resort development may arise from source organizations of one or other of the following types:

Private financiers

Private syndicates or consortiums

Joint venture between organizations

Government and private syndicates, or joint venture between the two

Design-construct companies who plan to sell the product to an investment group on completion

Different nationalities often form joint ventures or consortiums to finance and develop an international resort project in association with local investors, where there is a perceived opportunity. Indeed, this is usually a legal requirement of the host country, whose regulations may specify a mandatory percentage of local investment. Otherwise, the percentage of financial involvement between the parties varies.

The syndicates will have different corporate values, priorities, policies, and goals. They are subject to both international and national cultural influences which affect both the decision-making process and the requirements for different facilities and design factors in the hotel. An example is the contrasting process of decision making between Japanese firms, who make decisions by group agreement involving the whole company, and the process of decision making by one or a small committee of company directors, a system of decision making found in America and Australia.

Market influences. One of the main objectives of hotel or resort development must be to meet the needs and characteristics, nationalities, and expectations of the anticipated visitors and design room prices and quality for the project accordingly. The preparatory feasibility analysis, discussed in Chap. 3, forms a foundation for decision making based on market demand and future financial return. The information is correlated into a description of the scope of the work and used as a foundation and guide for design and for the selection of management models, incorporating social and technical environmental factors which form the constraints of the proposal. Market opportunities, geographic feasibility, and an appropriate choice of construction are identified through studies of these factors.

The hotel management group's analysis of the resource requirements necessary to serve market demand is also influenced by the location and availability of resources. The demands on management to administer an Ayers Rock Resort located thousands of kilometers from the nearest city, for example, are quite different from the demands of a downtown hotel (Figs. 4.2 and 4.3) and will have a major influence on forecast and actual long-term revenues. The hotel operator's input continues through all stages of the design, documentation, and commissioning processes in order that objectives for the future management and administration of public function and room housekeeping and maintenance are realized appropriately.

Constraints that are unique to specific projects will be discussed in more detail in the following chapter, and vary according to the physical and geographic location of the site and local culture and government regulations.

Designing the Model: Elements of the System

An appropriately designed model for a management and control system has the capability of realizing the desired outcomes of the project

Figure 4.2 A downtown hotel: The Hyatt, Adelaide. The Hyatt Hotel forms a central focus for the Adelaide Convention and Exhibition Centers, and a casino. The complex was partially constructed in the air rights over Adelaide's Central Railway Station, built in 1926, which was restored concurrently with the construction of these facilities. The station now contains an up-to-date retail center with boutique shops that serve the public, rail travelers, and the hotel's guests. John Andrews International, architects.

by balancing the project's needs and constraints, providing means to find acceptable solutions (with the assistance and support of each group in the production process), and coordinating all the various influences into an acceptable solution.

The plan for a management strategy includes activities that can be divided for convenience into two parts and together help to generate a statement of total scope of a project: (1) the identification of needs and (2) project scope management.[3]

Identification of Needs

The needs that are to be identified and satisfied include approvals by government authorities, physical and geographic requirements, environmental considerations, and budget and cost control.

Client needs usually require careful definition and clarification, as the project team receive them in terms that are difficult to interpret in the language of design and the structure of the management system. It is important, therefore, to clarify the client's objectives and obtain

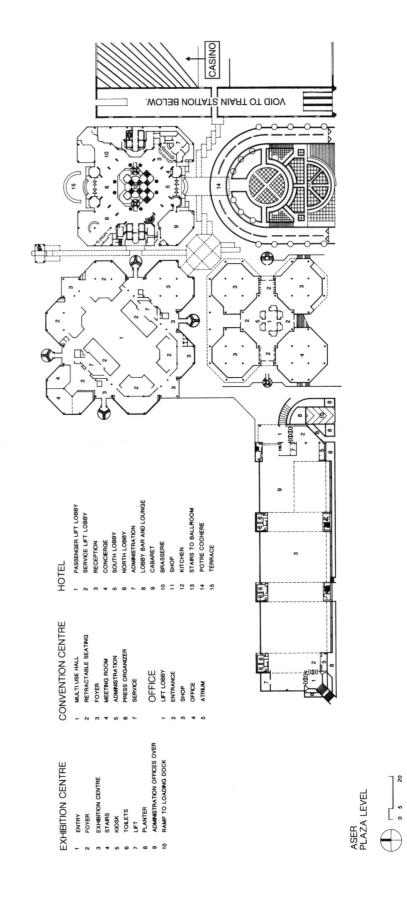

EXHIBITION CENTRE

1 ENTRY
2 FOYER
3 EXHIBITION CENTRE
4 STAIRS
5 KIOSK
6 TOILETS
7 LIFT
8 PLANTER
9 ADMINISTRATION OFFICES OVER
10 RAMP TO LOADING DOCK

CONVENTION CENTRE

1 MULTI USE HALL
2 RETRACTABLE SEATING
3 FOYER
4 MEETING ROOM
5 ADMINISTRATION
6 PRESS ORGANIZER
7 SERVICE

OFFICE

1 LIFT LOBBY
2 ENTRANCE
3 SHOP
4 OFFICE
5 ATRIUM

HOTEL

1 PASSENGER LIFT LOBBY
2 SERVICE LIFT LOBBY
3 RECEPTION
4 CONCIERGE
5 SOUTH LOBBY
6 NORTH LOBBY
7 ADMINISTRATION
8 LOBBY BAR AND LOUNGE
9 CABARET
10 BRASSERIE
11 SHOP
12 KITCHEN
13 STAIRS TO BALLROOM
14 POTRE COCHERE
15 TERRACE

ASER
PLAZA LEVEL

0 5   20

Figure 4.3   Plan at plaza level, the Hyatt Hotel, Convention and Exhibition Center, Adelaide, South Australia. John Andrews International, architects.

agreement at each key point in the process; to ensure that the project is not "locked in" to one design immediately and, as research progresses, adjust the program to meet emerging requirements.

The management strategies should be capable of balancing and supporting the efforts of professions and tradespeople who will contribute skills and expertise to the design, construction, and day-to-day management of the finished facility, and when complete, the project should satisfy the needs of sponsor and investor, hotel management, and guests, and government authorities. A difficult goal!

Project Scope Management

Management and control strategies provide an organizational framework from which to initiate and implement the plan, design, program, and schedule, and interface the project with its total environment. Monitoring procedures are continued throughout the project to determine whether the objectives of production quality and cost control are being met. If the systems and technologies do not reach these standards at any point in the program, they must be modified immediately. Within the general requirements for good management and control systems which allow the production process to flow smoothly, therefore, is the need to avoid or minimize risk factors caused by unexpected variations to the design and the program of development. The ability to respond promptly and flexibly to unexpected circumstances leading to variations during production is essential.

The following actions contribute to the detailed definition of the project: establishment of a comprehensive statement of scope of the project, programs and schedules needed to accomplish objectives, and design of the management and control system to suit the project and project constraints.

Procurement

It follows that the project goals and objectives and means for procuring these desired goals should be established in great detail to avoid confusion and misunderstanding.

At commencement, the project manager expands the project team according to perceived need and delegates duties and responsibilities. The project process is implemented by combining detailed design instructions, appropriate construction methods, available resources, and technology into the "statement of scope" document. This is very comprehensive and is expanded and detailed during Phase 2: development phase. The statement of scope is interpreted in three sections:

1. The physical element—materials and resources

2. The social element—outside the project: local culture, politics, and regulations, and the social elements internal to the project team, such as client and group relationships

3. Technical elements—professional and trade skills, techniques, and equipment[3]

More specifically, activities through which the project team prepare for the statement of scope documentation include

Detailed project definition and budget analysis

Analysis and preparation of strategies for scope management

Preparation of detailed design and documentation

Development of plans, programs, and schedules

Details of strategies for resource procurement

Establishment of quality assurance standards

Establishment of budget and cost-control programs

Methods for the control of variations and risk management[3]

Development and control of planning, programming, and grouping of tasks.   As the stages of the project are developed, tasks are grouped into work packages and divided into "work-breakdown units," and by this means the scope of the program is given definition. This task is assisted by the use of technological tools, such as bar charts, Gantt charts, network analysis, and precedence network planning, which enable the project management team to establish activities that are most critical to the program for the construction process.

The most common of these tools are the network diagram and bar chart and these are generally used at commencement of the programming procedure. Complex networks such as construction programs are designed by specialist programmers working in-house in the construction companies.

It is essential that the project management team cross-check and confirm dates and times of the construction programs according to their technical expertise and ensure that deadlines tie in with all the supporting activities. This will include, for example, the compliance with regulations and the acquisition of government approvals, as both must be confirmed before a program can proceed. During the project process, as each task is completed and a key date is achieved, the team must make an assessment to determine whether the quality of the work is acceptable and objectives have been met.

Resource procurement.   At concept initiation and during program development, the project manager and project team assess the human and physical resources which will be needed during the various phases, and calculate the quantity and the length of time required. Budget allowances are adjusted to meet these requirements.

Approvals.   The project manager must arrange progressive reviews of progress, so that delays are not incurred, and has the responsibility to make recommendations to the client to obtain formal approval at the completion of each major task. It is essential that the client give formal approval as each key point in the program is reached.

The tasks of monitoring progress and obtaining approvals are undertaken continually throughout the project and build one on another; therefore, an important part of the system design is the establishment of a process for obtaining approvals. Approvals confirm that an objective has been completed successfully, the standard and quality of work is acceptable, and the next stage of the program is able to proceed. Indeed, each contributor to the chain of activity is dependent on the previous trade, supplier, or contributor to provide materials, goods, or data of an acceptable quality on which to base his or her input.

Quality control. Total Quality Control (TQC), now a well-known system first developed by Toyoda Gosei in Japan, was designed to monitor and produce a desired quality outcome. It depends for its success on creating commitment in all members of the production team, who are then responsible for monitoring and quality control of their own work, and has the additional advantage of motivating and integrating team members.

Risk and Variation

All the planning methods that have been discussed above incorporate structures designed for smooth progression of the program toward the final objective of successful completion of the hotel or resort project. To avoid situations that put the outcome at risk, it is essential to establish a method to process unexpected problems speedily and efficiently.

Causes of variations. The management of variations involves the control of unexpected events in the program. There are two general causes of variations, although the sources are multitude: causes that are attributable to team members and are to be controlled at the operational level and causes that are a fault in the management system and affect the whole project team.

Both types arise for the five main reasons described below:

1. If a poorly defined project with insufficient data is initiated by either an individual or the team, contributors to the process will be unable to provide reliable solutions and recognize and provide alternatives for areas of uncertainty and risk. The poorly defined project is a general cause of failure and is self-generating.

2. The database is inadequate or has been maintained incorrectly.

3. Incorrect data has been provided to members of the team. This is a very common cause in the process of production.

4. The feasibility study has been hampered by an unsuitable management structure and management procedures.

5. Expertise is lacking among team members and delays occur.[2]

It is interesting to note that statistics show that causes attributable to team members constitute only 15 percent of all problems and arise from human error, but causes relating to a poorly functioning management system contribute 85 percent of all problems. These are almost impossible to remedy once the delivery process has commenced. A large percentage of failure is therefore attributable to poor management and control and underlines the importance of establishing a reliable structure and appropriate strategies at commencement of the project.

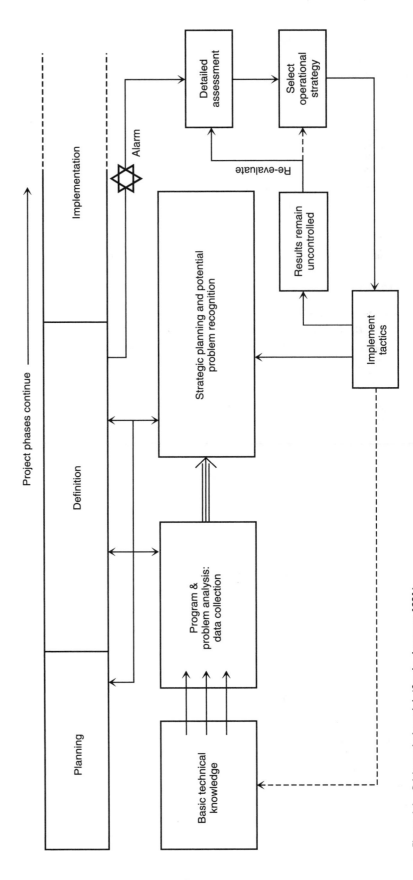

Figure 4.4   Crisis control model. (*Sawle, January 1991.*)

Control of variations.   Variations to the first proposals cannot be avoided, and, in particular, variations are likely to occur arising from a project's unique features. As development gets under way and more information is added to the general description of the project brief proposals for design, materials acquisition, and construction technologies and processes alter and have the potential to create uncontrolled and unwelcome effects which snowball throughout the project process life cycle.[4]

The important issue of variation management and control demands, therefore, the implementation of a strategy (with an alarm mechanism), that will recognize problems in the preliminary stages before crises erupt (see Figure 4.4).

Flexibility.   There are several means of regulating variations, once the causes are understood. The best means of achieving this objective is to design a system which can react quickly with the built-in flexibility to handle variations when they occur, thus providing the capability to maintain control. Flexibility is dependent on project definition and the availability of comprehensive data gathered in the early stages of the process. The more comprehensive the information and initial definition, the more likelihood the system will have of controlling variations. Project information should include comparative data gathered from past projects, which bear some similarity to the present concept, and their operating success.

Flexibility can be designed into the process with the help of various programming tools. In particular, the precedence network method offers an opportunity for sensitive analysis and recognition of alternatives, by assisting the establishment of the critical path of activity, the recognition of a "float" of time, first and last dates when all important events must occur, and provides an overview of areas where there is a potential for risk.

In summary, variations may often be turned to good account if areas that are susceptible to risk are recognized early in the project life cycle and appropriate alternatives selected. Some steps which may be taken to establish control are

1. Guarding against the unexpected by creating a sound monitoring and reporting system for progress.

2. Giving special attention to sensitive areas where variations are likely to occur. The experience of specialized team members should be used to identify these potentially problematic areas.

3. Giving all personnel the responsibility for the quality of their own contribution to the project process.

4. Designing a program to fit the project; for example, if a precedence network program is made for the process, it will highlight problems of scheduling for each link in the important series of events throughout the life cycle.

Team Building and the Formation of Team Relationships

The process of development and construction of each hotel and resort project involves a series of linked activities lasting on average between two and three years. The project manager and project team are appointed for the limited life span of each project. According to the size of the project, the project management team may include project manager(s), assistant project managers, project team members, and a temporary project "home" office.

The Project Manager

An experienced project manager may have one of the following profiles: an independent consultant nominated and appointed by the owner-client, or an officer delegated from the client's staff; a senior consultant from a firm specializing in project management; and a member of a design-construct organization.

Separate consultants, or project managers appointed from within a company specializing in project management, are sometimes selected by the client through negotiation. Most decisions, however, are based on the selection of a short list of consultants of known reputation, who are invited to submit expressions of interest, followed by competitive bidding.

Responsibilities. The project manager's responsibilities will vary according to the project owner, client, and hotel management group's characteristics; the market requirements of each project; geographic location; and potential for resource procurement. When acting as the investor-client's representative, the project manager will be responsible for the global management of "project delivery" from commencement to commissioning and handover.

During the project's life cycle these responsibilities may be divided into two parts: pre- and postformation of the head contract for construction. The project manager's involvement is usually most intense during the precontract and immediate postcontract phases. (See Fig. 4.5.)[3]

1. Precontract: The project manager is the project team leader
   General responsibilities in the precontract stage typically include

   Assisting the client's research of market and geographic conditions

   Establishing government authority requirements

   Negotiating preliminary approvals with government authorities

   Assisting the client to select a design team for the concept

   Monitoring the development of the conceptual design

   Assisting in negotiations with and appointment of a hotel management group operator

   Advising the client on the selection of the project team

   Supervising feasibility studies

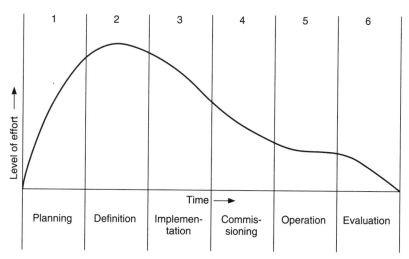

Figure 4.5 Project manager: spread of effort during the project life cycle. The main effort required of the project manager during the project life cycle occurs during the first two phases. The graph shows where the loading occurs with respect to the Project Delivery System. (Master of Project Management Notes, *1991*.)

Making recommendations to the client in the decision-making process

Supervising the preparation of the statement of scope and design documentation

Recognizing and defining risk areas

Supervising the initial research and scheduling for procurement of resources

Managing the bidding for and negotiation of contracts with head and subcontractors

Programming and obtaining commitments to the program

Organizing reviews, planning the management system and the reporting hierarchy

2. Postcontract responsibilities: The project manager's major post contractual responsibilites are to act as the client's representative with consultants and the head contractor, manage and supervise the project team, coordinate with the site management team, and monitor progress. Responsibilities are typically:

Developing, motivating, and coordinating the project team

Monitoring the program of detailed design documentation

Minimizing risk

Monitoring schedules and programs

Supervising the assembly of submissions for approvals from government authorities by key dates in the program

Arranging for tender submissions

Procuring and reviewing bids

Obtaining progressive approvals from the owner and clients

Arranging for approval of the appointment of subcontractors

Arranging for progressive reviews between the project team, client, and head contractor

Monitoring progress and schedules, cost, and quality programs

Monitoring procurement programs

Inspecting, supervising, and recommending for the approval of progress payments

Monitoring finishing phases of contract

These activities differ from the concurrent activities of design professionals, whose role at this time includes the development of design, monitoring of costs and budget control, compliance with regulations, and adding value to the product.

Skill and abilities. Clients' wish-lists for the characteristics to be found in a project manager often imply superhuman ability. There is no doubt, however, that the individual must be tough and energetic, have the ability to stand stressful situations over an extended period, and be willing and able to work long hours.[2]

In this author's experience, the most desirable skills and abilities can be listed simply (in no particular order) as

Good interpersonal skills, (with both client and team members)

Good communication skills

Good listening skills

Team building skills

Leadership

Planning and organizational skills

Flexibility of approach

Problem solving skills

Ability to make decisions

Ability to delegate

Ability to negotiate effectively

The project manager's key qualifications are summarized by Kerzner (1989) as the ability to demonstrate skills in the areas of interface, resource and planning, and control management.

Three factors contribute to this simple list: (1) prior experience, (2) ability to develop team skills, and (3) technical expertise.

Prior experience: Preferably, the project manager should have experience in hotel and resort development and be aware of the special requirements and problems that occur in this industry.

Ability to develop team skills: Team development is a very effective tool for building a strong team identity and encouraging group effort among team members. Development of individual team members and support of young persons entering the profession should therefore be included among the project manager's objectives and responsibilities.

Technical expertise: This is an important consideration in management and control for planning and programming, communication, problem solving, and the decision-making process.

Each of these skills is dependent on interpersonal communication and the project manager's personal characteristics and style. The project manager must be able to express ideas and intentions clearly and be aware of his or her own limitations in certain areas. The ability to delegate to the appropriate professional team members when necessary is very important, for the manager who is unable to do this and is interested solely in self-promotion, quickly loses the respect of team participants and eventually undermines the cohesiveness of the group.

There is usually more than one project manager appointed to a large project; for example, a general project manager who represents the client and forms a liaison between the client, the head contractor and other members of the extended project team, a design and/or construction project manager, and a project manager from the hotel management group.

The appointment of an independent outside general project manager to represent client interests is to be recommended. Often, when several project managers are involved, the terms and areas of responsibility and lines of reporting overlap and should be defined and established at the commencement of the project to avoid the conflicts of interest which often arise when different companies are represented on the team. Indeed, when a conflict of interest is seen to be a potential problem, it is essential that project managers establish trust and confidence among team members in their own abilities and manage the team with integrity. Promises of future favors or bonuses to individual members may be difficult to keep and will most certainly be very disruptive to team relationships.

The Project Team

The management of a large hotel or resort development project cannot be achieved by one person alone. The team, during the course of a project life cycle, may be composed of many different disciplines, with varying technical skills, according to the size, nature, and complexity of the project. Typically the team includes architects, engineers, planners, hotel managers, representatives from the client's office, and the construction team, according to technological requirements.

Appointing the team. Personnel may be recruited to the team by either the bidding process or by negotiation with the following options: (1) the individual consultant or members of a company are appointed to the team on a full-time basis, or (2) an outside company or individual consultant may work in cooperation with the team on a part-time basis, and contribute according to demand and progress.

Both individual consultants and companies, whether through successful bidding or negotiation, are appointed on a contractual basis for the duration of the project. It is desirable that they have experience in hotel and resort development and construction, and a successful company is likely to have an established reputation in the field.

Advantages and disadvantages of employing outside consultants. There are several advantages of selecting an external consulting company; for example, the firm will provide financial security, will already have established work practices philosophies and policies, and will be able to draw on support resources. However, there are a number of disadvantages to be considered. Responsibilities to the project may need the continuing experience and attention of a top-level officer who may not be readily available to fulfill program requirements at all times, because of other business commitments that conflict with the program. Part-time contributors may spend only a small percentage of their time working for the project, and problems of integration into the team may arise.

In the normal course of development, the project manager, specialists such as lawyers, accountants, hotel management consultants, a quantity surveyor, a head contractor, and a principal consultant are appointed at predesign stage. The principal consultant for hotel or resort development is usually, but not always, an architect. The selection of consultants must be appropriate to the type of development envisaged and geographic location of the proposed project.

A firm of architects is appointed in the planning phase (Phase 1 of the Project Delivery System), to assist in the preparation of sketch proposals which will be needed for the feasibility studies. [This architect may not always continue to develop the design (Phase 2: definition), and another firm may be appointed.]

The correct timing of team appointments is of great importance for both budget control and successful management. The requirements for personnel can best be assessed when a proposal for a program and schedule have been agreed on in outline. The project manager must estimate the correct timing and strength of the human and other resources that will be required. However, it is desirable to appoint specialists as early as possible in the process, rather than to be compelled to make an emergency appointment to solve unforeseen problems.

The principal consultants and the head contractor (if already appointed) should have a role in the selection process, and their preferences and biases should be considered in the initial stages of team formation. Later conflict may thus be prevented and greater confidence in team relationships established early.

Methods of Selection

The two basic methods of selection, bidding and negotiation, are often combined in some form or other. For example, a preliminary list of several well-known companies with appropriate experience and reputation is made for the first stage of a two-stage selection process. The first stage often involves bids on concept drawings with an emphasis on requirements and constraints applicable to the project. The most suitable submissions are then short-listed, and later a second stage of negotiation follows when discussions of any special technologies, the contract conditions, and price are continued.

Alternatively, the client may desire to negotiate directly with one well-known company and instruct the project manager to commence discussions. Fees and contract conditions for the work entailed are agreed on between the two parties. Companies or individuals are selected by reputation, or prior experience.

In any case, when bids are called or negotiations with selected consultants for work on the project occur, it is of crucial importance that all criteria be held constant, for, during the subsequent evaluation of the submissions, the project manager and team must establish a comparison which will be unmistakably equitable.

It is desirable that as much information as possible be made available in documentation form describing the project, although the amount of project definition and information may be limited according to the work thus far accomplished. This data is issued to the bidding-negotiating companies under the supervision of the project manager. The documents should define any special conditions and constraints, the client's project needs and desired special circumstances (which may include the appointment of particular persons to the team), backup requirements, market demands, the status of government authority approvals; environmental characteristics and conservation needs, and special design features related to the geographic location. The companies submitting the bid are invited to make proposals which suit their company skills and technologies, present an acceptable response to design criteria, and integrate the constraints of the project. Provision for team accommodation on location should also be discussed.

It will save time later if the project manager meets with each bidding company for questions and discussion when the documents are released. The documents are intended to serve primarily as a basis for pricing, but should be so designed as to clarify desirable aspects of the bidder's proposal, particularly in areas where problems can be anticipated.

In this author's experience, submissions received from consultants are often surprisingly disparate, even where the bidding document has been written with care and clarity and is considered comprehensive. When this occurs, it is recommended that further meetings be arranged with the consultants concerned and objectives discussed in detail.

Selection criteria. Important criteria that influence selection both in the bidding method and by negotiation are typically

Prior experience (either locally or internationally)

Type and characteristics of the proposed project

Cost and fees

Prior successful working relationships with other members of the team[3]

Appointment of international consultants. There are many advantages in the appointment of an experienced international company as principal consultant to a large and complex development. These include the company's reputation and experience to attract an international market, the company's knowledge and use of advanced technology in an international setting, and the existence of worldwide networks which can be utilized for the benefit of the project.

The International Division of Nihon Sekkei Inc., architects, engineers, and planners, usually establish local offices and form associations in consultation with local companies. For example, in recent years they have entered into a relationship with Leo A. Daly, architects and engineers of the United States. The two companies now practice as Nihon Daly, Inc. for joint-venture commissions in both the United States and Japan. Such an association gives the international company the advantage of access to local knowledge of working conditions and use of skilled local staff.

Problems of Staffing

The project manager will find that most difficulties of staffing and management of team personnel and relationships arise from the temporary nature of the project process. These problems are typically the achievement of individual staff identification and integration with the project and project team, and the management of the final phase of the project while the team member's attention is diverted to the problem of continuity of employment.[2]

Identification with the team. Work patterns that include sequential and unrelated temporary assignments have perhaps become more acceptable to individuals in the United States, where short-term consultancy is a more common employment pattern than in other Western business cultures. Project team members are often subcontracted away from the home or office environment for the length of the project life span, while contracting on location, and expect to return to the home office only at completion of their work on the project.

In both instances mentioned above, but particularly in relation to individuals on short-term assignments away from the contracting office, the following issues may challenge the project manager's skills in human resource management:

1. Team members who did not know each other previously or who may even have competed with one another may find it difficult to form good working relationships quickly.

2. Many employees find it difficult to adapt to constantly changing working conditions and to accept the uncertainties that arise in short-term employment.

3. The individual's well-known company support systems may be unavailable or inconvenient to use on location, and the estab lishment and use of temporary alternatives may be stressful.

4. Individuals differ in their ability to accept change between a functional "pyramid"-type management setting and the democra tic "horizontal" structure of the project management system, with different reporting hierarchy and expectations.[3]

Continuity of employment. During the final phases of completion of the project life cycle, the individual has several concerns that are related to the regular office and continuity of employment.

1. The individual may have been overlooked for promotion, or even have sacrificed permanence by joining a temporary team away from the home office. This anxiety is often detrimental to group performance, and the individual's working relationship with the project team becomes disrupted.

2. The subcontracting company may now wish to reassign the individual to another project which begins to take precedence over tasks in the final stages of the project work. The team member receives instructions from two different authorities (project manager and company line manager), and it is natural that the line manager will take precedence at this time.

To resolve these problems, the project manager must try to promote a good supportive working relationship among team members and encourage identification with the project and project team from commencement. Status and rivalries are less distinct in the project structure, and the quality of the individuals' contribution to the team is of greater importance. A well-planned program of work, an established hierarchy of reporting procedures, and regularly scheduled meetings all assist the individual to enter and contribute to the team and process.[3]

Actions to Be Taken at This Time

- Project manager:

    Defining client's project needs

    Assisting research of market and geographic conditions

    Assisting negotiations with government authorities

    Assisting with land negotiations

    Assisting with financial packages

    Developing procurement strategies

    Advising the client on selection and appointment of project team members

    Negotiating contracts

    Assisting the client to select primary consultant

    Managing design development

    Assisting with feasibility studies

    Defining areas of risk

    Initiating research for procurement of resources and logistics

    Preparing schedules and programs

    Assisting in the decision-making process

    Assisting with negotiations with hotel management groups

    Managing submissions for interior design contract

Obtaining commitments

Organizing progressive reviews, regular meetings, and reporting hierarchy

Team building

Managing submissions for construction contract

- Architect and engineers

Assembling information, producing initial conceptual design in accordance with client requirements, requirements of government authorities, location, and other requirements

Obtaining approvals

Assisting with feasibility studies

Assisting with procurement programs

Assisting with formulation of programs and schedules

Assisting with appointment of other consultants

References

1. *Project Delivery System,* Canadian Public Works Department, Ottawa, Canada, 1989

2. Harold Kerzner, *Project Management, a Systems Approach to Planning, Scheduling and Controlling,* 3d ed., Van Nostrand Reinhold. New York, 1989.

3. *Master of Project Management Notes,* University of Technology Sydney, Broadway, Sydney, New South Wales, 1991.

4. W. S. Sawle, "Concerns of Project Managers: Crisis Project Management," *PM Network,* Vol. V, No. 1, January 1991.

Bibliography

Project Management Body of Knowledge: Standards, Project Management Institute of America, 1987.

5

Influences and Constraints

Once the investor and developers are satisfied that the project is financially viable and have agreed to proceed, the project manager and the project team must develop the initial concept sketches into a definitive statement of sufficient detail to use as a basis for design and construction. For example, the project team needs to establish which specialists are needed and how long their services will be required, estimate quantities of materials and technological equipment, and locate the sources of supplies with first and last dates that are acceptable for delivery to the construction site. This data forms a basis for the construction program and schedule and allows major milestones to be established.

Special influences, options, and project constraints will exist in each different project. They are in general identified during the preliminary investigations made for the feasibility study and determine the characteristics of the development.

The program of activities which is now commenced to produce the definitive "project brief" is best managed as a miniproject management system, for there are many implications to be studied and incorporated. Production strategies must not only aim to correlate the various requirements and special constraints into an attainable program and schedule for construction but also provide an opportunity to generate and compare alternative courses of action.

The project manager has a responsibility to supervise this program of activity, and ensure that costs of procurement tie in with the agreed-on budget.

Origins

The sources of the special influences and constraints that are major contributing factors to each particular project and that are of concern to the project manager, may be summarized as follows:

1. Influences directly connected with the customer-investor, owner, or developer: perceived market demand, available budget, future anticipated return on investment

2. Physical influences: geography, materials, and resources

3. Social influences: the host culture, neighbors, and project team

4. Technical influences

Variations and risk may always be anticipated which arise from unusual conditions and requirements of the project, and, additionally, the constraints imposed by the requirements of each of the four sources may alter as new information is accumulated.

Customer Influences and Constraints

The customer-client groups fall into two categories. The first includes all those concerned with development and construction. These are typically: investors, financiers, government agencies, designers, and contractors. The second includes all those concerned with the business operation of the hotel or resort: hotel management chains and their in-house operators. Both groups influence the outcome of a project through their own special expertise and identity.

Project Budget

The design, project management processes, ongoing management techniques, construction, and technology utilized for a new development are influenced by the type of facility planned, the location, and the budget available. Maximum advantage should be taken of the site for every project.

The first category of customer, those who initiate and find preliminary finance for the project, have a major influence on the physical outcome. They perceive a market opportunity, select and purchase land that is considered appropriate, approve design proposals, and have the continuing duty of decision making throughout the process. Decisions are made, however, based on the advice received from many other professional participants, including the hotel management group who will eventually operate the business and coordinate the hotel or resort's resources into a product that will meet the characteristics of market demand. The two categories of customers are therefore interdependent.

Market Influences and Constraints

Classification of Market Demand

The final physical product must respond to market demand (see, e.g., Fig. 5.1) and give the hotel operator the capability to deliver the product and service required.

There are numerous different ways of classifying hotels that have many identical and overlapping features and functions. A simple classification used to distinguish the type of management, facilities, and support equipment offered is that of the division into commercial hotel and resort hotel. The division has become in recent years far from clear-cut, however. A group of hotel types has emerged in downtown areas that cater to the holiday maker's needs by providing many facilities that are characteristic of a resort, as well as the more traditional requirements of visiting business personnel.[1] This type of development can often be observed in cities and towns of great historical, commercial, or geographic attraction, such as Sydney and downtown Honolulu.

Other classifications are based on budget, economy, quality, location, and user groups, for example, the convention hotel, casino, all-suite, summer resort, winter resort, and other combinations and alternatives[1] (see Chap. 4, Hyatt Hotel, Adelaide, South Australia).

The commercial hotel. The commercial hotel has always been typically located in a downtown area of a city or town, near an airport, or on a major highway close to a business center. The hotel has in the past provided accommodation chiefly for the business person whose usual length of stay was one or two nights only. However, market demand and expectation has in recent years widened the scope of the commercial hotel to include facilities that are typical of resorts. A greater provision has been made for recreation and exercise facilities, and the original basic products such as clean and comfortable rooms, food and beverage facilities, and courtesy and service have been improved by the addition of full office facilities and communication technologies. The majority of hotels in the United States came under the heading of commercial hotels in 1988.

Under the commercial hotel heading we may now list the following types, for example, commercial or transient hotels, motels and motor hotels, all-suite hotels, and convention-exhibition centers.[1]

All-suite hotels have become increasingly popular over the last decade and offer accommodation in the inner city for guests who require a longer stay, and for the business person accompanied by

Figure 5.1 Jing Guang Center Hotel, Beijing (Peking), China. In Beijing, the supply of guest rooms to international standard has been inadequate to meet demand in the last decade. The large Jing Guang Hotel Center responded to market needs by providing 18 floors of guest accommodation and a shopping center. Designed by Nihon Sekkei Inc., architects and engineers, Tokyo.

family members. The all-suite hotel room is really an apartment. It is 30 to 50 percent larger than the average hotel room and has a dining space and some facilities for food preparation. Space devoted to restaurant and kitchens in the all-suite hotel is considerably reduced compared with the traditional city hotel, and the hotel operator's involvement in the supply of food and beverage is limited to serving a light breakfast to guests only.

The resort hotel. Characteristics of the true resort hotel originally were quite different from those of the downtown hotel. The most important difference was the typical guest's average length of stay. The purpose of the guest's visit to the resort—vacation—provided a clear-cut criterion for classification; however, the inclusion in many resorts of conference facilities has brought in a business purpose and again blurs the distinction between the two types. Nevertheless, while the most recently developed resort hotels continue to cater primarily to guests' pleasure and relaxation, many resorts offer both conference facilities and a program of meetings for delegates with opportunities to participate in traditional vacation activities during the guests' stay.

Resort visitors are attracted to the resort by its reputation, scenic attractions, and recreational possibilities. Part of the attraction of a resort may be its remote and scenic location. Depending on location, the many combined facilities that guests expect to enjoy in the resort typically include golf courses, tennis courts, skiing, swimming, shopping, theater, night life, hiking, horseback riding, and the observation of local history and cultural traditions.

Some common advantages of the rural location are:

Cheap land. The typical resort needs plenty of space for recreational facilities.

Availability of government financial support for their national tourist industry. This may take the form of assistance with the installation of infrastructure, such as international runways, and/or investment incentives.

A ready market.

Special local attractions.

Operator Influences and Constraints

The hospitality industry is labor intensive, and the availability of a reservoir of human resources for staffing purposes may be a major constraint in a remote district. The resort, while dependent on and becoming the major employment source for the local village, must also provide a comprehensive in-house training facility. In addition, it is nearly always necessary for the developer to provide staff housing and recreational facilities for permanent senior staff drawn from other areas.

The type of project influences the type of management required, and in turn, the hotel management's style will influence the character of the hotel and resort. For example, all hotels have the same fundamental requirements for guests: clean and comfortable rooms, safety and protection of guests and their property, and the provision of attractive meals. There is scope for many variations beyond these requirements, and other factors such as quality, amenities, decor, prices, location, and types of restaurants are subject to interpretation by management. It is this ability to diversify and exercise choice that permits the large hotel chains to establish their own international identity. In addition, like any organization, the hotel is influenced by the individual personalities of the hotel manager and senior management.[1]

Hotel and Resort Management Style

Owners, operators, and hotel managers are naturally concerned primarily with general business economics and profit, and the need to match and fit their services to the market, particularly in a highly competitive industry. One of the project manager's duties during the project process is to monitor and ensure that the finished product can be run as a successful investment, and especially during the planning and design stage, the project manager must therefore rely on the advice of experienced operators.

The style of management required for a commercial hotel differs from that for a resort. This variation arises from the differing characteristics of the two products. For example, the main product of the resort is recreation, relaxation, and pleasure. The operator undertakes to provide guests on vacation with opportunities for these kinds of experiences, and the physical planning and design of resort facilities should necessarily be oriented to promote this task. When conference centers are incorporated, management is expected to plan schedules so that delegates may combine business with pleasure and enjoy both types of activities.

The resort manager therefore has much more connection on a personal, face-to-face basis with guests and will endeavor to promote a feeling of warmth, hospitality, and rapport far more than is necessary for success in a commercial hotel. The hotel manager is required to be constantly involved in public relations activities not only with guests but with local residents as well. Personal style becomes an essential ingredient for success.[1]

Both physical and technical constraints arise from the organizational needs of management and administration. These requirements are conditioned by the hotel manager's previous experience of the essential facilities which are needed to keep the hotel running smoothly and economically, and by the hotel group's desired image for the project. For example, supplementary facilities may include special air-conditioned storage areas for supplies which cannot be readily obtained by the remote resort. The design team must make adequate provision for these needs during planning and preparation of architectural and engineering design.

Fortunately in resort development, the capital outlay for land is not so great as for the city hotel, and extraspecial requirements can be successfully balanced within the budget.

Figure 5.2 Radisson Plaza Hotel, Cairns. The Hotel, seen in the foreground of the photograph, is associated with a large retail shopping center and marina. The shopping center occupies two floors under guest rooms which are oriented toward the marina and harbor.

Recent changes. Most city hotels now include facilities which overlap with the concept of the resort. For example, those built recently incorporate a fitness center, holiday-type shopping arcades, and entertainment facilities within the structure of the building.

Radisson Plaza Hotel, Cairns, Queensland

A typical example, the Radisson Plaza Hotel, Cairns, has been constructed with shopping arcades both beneath and adjacent to the hotel. The operator intends to take advantage of this potential tourist market by providing facilities such as the type and quality of restaurants that are seen as part of the shopping activity and holiday experience elsewhere. These will attract not only hotel guests but also the outside community to the hotel. (See Fig. 5.2.)[2]

Each large hotel group with an international leisure image tends to concentrate on one particular area for development until it has established sufficient facilities in the region to satisfy projected tourist demand. There have been many recent changes in the composition of the international market, and further changes will come with the economic maturation of other Asian nations.

The nationality of the tourists who make up the larger proportion of the market also influence the type of facility developed in many small but influential ways. For example, the extensive Japanese tourist market appreciates a grand entrance lobby, accommodation with twin beds, and a large and deep bath.

The American market is very security-conscious, and card-key systems and room safes are provided. This market expects to have large, separate showers.[2]

Expectations may diversify again within the next few years as other national tourist markets expand.

Physical Influences and Constraints

The need to provide for the guest's demand and expectations raises many issues connected with the physical planning of the facility. The resort, especially when in a remote location, must be self-contained, providing transport for guests, an adequate supply of water, a supply of energy which must be generated within the resort, and adequate refrigeration and storage for the continuing provision of food and domestic items.

Within the different categories, each project demands a particular mixture of resources and technology which essentially influence the design, type, methods and program of construction, and form of the final product. These influences fundamentally affect planning and design, including the content and breakdown of construction tasks, the sequence of the critical path of activities, and the necessary strategies for supply and commissioning of the development program. The facility must be designed to include concern for future maintenance of buildings and grounds, for continuing productivity and return on the business is dependent not only on courtesy and service but also on the physical condition of the property. This factor may present problems in rural locations, and materials and finishes should be selected with this consideration in mind.

The operator needs and recommendations form a basis for design and selection of technological equipment during the planning and development phases. Their input should include suggestions for the type and extent of technical service necessary, for example, space requirements; planned energy conservation and heat exchange equipment; requirements for natural light and solar energy use for management offices; centralized computer control, to provide an "intelligent" hotel building (this is particularly necessary for the casino and convention hotel); easily maintained equipment and planned preventive maintenance; adequately planned kitchen and laundry facilities; provision of adequate space in public restrooms; adequate storage facilities for housekeeping and restaurants (there are never enough); and a planned work flow for staff and service.

Recreational facilities, such as a fitness center of adequate size for the establishment, are becoming increasingly common in the city hotel. Already fitness centers are being installed in most new projects, with size as an important factor. A fitness center which is too small may repel guests rather than attract them.

Other provisions that are gaining popularity for the city hotel market are squash courts and a billiards room. All these facilities serve to attract an additional market other than the traditional hotel guest.[2]

Geographic Influences

Many of the other physical influences and constraints that affect the design of a hotel or resort and consequently the final product, are imposed in one way or another by its geographic and site characteristics.

Wherever the environment is particularly sensitive, many important conservation issues must be considered. Damage to the local natural resources will eventually destroy the original attraction and therefore the market value of a resort project. An environmental impact study (EIS) first analyzes the current natural and social conditions and then becomes a tool which can be used by the project team to detect areas of risk and constraint so that alternatives can be developed to protect and maintain both the environment and investment. Some recent practical examples which are discussed in this chapter illustrate problems and solutions that have been made to deal with quite severe constraints imposed by the environment. It is recommended, therefore, that an EIS be undertaken during the planning or early development phase to assist design development and decision making, even if it is not a government requirement.

For convenience, the influences that are imposed on design development by the environment are discussed under three headings:

1. Development in urban centers

2. Environmental conservation

3. Developing the environment to meet market demand

Development in Urban Centers

In the urban setting, the project is in most cases a single high-rise hotel development or multifunctional high-rise facility. These may be a hotel with all-suite, serviced apartments; an associated convention center; shopping arcades; or any mixture of these in varying proportions to the whole design. Factors that influence the design and construction of a development in the urban location are typically

Traffic

Zoning—height restrictions, the ratio of total building area to the site, urban density

Local impact on services—sewerage, water supply, power supply

The need to conserve adjacent historic and heritage buildings

Shadowing of other buildings

The influence of, and need to coordinate with, adjacent buildings and their structure and functions

Local residents

Any solution to these urban constraints must also comply with regulations and meet with the full approval of the various government authorities. It is essential that the project manager ensure that time and money are not wasted by proceeding with design and documentation until all these obligations are met and approvals confirmed.

Major traffic flows and one-way streets in the vicinity of a proposed hotel often restrict the approaches and therefore the location where passenger arrivals and departures are permissible. The delivery of hotel supplies; garbage disposal and parking lot entrances must also be planned and cannot interfere with the flow of main traffic routes in the city, or with access to the hotel. Inner-city traffic flows also impose constraints on the planning and programming of construction site operations, such as the delivery of building materials, particularly very large items such as steel or precast beams, and large-scale equipment, such as cranes and air-conditioning plants. At times, these constraints determine the critical path of construction activities.

Both the hotel under construction and the operational hotel must be planned for these constraints. The agreement and approvals of the local government transport and traffic police departments seek to ensure that the impact of the increased traffic flow generated by the hotel is acceptable to the situation existing in the immediate vicinity prior to commencing construction.

Traffic Constraints: Nikko Hotel, Sydney, Australia[3]

The "Nikko Hotel" (also known as the "Corn Exchange Hotel"), recently opened in downtown Sydney, Australia, was developed in joint venture with a Japanese investor, by Civil and Civic Constructions Pty. Ltd. on a design-construct contractual arrangement.

The site partially consisted of air rights over major and minor roads. The development incorporates national heritage buildings which, forming part of the old Corn Exchange, were renovated and preserved as part of the condition for government approval of the development and the southbound lanes of the multilevel expressway. The site is bounded by an expressway and the harbor to the west. To the east, a narrow access lane, Day Lane, was in use behind the historic stone buildings which fronted onto Sussex Street. This usage had to be preserved. The Sussex Street frontage has one-way traffic flowing to the north only. (See Fig. 5.3.)

The constraints of traffic pattern and flow surrounding the development affected two general spheres of activity: hotel construction and hotel operation. The identical constraints, which imposed the need for coordination with the surrounding traffic flow on the construction process, were also judged, unless satisfactorily resolved, to severely limit the future operation of the hotel. They had to be resolved and agreed on and approved by the Department of Transport and Police Departments before planning approval could be obtained and construction proceed. (See Fig. 5.4.)

Problems with construction. Special problems encountered while creating a plan and strategy for the construction period included planning and establishment of the site, delivery and use of heavy equipment, materials storage, safety and protection of the public and construction crew, materials delivery to the site, and other vehicular arrivals and departures. The project management team were responsible for the clarification and subsequent planning, supervision, and continuous monitoring of the design solution, as well as safety procedures during the construction process.

Hotel operation. It was essential that the final design solution would also resolve operative problems including the coordination of guests' vehicular arrivals and departures, which are typically by taxi, tourist and airport buses, and delivery of hotel supplies with the flow

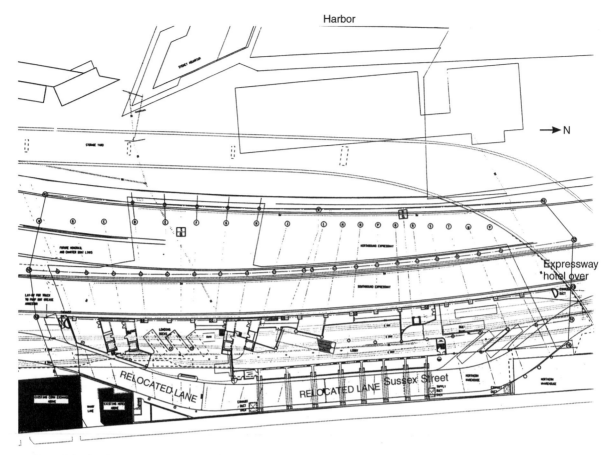

Figure 5.3 Site Plan, Nikko Hotel, Sussex Street, Sydney, Australia. The relationship of the hotel to the Bradfield Expressway (a freeway carrying north/south-bound traffic), Darling Harbor, Day Lane, and Sussex Street can be seen from the plan. Civil and Civic Constructions Pty. Ltd.: design-construct managers

Figure 5.4 Nikko Hotel, Sydney. A photograph of the hotel taken during construction shows the provisions made for public safety and protection, over the freeway. (Photograph by Civil and Civic Constructions Pty. Ltd., Sydney.)

of the neighboring traffic system. Further, strategies for baggage-handling systems and the delivery of hotel equipment and material supplies had to be resolved.

Solutions. The strategies thatwere developed for site planning, materials handling, delivery of equipment, and public safety during construction also assisted the resolution of the problems of arrival and delivery to the operational hotel.

1. *Rerouting of Day Lane:* (Fig. 5.5) A tunnel was replanned for the level under the stone warehouse buildings. Major services, such as sewerage, had first to be diverted and replaced under the new Day Lane construction. This project involved the demolition by numbered sections of some of the preservation buildings which were replaced after construction of the lane was sufficiently advanced. The structural brick and stone walls of other historic buildings were supported by reinforced concrete beams and columns. The tunnel provided a two-way vehicular approach to the construction site, solving the problem of one-way northern flow in Sussex Street and now provides access to hotel loading docks and contains a reception area for tourist coaches.

2. *The expressway:* The main hotel towers span the expressway and much of the major construction necessarily proceeded above the southbound lane. Heavy construction work had to be planned to take place during the night and early morning in order to ensure safety and minimal interference with normal traffic flow. The main hotel now spans the expressway with a major 2-meter(m) -deep posttensioned beam transfer system.

Figure 5.5 Nikko Hotel, Sydney. The original Day Lane now exists as an internal shopping arcade within the hotel. A new road has been built underneath the original to provide access for guest transport, hotel delivery, and through traffic to other buildings facing on to Sussex Street.

Environmental Conservation

At the present time, the natural environment in remote areas throughout the world is a major attraction for the tourist market. The ecological systems are usually very fragile and, if the environment is to remain unspoiled when the resort is fully operative, there is a strong need to preserve the environment by careful forward planning and detailed design of the final form and characteristics of the type of allowable development. Unique natural ecological systems in outback Australia demonstrate this fragility.

A recent example from Australia can be used to illustrate how the developer, designer, and hotel operator have reacted to and related the design to local environmental influences and constraints.

Seven Spirits Bay, Northern Territory, Australia[4]

An aboriginal community in the Northern Territory in Australia (see Fig. 5.6) wished to take advantage of the opportunities offered by the rare geography, flora, and fauna of their traditional land holding, to become less dependent on government subsidies. The community is part of a very old culture, markedly different from European culture, which traditionally occupied a land now designated as a nation-

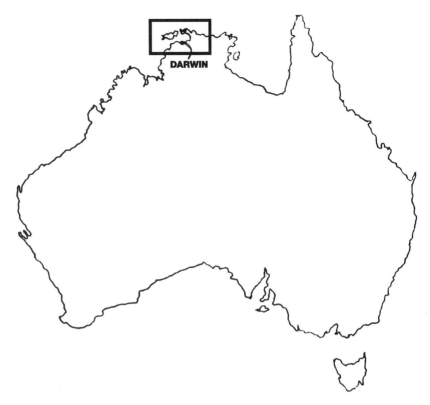

Figure 5.6   Seven Spirits Bay Resort, Northern Territory, Australia. Location map.

al wilderness park. The proposal for a resort originated with the Cobourg Peninsular Sanctuary Board, set up particularly to protect land belonging to the local aboriginal community in the far north of Australia, from exploitation. Local acceptance and approval was, however, essential before development could proceed. The Cobourg Peninsular Sanctuary Board accordingly invited interest from investors to lease a small area for the development of an adventure and cultural resort, and a concept was agreed on for Seven Spirits Bay on the Cobourg Peninsular. (See Fig. 5.7.)

Constraints.   It was recognized that the natural and social environments of the Cobourg Peninsular could not withstand visits from a large volume of tourists. A low-impact policy was essential. This proposal correlated with the Sanctuary Board's policy in general, and was upheld by the Conservation Commission of the Northern Territory, legislation such as the Aboriginal Sacred Sites Act, and the long-term distrust by the local community for European settlers based on historic events. A condition for the establishment of the resort therefore was the developer's sensitivity toward and ability to maintain a good relationship with the community while appreciating the spiritual significance of the connections between the local residents and the environment. The continuing success of this resort now depends on management's skills in maintaining a three cornered friendly relationship between management, guests, and local people.

An environmental impact statement was undertaken under the provisions of the Northern Territory Environmental Assessment Act.

Seven Spirit Bay

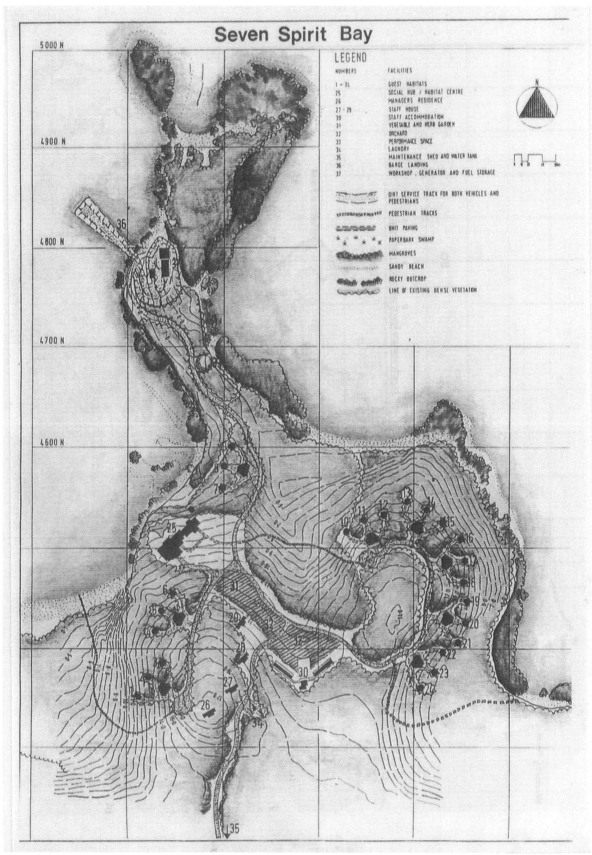

Figure 5.7   Seven Spirits Bay Resort. Site plan. (Drawing: Seven Spirits Bay Resort.)

Figure 5.8   Seven Spirits Bay Resort. Latitude 12. (Photograph: Seven Spirits Bay Resort.)

The site area, approximately 12 square kilometers (km²), with 6 kilometers (km) of coastline, includes stretches of eucalyptus and rain forests, melaleuca lagoons, and mangrove. (See Fig. 5.8.) There are white sandy bays and rivers, and many varieties of wildlife indigenous to the region, including a great variety of birds, porpoises, whales, and crocodiles. The ruins of the early European settlement of Victoria are about three hours' distance by boat. This historic settlement failed for lack of water, but now, imported herds of buffalo, deer, and ponies which were abandoned by the early settlers are flourishing.

Figure 5.9   Seven Spirits Bay Resort. View of prefabricated units from the restaurant.

Logistics: materials and resources. The coordination of supply of materials and resources with major events in the construction program was particularly difficult. The resolution of these problems turned on the provision of suitable transportation, efficient programming, and establishment of achievable delivery dates of supplies. Materials and resource supply and delivery is a constraint often encountered in the development of international resort projects and always demands efficient programming, scheduling, and timely placing of orders for materials and supplies. In many instances materials and supplies that are at first considered most desirable for use prove to be impractical because delivery times do not meet the critical path of the construction program.

Solutions: planning a construction program. The developers', park managers', and local owners' goal was to maintain the major part of the area in an original condition while providing an unusual experience for guests.

Environmental protection specifications were written into all the contracts issued to subcontractors and included penalties for failure to comply with requirements.

The buildings are designed in the form of 24 hexagonal prefabricated, lightweight, framed accommodation units which are planned around the central service core of the hotel (Fig. 5.9). This contains a restaurant, lounge, bar, kitchen, laundry room, and administrative offices and some other special facilities such as a darkroom for visiting photographers.

The site is utilized in such a way that individual units provide the maximum privacy for guests. The units are fitted with louvres allowing an airflow through the room and can be opened on the four sides that face away from other units and the hotel. The openings are protected by netting against insects, giving the illusion of camping in the midst of the wilderness. Air conditioning is not provided. The wilderness can also be enjoyed while using each unit's (semi-) outdoor bathroom (Fig. 5.10).

Two other major constraining factors had to be resolved during the planning stage: delivery of materials and equipment for construction, and the installation of services—energy, water, and sewage disposal—while achieving minimal impact of the environment.

Deliveries. Means of delivery of materials, equipment, and supplies for construction were necessarily limited to air and sea, and therefore plans were made to deliver the bulkiest sections in special barges. Prefabricated building parts had to be as lightweight as possible with easy methods of assembly. A special barge, designed and built to accommodate the requirements imposed by construction needs, was capable of transporting the maximum-sized equipment and is now in use for the purposes of delivery of fuel for the generator, materials, and supplies to the hotel, and for the of removal of waste materials. A special landing stage had to be constructed.

Energy. The immediate problems were the supply of power for construction equipment and a later supply for the operational resort. A

Figure 5.10 Seven Spirits Bay Resort. Outdoor bathroom. (Photograph: Seven Spirits Bay Resort.)

generator was therefore one of the first necessities to be delivered to the construction site. The hotel now relies on generated power, as solar panels are impractical for several months of the year during the rainy season of this latitude. The use of the generator must be limited to hours when noise will be of least inconvenience to guests. Power lines have been installed underground.

Water.   In this region, a readily available, constant, and adequate supply of potable water is a limiting and deciding factor in the location of the building. The old Victoria Settlement, which provides an historic example of failure through lack of an adequate water supply, was a constant reminder of constraints imposed on development in this region during the selection of the site for the modern resort. The site which was finally selected after geologic analysis of the region has a permanent underground supply of good water at a short distance from the resort.

The pipeline for bore water, as with other services, was laid underground with as little disturbance to the environment as possible. The resort is planned by the shoreline and sea water is utilized for other requirements such as flushing W.C.s.

Waste disposal.   A waste-disposal system can have a highly injurious impact on the environment if poorly designed. The resort's specific waste-disposal problems were solved by the construction of individual septic tanks for each group of three hexagonal units (eight in all). Other waste materials are removed by barge.

Supplies.   The resort continues to receive supplies once or twice a week by barge, although some provisions are flown in daily from Darwin, coinciding with the main method for guest transportation (light aircraft). The operators depend on a supply of fresh fish, caught by guests and employees of the hotel. It is possible to sample local meats, such as buffalo, crocodile, and venison, and the hotel operators have started a garden for the supply of fruit and vegetables.

Developing the Environment to Meet Market Demand

Ko Olina Resort, Oahu, Hawaii, USA[5]

The Ko Olina Resort project is located to the west of Honolulu. In 1990, a golf course and clubhouse had already been constructed and were in operation on the 640-acre [1,581.47-hectare (ha)] flatland which forms the proposed development site (Fig. 5.11). An analysis of market demand indicated an opportunity to establish a mixed-purpose resort with international standard hotels of 4000 rooms, residential facilities of 5200 rooms, a major retail center, and a yacht club, and appropriately expanded recreational facilities to complement the nearby golf course (already a major attraction). Among the new recreational facilities, the developers planned to include a marina to accommodate 500 boat slips and four swimming lagoons. (See Fig. 5.12.)

Figure 5.11   Ko Olina, Oahu, Hawaii. Golf Clubhouse, Ko Olina Resort. Leo A. Daly, structural engineers.

Figure 5.12   Ko Olina Resort, Hawaii. The 640-acre West Beach is a planned community. The resort will contain international standard hotels and resorts, private residences, and a shopping village which are all planned around the large marina and swimming lagoons. The marina and lagoons had to be specially constructed from land from the site and a rocky coast. Leo A. Daly, design engineers.

Figure 5.13 Ko Olina, West Beach Resort, Hawaii. View of recently constructed lagoon.

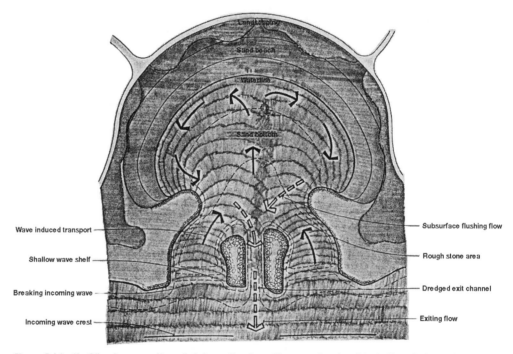

Wave induced transport

Shallow wave shelf

Breaking incoming wave

Incoming wave crest

Subsurface flushing flow

Rough stone area

Dredged exit channel

Exiting flow

Figure 5.14 Ko Olina Lagoons, Hawaii. Schematic plan of lagoon, showing the shallow shelves which were built to control wave forces and the flow of water, and to promote a flushing circulation. Leo A. Daly, design engineers.

Constraints. The rockiness of the nearby shoreline initially placed major constraints on the potential for the new resort concept and marina. The construction of sandy lagoons which would be appropriate for sunbathing and swimming and a deep, safe haven for yachts were essential to fulfill market demand and particularly to compete for customers with other resorts in the Hawaiian Islands.

Solutions. A 37-acre (91.39-ha) marina has been carved out of the plain, and four swimming lagoons containing beaches of white sand

Figure 5.15 New Inhali Hotel, West Beach Resort, Ko Olina, Hawaii. Leo A. Daly, structural and building services engineers.

have been constructed along 2 miles (mi) (3.25 km) of coast where large rocks once met the ocean.(See Fig. 5.13.)

The marina shares an ocean access with a nearby commercial harbor, and includes a yacht club, temporary berths, a public boat ramp, boat services and fueling dock, and other facilities and services to serve visitors and the boating community. The lagoons were modeled on the wave action and wave flow of the nearby Paradise Cove lagoon system. The design required extensive local environmental analysis into the conditions of soils, tsunamis, storm wave conditions, and longshore currents. A major design problem was the reduction of wave size, and the creation of flushing and circulatory water action in the crescent-shaped lagoons. Study models were first made, and the objectives of wave action control were achieved by means of the careful design of the lagoon mouth, the shaping of the lagoon section, and closely monitored construction procedures. (See Fig. 5.14.) A landscaped promenade has been made for guests along the edge of the beaches.

There were few problems connected with the delivery of equipment and supplies to the construction site in the case of this project, as there is an existing nearby four-lane highway serving the west of the island. Waste disposal, however, had to be carefully considered and planned so as not to destroy the natural and artificial environment.

The 383-room luxury hotel "Ihilani" was one of the first to open (Fig. 5.15).

The Creative Solutions to Constraints: Summary

The discussions of the current examples above serve to illustrate solutions to some very difficult environmental problems that have placed constraints on the design and development of different types of resorts. Many other modern examples could be used for illustration, especially in a country such as Australia, where the tourist industry is currently expanding rapidly, and designers are only just beginning to gain experience of the interface with the very fragile and unique ecological system.

In the projects illustrated, the original concepts, first stimulated by market interest and demand, have been met in such a way that the physical environment has been preserved and even enhanced in a manner that can be maintained and will contribute to the success of the resort operation.

Problems that arise from commonly encountered general constraints always have special attributes arising from the unique total environment of each project, which make them project specific. Solutions must be "tailor-made" for each project, as the examples presented above illustrate.

It is essential that the project manager and the project design and construction team be prepared for creative "lateral" thinking in order to solve these problems efficiently. During the design development and documentation stage every team member, including designers and technical, construction, and trades personnel must participate in problem-solving activities and contribute to the solutions from their specialized knowledge. Contributions that arise from team sources will help provide an efficient resolution for major issues and develop a choice of cost saving and contingency alternatives for development of the main program and process.

The early involvement of team members has the additional advantage of encouraging "ownership" attitudes that will continue through the life cycle of the project. These will be a valuable asset for the management of quality assurance, cost control and commissioning procedures as the process of development proceeds.

Actions to Be Taken at This Time

- Project manager:

    Establish project management system

    Plan programs and schedules

    Acquire information

    Establish communication system and database

    Procure specialized technical resources

    Coordinate specialists with project team

    Prepare EIS

    Supervise preparation of required design and documentation

    Supervise submissions for approvals from state and local government authorities

- Architects and engineers:

    Produce creative input for problem solving

    Design and document solutions

    Plan programs and schedules

    Acquire information

    Establish communication system and database

Produce specialized technical resources

Coordinate specialists with project team

Prepare EIS

Supervise preparation of required design and documentation

Supervise submissions for approvals from state and local government authorities

■ Architects and engineers:

Produce creative input for problem solving

Design and document solutions

References

1. Chuck Y. Gee, *Resort Development and Management*, 2d ed., The Educational Institute of the American Hotel & Motel Association, East Lansing, Michigan, 1988.

2. Alan Featherby, Deputy Managing Director, Radisson Hotel Group, Australia, and Art Kreiger, Manager, The Radisson Plaza Hotel, Cairns, *Discussions: Radisson Hotel Group*, 1992.

3. J. Frost, Project Director, Civil and Civic Constructions Pty. Ltd., *Discussions, Nikko Hotel, Sussex Street, Sydney Development*, Sydney, Australia, 1992.

4. S. Noonan, Manager, Seven Spirits Bay Resort, *Discussions: Resort Development*, Seven Spirits Bay Wilderness Pty. Ltd., Cobourg Peninsular, Northern Territory, Australia, 1991.

5. E. Cambridge, Senior Vice President, Leo A. Daly International, architects and engineers, Honolulu, Hawaii, *Discussions, Ko Olina Resort Development*, 1991.

6

Development: 2 Establishing a Strategy for Implementation

During Phase 2 of the development cycle, the general parameters of the project management system are brought together in order to support the commencement of detailed technical documentation of the project. Strategies for planning and control are planned and established. There are many diverse factors to study, clarify, coordinate, and document, especially in hotel and resort development, and these combine to produce management tasks of great complexity. It is inevitable, therefore, that a large project be divided into many subprojects for management and control purposes and responsibility delegated by the project manager among senior team members. Indeed the tasks that contribute to this phase demand from the project manager the most concentrated effort of the entire process.

The project management system is the most suitable management system for a complex project with a short-term life cycle of development because it has a broad-based hierarchical structure. This type of structure promotes flexibility of control, free flow of information, and the capability to determine an appropriate balance between innovative and supportive actions on one hand, and the payoff to be gained from each according to the current situation and project characteristics on the other hand.

Translating Client Needs into Technological Criteria

In addition to many different functional needs, hotels have many different customers whose requirements must be satisfied. Some have already been discussed in detail in other chapters. A resort development offering a mixture of market opportunities, such as relaxation, recreational, and business services, will need technical expertise and input from different professions and trades during project design, documentation, and construction.

The prime activities in the development phase are the translation of client needs into technical criteria that will satisfy the constraints imposed on the project by the total environment and the distribution of this information to participants for processing and development.

Some tasks to be addressed in this phase of the project are translation of the client's needs into technical criteria; appointment of design teams; development of design, documentation, and procurement strategies; incorporation of constraints within design solutions; evaluation of proposals within budget limits; determination of risk and evaluation of alternative courses of action; development of programs and schedules; resource allocation and programming; design of quality assurance and cost-control programs and schedules; development of programs for commissioning; balancing and validation of documentation and logistics; and acquisition of approvals.

Developing Strategies for Management and Control of the Process

At the start of the project, there are two essential tasks among the diversity of duties that the project manager must execute immediately: (1) establishment of a management hierarchy for responsibility and accountability and (2) implementation of information-processing methodology (Fig. 6.1). These two play a basic part in both initial planning activities and ongoing management and control of the process; the technology of one becomes a supportive tool for the function of the other.

The management hierarchy establishes channels for reporting and securing approvals and a method for allocating tasks among the team members.

An information-processing system, by providing an easily accessible source of project data, links each member of the extended team into the project's channels of accountability; assists the spread of project data and status reports, and identifies members of the group to others as specialists in fields of technical expertise.

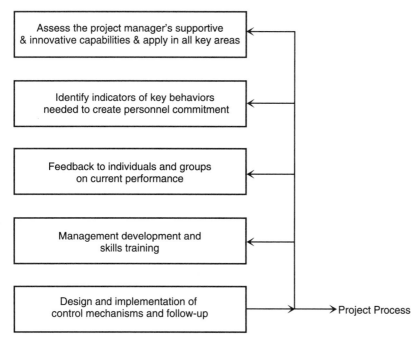

Figure 6.1 Cultivating a commitment among team members. The translation of the objective of team commitment into everyday behavior patterns requires a systematic approach. Project leaders need skill to assist the implementation process, and training may be necessary for the team. (After *Rossy, June 1992.*)

Hierarchy of Accountability

The channels and direction of reporting should be especially created to suit each unique project concept. Reporting channels are short in the project management system, and so greater responsibility is borne by each member of the team. The project manager must submit major decisions to the owner-client for formal approval, and team members contribute reports to the project manager with responsibility for the quality and correct performance of their area of expertise. Moreover, the system that works best is an open, two-way process capable of disseminating new ideas and information and giving feedback data quickly. It must have the flexibility to serve any unexpected situations that arise in the development process.[1]

Information Processing

From concept phase onward, good communication between team members plays a vital part in information processing and the distribution of data for successful management of the project process. (See Fig. 6.2.)

A summary of the objectives of a good system of information processing would typically include the following:

Familiarizing the team with project goals and objectives

Coordinating designs, programs, and schedules

Providing data and an approval mechanism on which to base design and documentation development

Providing a source of easily accessible information for decision making and approval processing

Data item distribution matrix		Project manager	Project team	Team member	Owner & operator	Construction manager	Resource source companies
Item	Description of data						
1	Monthly progress reports	X	X		X	X	
2	Monthly cost summaries	X	X	X	X	X	
3	Inspection & milestone reports	X	X	X	X	X	
4	Request for approvals	X		X	X		
5	Requests for progress payments	X			X		
6	Commissioning & test results	X	X	X	X	X	X
7	Requests for variation	X	X	X	X	X	
8	Scheduling summaries	X	X		X	X	X

Figure 6.2   A data distribution matrix. This matrix diagram illustrates a very simple format for data distribution among the extended team and must include the owner-client's decision makers. A similar matrix, with fully defined and detailed distribution, should be made for each project.(*After Kerzner, 1989.*)

Providing a method for maintaining continuous control and direction

Gaining team commitment to the project and the process of production

Providing a common basis of information which can easily be referred to by all team members during the performance of their project tasks

Monitoring progress and ensuring areas of uncertainty and risk are recognized[2]

Developing Technological Tools to Assist the Process

Communication systems networks. Communication systems networks are technological tools which serve information processing in all management systems. They are particularly important to the short-term project with a wide-based management structure, because the output of many skilled employees, who function at the same level, must be interconnected. One of the major team objectives during the development phase, therefore, is to plan and implement a communication network system that links the project owner, project manager, user group, project team, and construction teams.

The design of the communications system is dependent on the verification of the delegation of responsibility and authority within the hierarchy. It is therefore best to plan a strategy for the use of the system, once reporting hierarchies and team responsibilities have been allocated. (See Fig. 6.3.)

The network system must provide the team with detailed information about project resources, technical data, schedules, and programs at any point in the project process and assist decision-making procedures by providing immediate access to relevant information for dis-

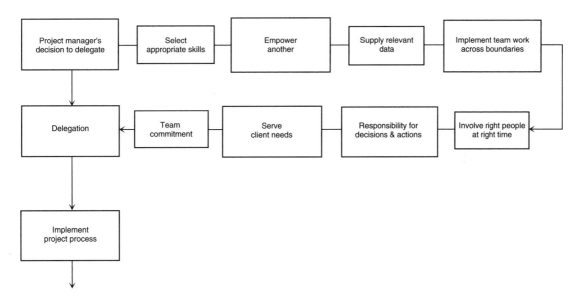

Figure 6.3 The process of delegation. Once the project manager decides to delegate specific project management tasks, a loop process takes place. The newly delegated officer assumes responsibilities to the project manager and main and subsidiary project processes, counting on the support and assistance of all team members. (*Dessler, 1987.*)

cussion and action. Lack of data may enforce uninformed compromises which are very likely to affect the budget, schedule, and overall success of the project. Moreover, it must be remembered that it is a two-way process which not only circulates data to the project team members, but feeds back information that allows approvals and decisions to be made.

A communication system that provides for daily exchange among project team members ideally has the capability to make information readily available through discussion and contact, control and maintain the circulation of information to each team member, ensure that relevant information is supplied to each specialist, update the team with new information, plan and report meetings, encourage participation in problem solving, issue unambiguous instructions based on up-to-date information, and obtain feedback from the team.[2]

Training programs in the use of the communications network will most certainly become necessary for some groups, and allowances of budget and time should be made during the process of planning information-processing strategies.[3]

It is recommended that information processing and the communications network system be implemented by means of a supporting miniproject within the main project process. The program should have the same phases and stages of all project management systems, and be designed especially to suit each project's needs and characteristics.

Delegation of responsibility. Although a team member is usually delegated by the project manager to undertake the responsibility of planning and establishing the network, it is important that the project manager remain closely involved in the process, for the implementation of this program offers the project manager an early opportunity to establish personal leadership and other management skills and qualities, and in addition assists the promotion of team commitment, identification with the project, and encouragement of group interaction. Once the network is established, it will continue to serve the project throughout the life cycle of the process.[1]

The following information-handling strategies are used to establish a workable system and to provide the project manager, all team members, and clients with information when required:

Delegation of a team member to develop a plan and control the system

Appointment of other team members for specific responsibilities at focal points in the process or system

Reconciliation of the first plan for information processing with the specific needs and requirements of the project

Establishment of programs and schedules for meetings and methods of record keeping

Design of information handling units of suitable capacity to avoid overload (taken from the definition of major work elements of production)

Selection of technology to be used, including methods and computer programs

Implementation of the communications network

Scheduling of training programs

Training the team in clear communication techniques and responsibilities

The system should be flexible in order to support, initially, documentation and procurement and subsequently the ongoing work of management and control. It must be continuously monitored to ensure that data is supplied in accordance with the main schedule and is appropriate for the special areas of concern.[2]

The establishment of a communication system is also a prerequisite for obtaining data for cost planning, time and quality assurance programs, and reporting procedures.[4]

A Practical Example of Delegation. A team member was delegated for the management and control of costs on a resource procurement team for a downtown city hotel. This officer was responsible for the scrutiny, monitoring of quoted prices, and comparison of costs with budget estimates. He made regular weekly recommendations and reports that were circulated to the project and construction teams. The contribution enabled problem areas to be recognized at the time of tender, which was sufficiently early in the process to allow alternatives and opportunities to be discovered and integrated with the program and schedule. Many cost savings were made and problems forestalled.

Meetings and record keeping. Meetings can be a strong foundation for communications if well planned. It is important to the success of the communication process, therefore, that meetings be scheduled according to the need for discussion and the program of project development. Activities will include planning to meet schedules, which should be regular in the first stages of the process and become more flexible to meet requirements as the work proceeds, and record keeping. The records should be distributed according to attendance, on time (with assistance from other specialists), and circulated to other members of the team on a need-to-know basis. Team members who are responsible for special technical areas should be consulted.

In summary, the detailed tasks that implement information flow and responses include programming and scheduling regular project meetings, and arranging informal meetings on request; record keeping; report writing; planning and supervising circulation lists on a need-to-know basis; monitoring of documents, revisions, and revision dates coordinating PCs (personal computers), with main computer program; and monitoring of contributory programs for content and clarity.

Information transmission. During the development phase, the communications network functions to transmit information to support programming and the architectural and engineering design work which is part of the documentation activity. The easy-access system will transmit up-to-date information in one of two ways: visual or oral.

A communications model. A model of the function of communication was developed by Shannon and Weaver (1949) which shows (1) an information source, (2) a transmittal device, (3) an outgoing signal, and (4) a destination and receiver. (See Fig. 6.4.)

Shannon and Weaver draw attention to the "filter" or outgoing signal as the point in the system where a communication breakdown is most likely to occur, and demonstrate that information is often distorted at the filter point by several factors which typically arise from the characteristics of the policy set by management for control of the process. Distortion may also arise from problems of sender and recipient.[5]

Management policies which adversely affect communication and information processing. These policies are likely to include the following factors:

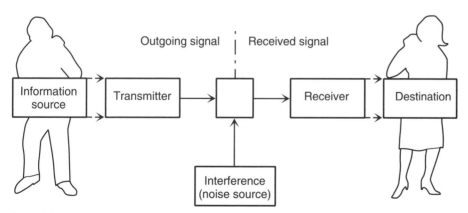

Figure 6.4 Communication. Information may arise from a single person, team, or company. The means of transmittal may be by face-to-face conversation, facsimile transmission, telephone, written reports, or other technologies. Misunderstandings and misconceptions often arise at the interface between transmitter and receiver when "noise" or interference has many causes. (*Shannon, 1949.*)

Information is insufficient and unavailable

No strong team commitment has been established

Reporting channels have not been clearly defined

Individual responsibilities have not been clearly defined

Working relationships of trust and respect between project manager and team, and among team members have not been established

Channels of communication and capacity for handling and information exchange are unplanned and inadequate

There is information overload

Some practical solutions. The project manager has the responsibility to assess project needs and decide how much data will be included in the information-processing network for each profession and trade. This is a difficult task and involves balancing conflicting objectives. Lack of time and appropriate education can confuse and inhibit understanding of technical information outside the participants' own field, and a balance must be made between sufficiency and oversupply. Training programs which enable the worker to understand technical drawings, for example, may have to be established.

Solutions to these problems require a flexible and open management approach adapted to the characteristics of each particular project. For example, the effects of a controlled increase in information flow to project workers was recently illustrated by the management policy of a large construction company who implemented a program for "multiskilling" of trades. Programs were set up for workers which included training outside their own regular trade skills. After successfully completing the program, workers were able to contribute to the process on a more continuous basis, and some enforced idle time was eliminated. The results of this initiative supported the premise that the dispersion of additional information not only increases understanding of the total process, motivates, and builds commitment but also encourages participation by way of valuable suggestions for alternative methods.

Problems of sender and recipient. An understanding and awareness of these problems are of importance to the project manager, for otherwise the management and control processes can be adversely affected. Such problems therefore warrant some detailed discussion.

Problems of communication which arise from either sender or recipient are similar. Those caused by the sender include the following:

The sender is unable to communicate clearly, causing ambiguity in the message itself

Information is transmitted only partially

The sender withholds information, and does not consider the information to reflect well on her or his abilities and professional standing (this is often the case in the transmission of bad news)

Problems at the receiver's end may arise from the following:

The receiver has preconceived notions of the nature of the work or problem under discussion

The receiver forms an incorrect opinion of the value of the information source and adjusts his or her understanding of the information accordingly

The receiver ignores conflicting or difficult information and hears only what she or he wants to hear

There may be a language problem[2]

Problems of language and trade use. Language differences present a problem for communication management especially in international hotel and resort work. For this reason, the client and project manager usually form an association with local professions (architects and engineers) who can assist with translation and site supervision. Trade expressions can also be a fertile source of misunderstanding, as the use of trade words varies considerably throughout the construction industry. Use varies between the United States, the United Kingdom, and Australia, and even between closely associated regions in the same country.

Project management software and the technology of communication. The use of project management computer software forms only a part of the technology of communication, by linking many of the functions of the system. A wide variety of computer programs used in project management have come onto the market in the last few years. Most are used for tasks such as feasibility studies; cost estimating; task scheduling; control of cost, time, and resources; the formation of databases; and the familiar computer-assisted design (CAD) programs which are used as an aide to architectural, engineering, and landscape design. (See Fig. 6.5.)

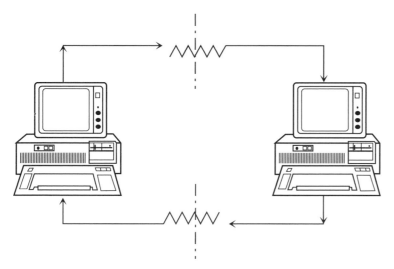

Figure 6.5 Communications technology: interteam-group data exchange. The project team and extended team may be linked by computer software management programs, CAD, and other means, for information processing and data transmission, if budget allows. In this way, team members can be quickly advised of new data; however, responsibility for keeping records up to date demands careful control and monitoring. It is often difficult to take advantage of these technologies on location, as initial installation costs are high.

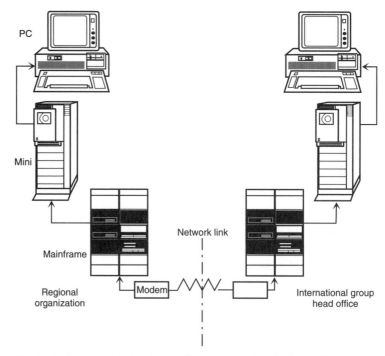

PC

Mini

Mainframe

Network link

Regional
organization

Modem

International group
head office

Figure 6.6   Data exchange network. Nowadays, the head offices of large companies and their national and regional offices are connected via satellite to private data center terminals. This technology permits immediate information processing and decision making, delayed only by world time zones.

During the course of a large project, it is difficult to monitor and maintain control of small additions and revisions and to constantly update information, especially if contributions can be made to the program from independent terminals. A team member (or members) should be appointed with the special responsibility of creating a system to manage and control input and, if budget allows, to ensure that all revisions are confirmed before circulation. (See Fig. 6.6.)

The installation and use of computer software programs may be over budget limits, especially for on-site development work in remote locations where hardware is unavailable. The project manager and team should study the computer program options in relation to the specific needs of budget and the characteristics of each project.

Creating Team Commitment: The Project Manager's Responsibility

A major challenge for the project manager is to devise a method of achieving team commitment to the project, and ensuring that these commitments are fulfilled during the project life cycle. The successful establishment of team commitment is a human relations management process and is always dependent on the clarity of communication between the extended team. (See Fig. 6.7.)

The team participant develops commitment by achieving a clear understanding and set of beliefs, values, and goals about the project. This development continues throughout the life cycle of the project and encourages the perseverance to complete assigned tasks while carrying out the participant's belief and values. The tasks that contribute to the development of commitment can be divided into two

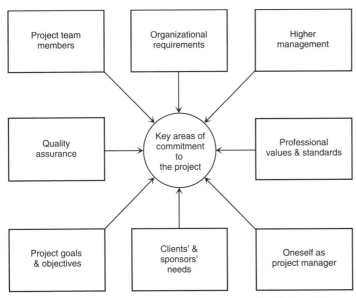

Figure 6.7   Key areas of commitment. The key areas of project activity which demand the project manager's and project team commitment are personal responsibilities, the owner-client's interests, project goals and objectives, the quality of production, team commitment, project management system requirements, and professional values and standards. *(After Rossey, June 1992.)*

categories: (1) team planning and control and (2) the project manager's leadership skills.[1]

These two factors cross the functional lines of management which unite team members with their permanent employer. This crossing of functional management lines often causes confusion regarding responsibilities and authority and goals and priorities.

Team planning and control.   This involves setting recognizable project goals and objectives; developing plans, schedules, and programs for the use of human resources; monitoring strategies of delegation; achieving the best utilization of available resources; and setting budgets and performance quality standards. Well-designed staff planning, programming and scheduling, and task definition are important requirements in gaining commitment, for no one can identify with a task which is ambiguous. If roles are not clearly defined, conflict will occur. All team members must fully understand their roles and responsibilities in relation to the overall program.[6]

In general, team members must know what is expected of them and the state of progress at any point in the schedule. Achievement of these objectives is assisted by facilitating the flow of information and ideas among the team; providing reliable and sufficient data to make the team member's contribution understandable in the overall program of the project; providing a basic method for monitoring the program, schedules, costs, and quality; and ensuring that continuing interaction takes place among team members and obtaining input from all team members so that creative alternatives are generated and solutions are provided quickly.

Leadership.   This involves influencing by example, giving direction and support. Commitment is unlikely to develop without demon-

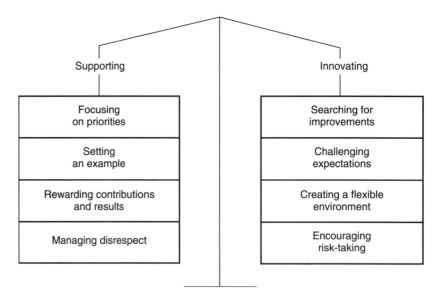

Figure 6.8 A comparison of supportive and innovative behaviors. The final goals and objectives of supportive and innovative behavior are complementary, but require different project management strategies to elicit each type of performance. Both these behavior patterns are necessary for the success of the process, and therefore must be balanced. (*After Rossy, June 1992.*)

strated leadership and personal commitment of the project manager, best shown through the key behavior described below:

Supportive behavior: The project manager exhibits supportive behavior by concentrating on the focal issues of project management and control, setting an example of commitment to the project, rewarding contributions, and managing instances of disrespect for other participants. By focusing on important issues, supportive behavior promotes the discovery of alternative opportunities in the project process, and gives goals and objectives priority. (See Fig. 6.8.)

Setting an example: The project manager must set an example of commitment to the project, which will effectively influence others to do likewise.

Rewarding contributions: It is recognized that praise and encouragement achieve far more than blame.

Managing disrespect: It is important for the continuing morale of the group that any negative comments or actions be discouraged. These may be derogatory comments about the client, other team members, the organization, or the team member's own task. Although this kind of comment is often meant to be facetious, it can easily undermine commitment.[2]

Innovative Behavior

The best time to build team allegiances and interaction between team members is during early documentation. This is also the time to discourage the rivalries and competition that often threaten to disrupt the smooth running of the project management system. Valuable creative responses to problematic issues arise when team members are committed to the project and are encouraged to challenge accepted work patterns and design solutions through open and relaxed discussion. Emphasis should be placed on the value of every contribution and the complementary nature of its function to the global process.[6]

It is traditional for the Japanese work force to participate in group discussion. Team members' suggestions are given consideration through a traditional business custom called *ringi-sei,* a custom which gives a format for planning and decision making through group consensus. However, in Western countries where a more rigid "functional" system of management has been prevalent until recently, the team may need some training before these techniques can be translated into operational behavior.[7]

Development of the Statement of Scope of Work

The statement of scope of work (project brief) is a detailed written description of the work that must be produced before execution of the project process can commence. Two major tasks contribute to production. First, both the client's intention for the concept and market requirements must be translated into detailed technical definition in order to establish a body of information on which to base design and documentation. This work is followed by the development of specifications for construction that will fall within budget requirements. Contractual agreements for procurement are based on the completed description.

Documentation

The planning process for the delivery of a large construction project is not only very complex in itself, but in addition, the owners' and users' original concept, being descriptive, must be translated into technical instruction. The initial concept of the completed physical design outcome is likely to be ambiguous and lack sufficiently well-determined objectives to use as criteria for technical detailing. The special constraints imposed by location and other factors unique to the project must also be taken into account.

With regard to the management of complexity and development of project definition and documentation, the process is divided into a collection of many smaller projects by adoption of a strategy of delegation. Work packages are established [termed *work-breakdown structures* (WBS)], for the purpose of implementation.

Defining Project Goals and Objectives

The communications–information–processing network links the evolution of the work packages of the WBS. It is used to assist coordination, integration, and the preparation of programs and schedules; and for transmitting the instructions conveyed in design drawings, quantities and specifications, and technical reports. Requirements must be

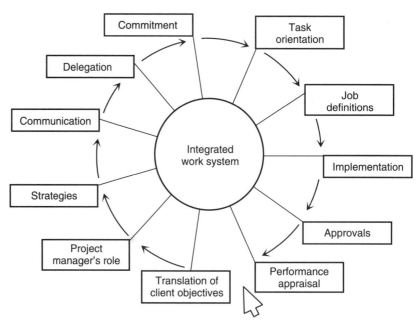

Figure 6.9 The integrated work system. Commencing with the translation of objectives into the statement of scope, the project manager initiates a program for task processing that connects all subsequent dependent tasks into the total process.

communicated with simplicity and clarity, together with adequate supportive background information. Management, control, coordination, and decision making all depend on the capability of the communication system to disperse data. (See Fig. 6.9.)

The exercise of fact-finding meetings that are held within the client's company or on location in one of the client's facilities have several advantages; for example, relationships can be established with the client and company employees from the start of the process, and suggestions and ideas for improvements for ongoing business procedures can arise. The use of questionnaires is very helpful for clarifying requirements.

The extended project team should be closely involved, for their advice and contributions are necessary. Team contributions should be prepared by architects, engineers, and landscape architects, for design; surveyors, for quantities and geotechnical data; lawyers, for advice on contracts; interior designers, for design and interior details; and the hotel operator, for hotel management strategies.

Current prices and the availability of supplies and delivery schedules must be obtained from suppliers of materials and equipment in order to assist the initial direction of ideas and formulation of design details during the documentation process. These must be defined in sufficient detail to enable bids to be called and realistic quotations to be received, so that contracting firms may be selected.

Communication breakdown and misrepresentation. A breakdown in communication between the owner, clients, and the project team at commencement results in issues which are disregarded or misrepresented during the development phase. These will surely cause variations later in the project life cycle, becoming very costly and taking the project over budget. Clear design criteria are essential.

Common causes of misrepresentation and breakdown during documentation and implementation of the delivery process are lack of clarity and definition in the statement of scope of work or in programming and description of work-breakdown units; failure to obtain reviews and approvals at the correct level, imprecise technical language and description; the specification of tasks being left open-ended, to be done "as necessary"; work-breakdown units too large to achieve precision; and variation in the quality of preparation of documentation and detailing.[2]

Project Design Criteria

The criteria which are used to evaluate resort or hotel products must be addressed within the design context. These are both general and specific to the project and influence both the outcome and the period required for production. The main criteria that are used are typically: the degree of satisfaction of market requirements that has been achieved (and therefore also concern actual and potential revenues), and the degree to which the project has fulfilled the owner and user's original concept and conditions.

Evaluative criteria which are general for the design of all buildings include suitability for purpose, safety, security, budget, and resource procurement. Some of these acquire particular importance for the detailed design of hotels and resorts, for example, safety of guests (especially evacuation in the event of fire), security of guests' belongings, capability of in-house service facilities, appropriateness and durability of finishes for hotel use, source and delivery of hotel supplies, and availability and coordination of guest transportation.

Elements of documentation. The essential elements of the documentation emerge from the conceptual sketch designs. Typically these are the work-breakdown structure; a definitive analysis of work content in the form of drawings, graphs, and reports; written specifications; major and auxiliary construction programs; and schedules of work duration and critical events.

The first sketch designs have already been approved by the owner. During the preparation of the documentation that defines and describes the scope of work, frequent reviews must be held with the clients and technical members of the project team to ensure that conformity of content is maintained with client and market needs, that the design objectives are feasible in the proposed form, and that sufficient information is available for the technical translation.

The client's formal approval must be obtained for each major decision. The importance of obtaining approvals from the owners and clients at frequent focal points throughout the development of documentation cannot be exaggerated, and the project manager should establish a schedule for approvals which equates with the major events in the documentation process and later during the program of construction.

In summary, the activities listed below are undertaken by the project manager during the execution of documentation:

1. Assign team members to specialized duties, including responsibilities for cost control; main and auxiliary construction programs; schedules; quality assurance, communications; logistics, labor relations, and safety and control strategies.

2. Prepare to coordinate input by establishing communications strategies and network for information exchange, approvals, and reporting.

3. Review all existing documents relating to the concept and sketch proposals, feasibility study, and approvals.

4. Identify tasks in relation to design criteria, documentation requirements, and special requirements of the project.

5. Establish a preliminary work-breakdown structure.

6. Assign specialist members of the team to the supervision of work-breakdown units and associated responsibility for document preparation.

7. Prepare a checklist showing the mandatory content for the preparation of technical documentation and the format of presentation.

8. List authority requirements and the approvals needed, with dates.

9. Identify critical dates and deadlines.

10. Establish schedules for submission of documentation.

11. Plan the schedule of meetings for briefing, coordination, and reviews. These will be adjusted later in accordance with the needs of the process, program, and schedules.

12. Determine the format of meetings.[2]

Working to budget. In the concept phase of the project, the project team investigates the financial feasibility of project development. At this time, the investor-client approves limits to be set for a budget based on the production of an acceptable return. During the development phase, the team proceeds to the task of clarifying and defining costs associated with different work-breakdown units and tasks, balancing costs of one unit against another and relating the aggregate to the budget allowance.[4]

The first budget, made at the concept-sketch design stage, is only an estimate of costs, and at the time, for reliability, the estimate is related to current prices in the building industry. Other projects are often used for comparison based on similarity of architectural details.

Plans for the allocation of monies to various work-breakdown units can commence only once the project enters the development phase with the start of detailed documentation. As design and documentation proceed and tasks are more clearly defined, the cost and quantities of resources can be calculated with increasing accuracy.

Total costs of development. The total costs of development are much higher than the cost of construction of the buildings and include

Acquisition of land, including legal costs

Legal fees associated with contract work

Preliminaries: costs of preparing the site, including demolition; costs of installation of infrastructure, (sewerage, roads, water supply lines, etc.)

Consultancy fees

Costs associated with obtaining government approvals

Holding costs on investment

Construction costs

Landscaping costs

Fit-out costs (high in hotel work)

Management and commissioning costs

Costs associated with client's special needs

Costs associated with the hedging of risk

Promotion and marketing costs

If any of these costs is abnormally high, other costs may have to be cut and the budget balanced accordingly. For example, some important client needs and requirements which affect costs and cost planning in hotel and resort development are staged completion, low maintenance requirements, meeting a guaranteed early opening date, importation of special materials and resources, and timing of cash flows.

The development of design detail, that meets the requirement of project needs and standards, places considerable responsibility on the project manager, architect, and engineers during the development phase. Details must be completed before bidding proceeds, as measurements will be taken from the documentation in order to calculate quantities and later, reliable comparisons between different bids are needed. These quantities and prices include costs of labor. Furthermore, the work of developing the documentation must usually be completed in a very limited time frame.

The documentation has yet to be handed to the trades and undergo the refinements given to shop drawings and may often still be quite a hypothetical construct within which later changes will occur. Bidding prices, therefore, rely to some extent on each bidding company's expertise and experience as well as the details of the documentation, to reflect a true price of project works.[4]

As bids serve as the basis to recommend acceptance of a contractor to the owner, and must be compared, in some countries the services of quantity surveyors are commissioned separately, and a "bill of quantities" is prepared as the preliminary to issuing documents. These consultants are commissioned by the project manager or architect, and appointed directly to the project team.

When a large construction company is appointed on a design-construct basis with in-house expertise, the professional quantity surveyors are usually permanently employed on staff. This situation has an additional advantage, as they are able to introduce cost savings into their calculations, both from experience gained on similar projects and from their knowledge of the company's technological capabilities.

International developers. In recent years many large international construction companies have turned to development in addition to their normal business activities. In general, the company brings the hotel or resort into full operation and, following commissioning and completion, sells to another investor. These construction companies employ professional personnel in house or have a direct association with subcontractors and suppliers.

The management method which is used in this situation is the *matrix system*. Company structure and existing company business associations and relationships have the advantage of broadening available options for the procurement of materials and resources, can cut costs through economies of scale, and can reduce the number of focal points where misunderstandings and misinterpretation can occur. Close liaison and cooperation must nevertheless be maintained between the developer and future hotel management and user groups.

Cost-Benefit Analysis and Upper Limits of Investment[4]

"Life-cycle costing," "value engineering," "cost-benefit analysis," and "upper limits of investment analysis" are tools that are used to balance and compare quality and cost.

Life-Cycle Costing

Life-cycle costing is concerned with the comparison of alternate design solutions within the budget rather than, as is often thought, the prediction of life-cycle costs. It should be carried out early in the project process while design development and documentation are still in progress. The techniques aim to discover and evaluate alternative opportunities, and promote a general improvement of design solutions, through team discussion, taking into account functional as well as financial criteria.

Value Engineering

The issues of life-cycle costing and the evaluation of intangibles are brought to the design process by means of value engineering technology, and are related to improvements in building design. They require an explicit approach to the consideration of alternatives, both functional and financial.

Both life-cycle costing and value engineering technologies can be used as tools to enhance design proposals. Although the greatest period of activity for both takes place during the development phase, these technologies should be continued during subsequent phases of the life cycle while other monitoring procedures are carried out in order to take advantage of any opportunity to enhance cost savings and quality assurance.

Cost-Benefit Analysis

Cost-benefit analysis is closely tied to perceived opportunity at the design stage. The price quoted to achieve each project objective is compared with the expected benefits given to factors such as marketing requirements, future returns on investment, operating costs, and maintenance of the facility over the total life expectancy of the project. The comparisons are analyzed to determine the best outcome, and this involves continuous examination for opportunities for improvement. Professional time has, of course, to be given to discussion and meetings. The project manager must evaluate the expected advantages of cost-benefit analysis against professional costs and tailor the schedule to suit the project's budget.

Practical Cost Savings

In the hotel industry, quality of product is very important for long-term business success. Developers who plan to sell the project on completion prepare a very tightly controlled budget. However, the quality of fittings installed must be considered. If these are of inferior quality, they may have to be replaced within a short time. Initial savings on cost will be outweighed by replacement values, and future value is therefore placed on present quality standards. The input of the hotel management professional's advice is particularly important to ensure that the long-term costs of service and maintenance are acceptable and the final product meets a standard and quality that will give service over the planned life span of the facility. It is obvious that the ruthless cutting of up-front costs during fit-out dramatically shortens the productive life expectancy of the project.[4]

Decisions regarding size and amount of space devoted to storage and service areas also serve as another example. The saving of staff time and labor, by conveniently planning facilities of workable size, must be compared with the disadvantage of loss of this space to additional guest room revenue. In the long run, the benefits derived from the allocation of space to extra guest rooms must be justified in relation to overheads and to the time and labor spent traveling between guest rooms, storage rooms, kitchens, and other service centers. Such allocation may not always produce maximum revenue in comparison with the charge for local labor.

Cost savings may be achieved through expert advice, for example, for the installation of highly specialized equipment such as elevators. The success of this installation depends on team effort and the close coordination of data obtained from elevator technicians, hotel management professionals, architects, structural and electrical engineers, and interior designers. Capacity, computerized speeds, operation, and timing must be planned according to expected passenger and/or guest periods of maximum and minimum use and will influence the number of elevators installed. As documentation proceeds, specialists from the contractor's staff are temporarily appointed to the immediate project team and attend meetings as required.

Each company participating in the bidding process may be asked to suggest alternative methods for the economical use of their own techniques and resources and submit cost benefits resulting from employing their in-house expertise. These requests must always be very clearly defined and communicated in the bidding documents so that each company has equal advantage.

In any case, shop drawings must always be produced for approval. These must be reviewed by professional members of the project team prior to submission to the client.

Alternatives and Optimal Solutions

In summary, a program of life-cycle costing and value analysis is likely to create savings in costs by promoting the discovery of opportunities for choice and for alternative solutions to problem areas. The active participation of team members in discussion is an important part of this process. Techniques of Total Quality Control (TQC) and quality assurance, which are similar, also depend on group discussion for success and can be combined within the program.[8] Companies in Japan (where TQC techniques originated), and later in other countries, have found it necessary to provide a short training program to encourage a relaxed atmosphere within which suggestions can arise spontaneously.

Contractual Arrangements

In all forms of contract, it is essential to obtain approvals from the owner and client for variations to the established program. Several forms of contractual agreement can be made between owner-client and the construction company or supplier. The most common are described in the following paragraphs.

Price in Advance

The "price in advance" system is a price agreed on with a general contractor before construction commences. It secures a firm cost commitment and is a system which has been used traditionally in the construction industry to establish the price of resources, materials, and supplies and as a check on later bids from subcontracting trades. However, in recent years, as the size of major projects has increased, the construction process has become much more complex to administer. Additionally, the reliability of a fixed quotation is affected by the uncertainty of international exchange rates, inflation, and problems that are linked to international investment, local social and political factors, and new technological processes that are imperfectly understood and that may cause risk and unexpected contingencies during the program at the execution phase.

Other forms of contract have therefore been developed.

Fixed-Price Contract

The "fixed price" design-construct contract places responsibility to hold the quotation firm throughout the process of procurement on the contracting company. However, the "fixed price" contract type gives the extended project team, which includes the head contractor, the flexibility to use cost-benefit analysis and value engineering of trade qualities and prices, resources, and materials and so obtain cost benefits and reductions. These procedures demand very close coordination between all project team members, with good, clear channels of communication and a reliable flow of information about the current socioeconomic situation and procurement opportunities. If relationships are not well established, a breakdown can easily occur in this form of contract and lead to litigation.

Actions to Be Taken at This Time

- Project manager:

    Clarify owner and client's needs and intentions

    Appoint project team, and arrange contracts

    Create database

    Arrange delegation and reporting hierarchy

    Inform team of tasks and responsibilities

    Foster team relationships and commitment

    Appoint team members to specific tasks, such as cost and program control

    Supervise control strategies

    Supervise the development of design documentation, the main program and schedules, subprograms, and work-breakdown structure

    Schedule regular meetings, formal and informal, and required attendances

    Schedule approvals acquisition: client and government

    Plan commissioning program

- Architects, engineers, interior designers, and landscape architects:

    Commence and develop design documentation for project

    Coordinate with project manager and other team specialists

    Advise project manager of all specialist input that will be necessary (kitchens, elevators, etc.) and coordinate with program

- Hotel operator:

    Clarify management needs, work in coordination with architects and engineers

    Plan supplies and commissioning

References

1. Gerard L. Rossy and Russell D. Archibald, "**Building Commitment in Project Teams,**" *Project Management Journal,* Vol. XXIII, No. 2, June 1992 (publ. Project Management Institute).

2. H. Kerzner, *Project Management: A Systems Approach to Planning, Scheduling and Controlling,* 3d ed., Van Nostrand Reinhold, New York, 1989.

3. Harvey A. Levine, **"Implementing Project Management: Commitment and Training Ensure Success,"** *Project Management Journal,* Vol. VI, No. 1, January 1992, pp. 35–37 (publ. Project Management Institute).

4. Douglas J. Ferry and Peter S. Brandon, *Cost Planning of Buildings,* 4th ed., Granada Press, London, 1981.

5. C. E. Shannon and W. Weaver, *The Mathematical Theory of Communication,* University of Illinois Press, 1949.

6. G. Dessler, *Organizational Theory: Integrating Structure and Behavior,* Prentice-Hall, Englewood Cliffs, N.J., 1987.

7. Chie Nakane, *Japanese Society,* University of California Press, Berkeley, 1972.

8. M. Nemoto, *Total Quality Control for Management: Strategies and Techniques from Toyota and Toyoda and Toyoda Gosei.* Prentice-Hall, Englewood Cliffs, N.J., 1980.

7

Documentation: Design, Planning, and Scheduling

One of the fundamental characteristics that influences a hotel's business success is the standard of quality and detail of the design of the interior. The attraction and serviceability of public and private guest spaces, service areas, materials, fixtures, and finishes must all support the desired standard, which helps establish and sustain the continuing reputation of the hotel or resort. The project manager and team should therefore understand the special requirements of the functional areas of a hotel very well, if the goals and objectives of the project are to be attained, expenditure controlled, and fit-out satisfactorily implemented. The content of the documentation must be planned to take account of these inherent needs.

Developing Detailed Documentation: The Influence of Hotel Functions on Design

The Downtown Hotel

The provision of an environment conducive to relaxation and enjoyment has long been one of the recognized functions of the hotel. These are found in good food, comfortable accommodation, entertainment, and convivial company. Hotels have always had the potential to provide a setting for these functions; however, if the hotel is to operate efficiently, well-planned back-of-house support facilities (staff offices, etc.) and work flow patterns are as essential as well-equipped guest rooms and public spaces. In many countries the downtown hotel has often been used for political as well as business functions, and now the provision of special conference and convention facilities, office facilities, audiovisual entertainment and recently gyms and saunas has increased business opportunity in the industry. Large, eye-catching international-standard hotels have also helped to attract associated secondary industry and employment to many cities.

The Resort

Guest satisfaction and enjoyment are found in many forms of athletic activities made possible by the geographic location of the resort. These are often associated with one or two outstanding natural or cultural environmental features which have additional attraction for visitors. The external environment, therefore, influences the design and orientation of guest and public rooms, and the desirability of obtaining views from every room becomes an additional planning consideration.[1]

Breakdown of Project Professional, Technical, and Skilled Trade Work into Units by Association

As the translation of technical instruction progresses into design and documentation, the tasks that go to produce the completed work are correlated and divided into individual "work packages" of a size convenient for design and development activities of program and schedule and later for management and control.[2]

The work packages each contain contributions from many trades and resources. Interdependent functions within the work packages will become clear when the project design intent has been defined in such detail that lists of tasks can be made and work packages created. The team programmers correlate the interdependent functions of the construction process, and these are programmed into the schedule in order of performance. While these activities continue, the schedule and program are again analyzed for areas of risk and uncertainty, with the intent to substitute alternatives. A major part of the work package breakdown in hotel and resort development is concerned with interior design and fit-out.

Interior-Design Needs, Variables, and Constraints

Planning and design for the modern variations on hotel and resort themes must take account of the amenities that are needed to support different functions. For example, the need to serve guests of the all-suite hotel, motel, convention center, casino (a very powerful attraction), conference center or superluxury and mixed-use hotel requires different space configurations, functional allocation, and technical equipment. These differences are often quite minimal but nevertheless important. In general, the major interior areas that need detailed design definition are

Guest rooms—planning, security, guest facilities

Public areas—lobby, main and other entrances, baggage handling

Guest transport—tour buses, taxi arrivals

Public areas—reception, lobby, ballroom, conference room

Restaurants

Storage and service areas, including liquor stores, room service, refrigerated storage

Shopping arcades, and provision of facilities such as a medical center and pharmacy

Laundry facilities

Deliveries

Garbage and waste disposal

Back-of-house functions—offices, staff facilities

Influence and Constraints of Hotel and Resort Rating on Space, Dimensions, and Contents

The budget category, standard, or rating (e.g., three-, four-, five-star, or luxury) is determined by the design and dimensions of space allotted to various functions (especially to guest rooms), the quality and diversity of facilities available to the guest, the quality of interior materials and finishes, and the standard of restaurants and kitchens. Precise dimensions and standards vary for each and every type of hotel and resort. They include the preferences of the owner and the operator and are influenced by the designer's prior experience and expertise.

There have been many variations on hotel building floor plans; however, an analysis of the different configurations of the high-rise hotel indicates only a relatively few efficient solutions. As illustrated in Fig. 7.1, the most commonly encountered plans are the double-loaded slab, the rectangular tower, and the atrium (Fig. 7.2).[3] According to configuration, guest rooms increase in size from 43 to 53 m² (462.85 to 570.49 ft²). A well-planned guest room floor can save 20 percent gross area and achieve efficiencies throughout the whole design of a possible 15 percent on the total building.[1] Companies with experience in the design and fit-out of hotels keep

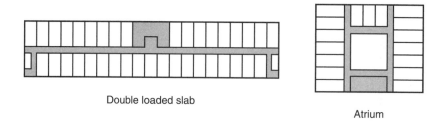

Double loaded slab

Atrium

Rectangular or square tower

Figure 7.1   The most commonly encountered hotel floor plans. These types are the double-loaded slab, the rectangular or square tower, and the atrium. The three are illustrated here in a simplified form, modified and adapted to suit the hotel type, environment, and desired characteristics. (Architects Journal, *1974 and Rutes and Penner, 1985.*)

Figure 7.2   The atrium in the Tokyo Bay Hilton, Tokyo, Japan. Nihon Sekkei Inc., architects, engineers, and project managers. (Photograph: Kawasumi Archi, Photograph Office.)

their own carefully guarded records of standards that have been used with success in other projects.

Space planning and circulation patterns. Space planning must satisfy the demands for different spatial needs, circulation, and the staff servicing of these areas. The efficient use of space, the provision of high-quality interior environmental control, and resource and energy uses, are all major factors to be considered in the development of the design; while provision for the safety of guests and staff in the event of fire or other disaster is a vital requirement.

Minimum space standards. The percentages of floor area allocated to revenue-producing functions should be maximized whenever possible, and circulation and non-revenue-producing space kept to a functional minimum. The designer must balance these needs, for example[1]

The proportion of space and dimensions of the space allocated between public and private areas and back-of-house functions (See Fig. 7.3.)

Circulation—vertical and horizontal circulation patterns for guests, walking distances for guests and service staff, staff work patterns and work flow, guest arrivals, departures, deliveries

Fire safety and escape provisions

Restaurant and kitchen planning, work flow, patterns of service

Delivery, food storage, food preparation, waste disposal

Guest room planning and servicing

In addition, other factors such as the operator's management and administration policies and practices also influence the design of space, type of construction, and quality of materials and finishes. The operator's advice and input should be incorporated, especially in the areas of housekeeping customs and procedures, the computerization of hotel management and control systems, maintenance services, and provision of closed-circuit monitoring or other devices to ensure guest room security and attention if required for medical emergency and theft.

Various space and other criteria are used to create functional relationships between areas and departments. These are quoted in many references and differ across cultures (Americans are renowned both for their desire for spacious bathrooms and for guest room security), although there are minimum acceptable standards for an international hotel, worldwide. Certain standard components and technologies are mandatory for public, private, and service areas which in general vary little in size.

Because the space is planned in four dimensions for the functioning hotel (the time factor becomes important for circulation and service), the configuration is influenced by such major space requirements as vertical riser ducts which contain air conditioning, electrical and telephone services for guest room supply, elevator banks, the uninterrupted spans of conference and convention halls, restaurant areas (and their necessary visual enticements), repetitive guest room

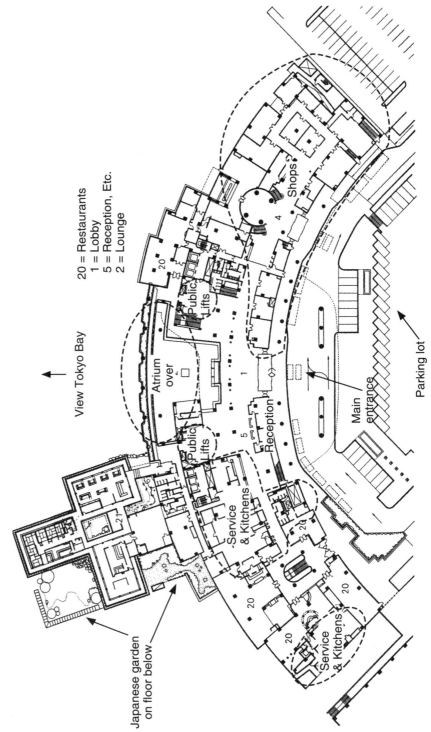

20 = Restaurants
1 = Lobby
5 = Reception, Etc.
2 = Lounge

View Tokyo Bay

Atrium over

Public Lifts

Public Lifts

Reception

Main entrance

Shops

Parking lot

Service & Kitchens

Service & Kitchens

Japanese garden on floor below

Figure 7.3   Plan of ground floor, Tokyo Bay Hilton. Nihon Sekkei Inc., architects, engineers, and project managers.

Figure 7.4 City hotels: Maihama urban resort area, Tokyo Bay. Disneyland becomes a central focus for a group of hotels of sculptured form located along the edge of Tokyo Bay. The repetitive planning of guest rooms is echoed by the windows. Nihon Sekkei Inc., architects, engineers, and project managers. (Photograph: Kawasumi Archi, Photograph Office.)

geometry, and other spatial relationships. Exterior elevations therefore reflect guest needs and hotel functions through both the plan and the influence of the plan. (See Figs. 7.4 and 7.5.)

The Guest Room

The holiday guest buys, for a short time, a standard of luxury that may not exist back home. The hotel visit should therefore become for many guests a happy and memorable experience. (See Fig. 7.6.)

Figure 7.5 Sunroute Plaza Hotel, Tokyo Bay. Nihon Sekkei, architects, engineers, and project managers. (Photograph by *SS Tokyo*.)

Figure 7.6 The Hyatt Hotel, Adelaide, South Australia, guest room. The hotel has five-star rating. John Andrews International, architects.

The quality and degree of luxury is demonstrated in the room width and circulation space, lounging facilities, and bathroom space and equipment. Bathrooms attached to luxury suites are very spacious and often palatially appointed with marble and other costly finishes on all surfaces, centrally placed baths, and gold-plated faucets. Indeed, such facilities, room contents, and equipment of equally glamorous nature have come to be expected by hotel guests.

The private bathroom is a normal adjunct to the guest room in all the varying types of four- and five-star hotels, including the all-suite hotel and the motel. It is quite unusual to build a hotel in the three-star category without this facility, unless there is some constraint or characteristic that has had a major influence on the design. The Yullara Maisonette Motel, at Ayers Rock Resort, Central Australia, was built to provide accommodation for the touring family group. Guest rooms share bathing facilities, but this lack is compensated by a generous kitchen and dining area in each guest room, with microwave oven, refrigerator, and tea-making facilities.

Public Spaces

The main spaces devoted to public use in a hotel may be summarized as follows:

1. Lobby—front desk, administration, retail shops, concierge, guest arrivals and departures, circulation

2. Food and beverage—coffee shops, restaurants, speciality restaurants, bars

3. Meeting rooms—ballrooms, conference rooms, lounges

4. Recreation—shops, gym, swimming pool, billiards, table tennis, bridge

5. Transport—arrivals and departures and parking for tourist buses, axis, guest cars

Other special public spaces such as convention halls and casinos may be incorporated into the main hotel building, or have a separate, but connected, identity.

1. *Lobby.* A well-designed lobby (see Fig. 7.7) has the ability to promote the hotel's business both psychologically and also through the guest's response to physical use of the space.[3] As the main entrance to the hotel, the lobby decor creates the first impression of the quality to be expected in other interior spaces. It is a control point where staff are located to offer assistance, and in this way they add to the guest's first impression of the standard of service and efficiency to be anticipated. It is the place where the guest makes business contact with hotel management by checking in and settling accounts before departure. It is also, usually, the main circulation area and an informal meeting place for guests. Dimensions of the area must be designed according to the number of people who will occupy the space at key times. It is inevitable that the lobby will sometimes become congested at peak periods when guest groups are arriving or departing; however, the designer's objective must be to modify the plan so that as little inconvenience is caused as possible. Clear direction signs should be provided to indicate useful facilities such as the front desk and concierge, for who has not spent several minutes searching for elevators or reception?

2. *Restaurants.* Hotel restaurants aim to increase their revenue by attracting many outside patrons as well as the guests staying in the hotel. The quality of the design is therefore of great importance and offers an opportunity to express the theme of the menu, and create an effect of glamour and "theater." Indeed, the client often requests that the interior designer provide not only plans and designs for color schemes and motives for furnishings and special fixtures and fittings but also staff uniforms, tableware, china, and napkins, in order to carry the special theme throughout the decor. All the restaurant's functional needs, characteristics, and operation must be defined and agreed on at the beginning of the interior-development phase. The design of restaurant character, type, and even menus may be constrained by the prior design of other areas. For example, if restaurant designs are delayed until after the lobby is completed, the opportunity to install special features and change entrances or change floor levels may be forfeited.

The planning of guest circulation, table layout, lighting, service flow, and entertainment space reflect the characteristics and theme of the restaurant. The coffee shop seating density is much higher than the upscale restaurant catering for dinner service. It is usually desirable to have flexible seating arrangements in both types; however, the speciality restaurant will usually have an adjoining bar and lounge, and a feeling of intimacy should be created around the tables and seating. (See Fig. 7.8.) The project manager and members of the team should recognize that problems and delays often occur during fit-out because special materials and supplies must often be ordered from distant sources. It is important that schedules take extended delivery times into account to ensure that all such equipment is

Figure 7.7 The lobby, Nagasaki Prince Hotel, Kyushu, Japan. The design of this popular hotel meets the demand for a sumptuous venue for meetings, weddings, and other celebrations held in the provincial Japanese city of Nagasaki, Kyushu. Nihon Sekkei Inc., architects, engineers, and project managers.

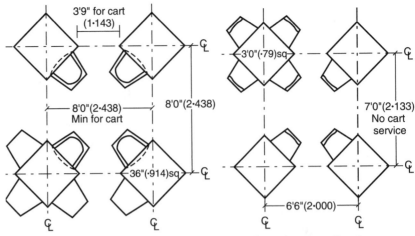

3'9" for cart
(1·143)

8'0"(2·438)
Min for cart

8'0"(2·438)

36"(·914)sq

3'0"(·79)sq

7'0"(2·133)
No cart
service

6'6"(2·000)

Dimensions of seating for dining rooms   Dimensions for coffee shops

Figure 7.8   Restaurant seating plans compared. The dimensions of the table and seating plan for restaurant dining are spacious and allow comfort and attentive service, including cart circulation among the tables. It is more spacious than the plan for a coffee shop, which, although comfortable, intends to promote a faster turnaround, in hopes that guests will not dally over their coffee or meal.

ordered from suppliers in ample time to meet the construction program and well in advance of planned opening dates. This is especially important for resorts in remote rural locations.

3. *Kitchens.* There is a rule of thumb regarding the proportion of kitchen space to restaurant area. The traditional recommendation is for the kitchen area to be approximately 60 percent that of the dining room, given an allowance of 0.9 to 1.0 m² per seat (9.68 to 10.76 ft²). This rule is inclusive of circulation space, but exclusive of storage area. A separate kitchen is usually provided to serve each restaurant area, although kitchens may often be combined to serve a "back-to-back" restaurant configuration. Spatial economies can be effected in this way. Kitchen design is very specialized, and kitchen design experts are usually appointed by the project manager on the recommendation of the operator, architect, or interior designer, with the approval of the owner and the hotel management group. This is particularly important when speciality restaurants, such as Japanese, Chinese, or Thai are planned. (See Figs. 7.9 and 7.10.)

4. *Meeting rooms.* Plans and designs for meeting rooms and ballroom space need to be flexible and adaptable so that the space can be converted to many different uses, such as for small and large conferences, balls, business luncheons and dinners, theatrical performances and floor shows, and exhibitions. Interior fit-out problems are generally those of delivery of materials and equipment, such as floor-to-ceiling temporary folding or sliding doors, stacking chairs, special material for wall panels, and the installation of suspended floors. Hotel meeting rooms and ballrooms always seem to be the last spaces to be completed in the interior, because the main activities of the hotel can be commissioned and opened without this facility.

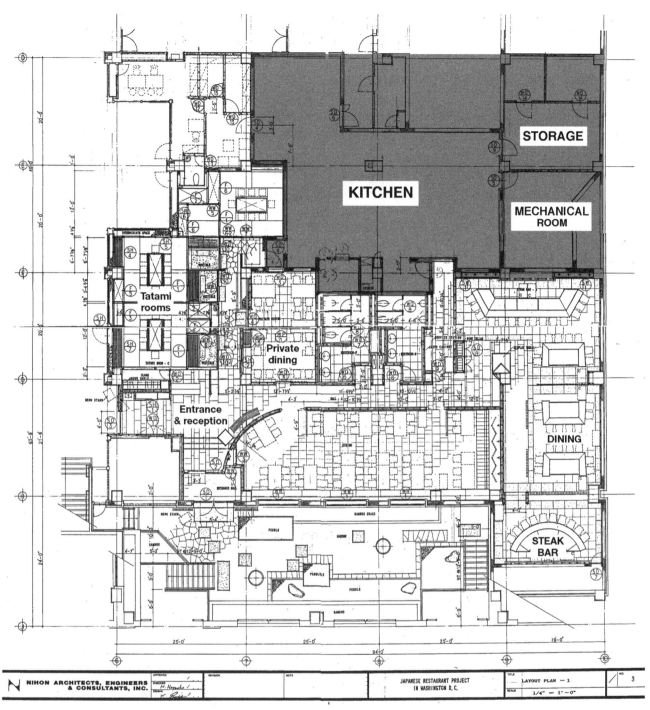

Figure 7.9 Plan, Japanese restaurant, Washington, D.C. The kitchen area is roughly 62 percent of the dining area, although the traditional entrance and vestibule increase the overall proportion of public-to-service space allowances in Japanese style restaurants in favor of the diners' accommodation. Nihon Sekkei Inc., architects, engineers, and project managers.

Figure 7.10 Japanese Restaurant, Washington, D.C. (*a*) Sushi bar; (*b*) main dining area. Nihon Sekkei Inc., architects, engineers, and project managers.

More Technological Tools for Management: Quality Assurance

The technology of "Quality Assurance" has recently been developed to ensure the production of acceptable standards of skills, materials, and finishes. Some measures that make up the technology of quality assurance have been discussed in an earlier chapter. Team commitment and team feelings of ownership toward the project encourage participants to give their best effort and undertake responsibility for evaluating their input. The process of creating task interdependence and cooperation among the team during the production process is an important part of this technology. Quality assurance programs are best implemented through regular meetings, discussions, inspections, and approvals when observations, opinions, and suggestions can be exchanged.[2]

The development of a strategy for monitoring output and the production of comprehensively detailed instructions in the form of design drawings and specifications is essential for the achievement of quality performance. Indeed, quality can be assured only if the standard and level desired are specified and verified with precision. A quality control program should constitute a subsection of the main program, and key team members should be appointed to report on the progress of their own related tasks.

The standards and quality of interior fit-out, including fixtures, fittings, materials, and finishes, must be the best that can be obtained within the budget. Management and housekeeping are dependent on quality to maintain the standard and image of the hotel environment for several years. Their success depends primarily on quality and design of building services, fixtures, materials, and finishes.

To recapitulate, the tenet, that the translation of the client's original concept into clearly defined design instructions requires experience and commitment, is valid not only for the global development of the project process but also for the specific design of the interior environment. Certainly, the level of skills and expertise needed for the design of the hotel interior could be compared with those of a hospital or research laboratory and require technical knowledge that exceeds that of many other forms of commercial construction and development. For this reason, most owners and clients prefer to commission a company with demonstrable international design experience and standing, especially for development of top-class international hotels and resorts.

Methods of Project Programming and Control[4]

There are several methods of recording all the activities and tasks necessary to complete the process of development against a flow of time.

Bar charts and precedence networks. The bar chart is perhaps the best known of these methods, and has an uncomplicated format. It can be used for simple programs or as a first step in the analysis of more complex network systems. All tasks necessary for processing of the project are listed and shown against regular time intervals, usually by week (week 1, week 2, etc.) in the construction program. (See Fig. 7.11.) It is not possible to record completed work in this form of chart. Progress can instead be recorded on the Gantt chart, which is a very similar system. However, milestones (key dates) can be recorded and the interdependencies of tasks can be shown on the bar chart with a superimposed system of lines and arrows which indicate the direction and flow of work over time.

The simpler systems, such as the bar chart, have the limitation that they use time as a measurement against which to plan activities. The commencement and completion of an activity is rarely forecast completely accurately, and an error in estimation will necessitate the complete reprogramming of the chain of dependent events: a complex

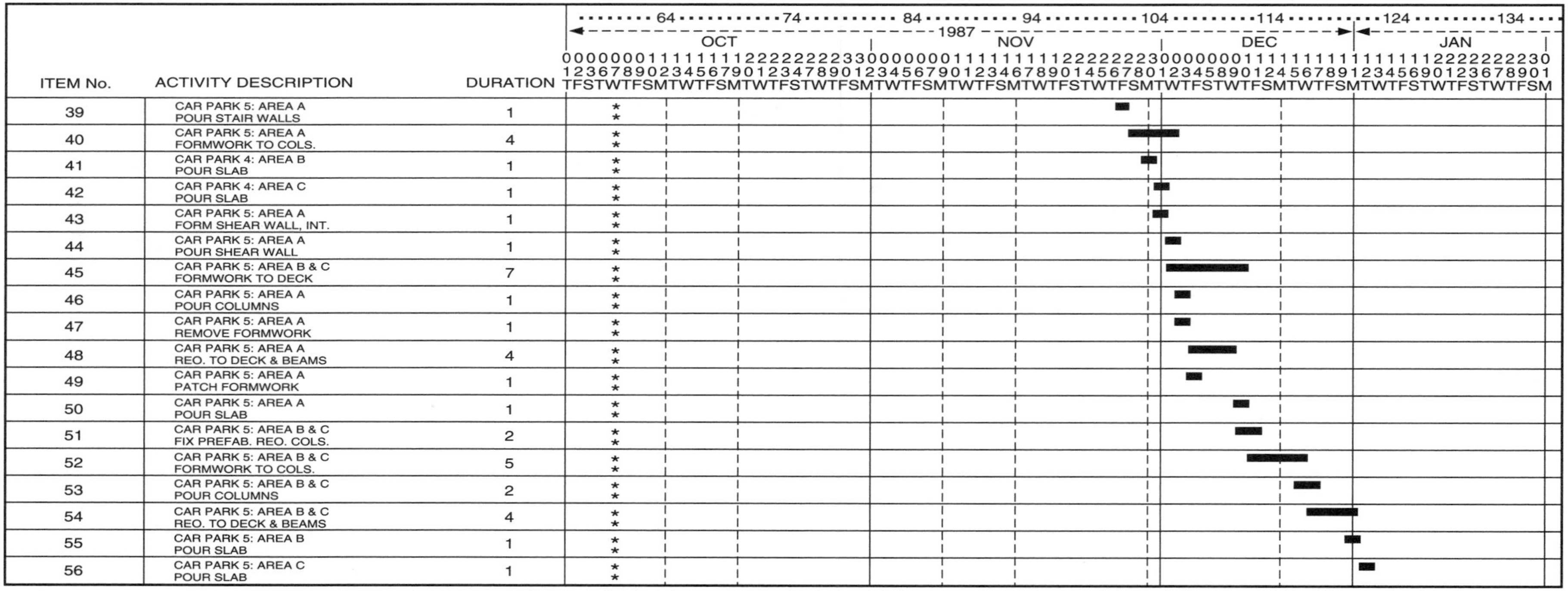
64 74 84 94 104 114 124 134
1987
OCT NOV DEC JAN
ITEM No.
ACTIVITY DESCRIPTION
DURATION
39 CAR PARK 5: AREA A POUR STAIR WALLS 1
40 CAR PARK 5: AREA A FORMWORK TO COLS. 4
41 CAR PARK 4: AREA B POUR SLAB 1
42 CAR PARK 4: AREA C POUR SLAB 1
43 CAR PARK 5: AREA A FORM SHEAR WALL, INT. 1
44 CAR PARK 5: AREA A POUR SHEAR WALL 1
45 CAR PARK 5: AREA B & C FORMWORK TO DECK 7
46 CAR PARK 5: AREA A POUR COLUMNS 1
47 CAR PARK 5: AREA A REMOVE FORMWORK 1
48 CAR PARK 5: AREA A REO. TO DECK & BEAMS 4
49 CAR PARK 5: AREA A PATCH FORMWORK 1
50 CAR PARK 5: AREA A POUR SLAB 1
51 CAR PARK 5: AREA B & C FIX PREFAB. REO. COLS. 2
52 CAR PARK 5: AREA B & C FORMWORK TO COLS. 5
53 CAR PARK 5: AREA B & C POUR COLUMNS 2
54 CAR PARK 5: AREA B & C REO. TO DECK & BEAMS 4
55 CAR PARK 5: AREA B POUR SLAB 1
56 CAR PARK 5: AREA C POUR SLAB 1

Figure 7.11 Bar chart of construction sequences. This simple model is part of a bar chart for the construction of formwork, reinforcement, and concrete pour of the lower parking lot (level 5) in the basement of a city hotel in Sydney. The chart is a subprogram loop in the total program and connects to consecutive and simultaneous activities at items 38–39 (construction preliminaries) and items 56–57. Many activities shown, for example, items 52 and 53, are on the critical path of construction.

and time-consuming task for a large project.

The bar chart is an excellent tool when used as a first step on which to list and correlate information and build a more flexible network to overcome some of the limitations of the simple programs.

Network analysis. The rapid increase in construction costs, competition, and the necessity to reduce interest payments on loans and obtain revenue on investment have demanded new skills of project management. Network analysis techniques are a group of skills which have been developed since the end of World War II in order to assist the management and control of large projects and have the capacity for time-factor manipulation. They are linked with techniques of decision-making theory, statistical inference, research techniques, and computerization to produce a powerful tool for regulation and monitoring purposes.

Programming for documentation. Steps in the process of creating programs and schedules are typically

1. Objectives are defined and established.

2. The project concept and objectives are translated into technical criteria.

3. Areas of risk and uncertainty are identified and alternatives found.

4. Detailed documentation is produced.

5. The overall work process is divided into work packages.

6. Time allowances are calculated.

7. Intertask influences and dependencies are identified.

8. Priorities are set and agreed on.

9. Organizational nodes are established (maximum time allowances, reviews, approvals).

10. Project review dates are set and agreed on.

11. Milestones are established for the completion of key tasks.

12. Work packages are brought together in a network of related functions and activities.

If the time period necessary for a task cannot be precisely estimated, a time allowance or "float" is incorporated into the program during the design of the network. As the program develops, a critical path of activities can be identified. The critical activities are the set of tasks that must be completed before the process can progress and on which all other tasks depend. Tasks that appear on the "critical path" of the network must be controlled by the allocation of an extra time allowance, so that the commencement of later activities and the planned date for completion is not delayed by unexpected occurrences.

The operational success of the program and schedule is completely dependent on approvals being obtained on time.

Designing a program and schedule. Programs and schedules are intended to function as a means of communicating vital information, such as task sequences and key dates, to the wide variety of professions and trades who make up the project team. First, a main control program must be made to clarify and define sequences and to locate the critical path of activities for the overall program of development.[2]

A large project such as a hotel or resort is composed of many hundreds of interrelated activities, and many subsidiary programs are necessary to best describe and clarify the whole. The building construction program forms one of these subsidiary programs. It is usually designed in house by the head contractor and must be made to correlate with the main program by being based on information contained in the global documentation and programs received from the project team. The project teams' main program of control must in turn be flexible for adjustment in terms of needs of construction and other subprograms, entailing a process of close cooperation, by discussion, monitoring, and feedback while programming proceeds.

Planning a network. Planning a network requires a great deal of intellectual input. Although one team member, usually a planning specialist, must coordinate the effort, this officer relies on the cooperative endeavor of the whole project team. Indeed, the programmer must consult with all team members with regard to their speciality, sequences, dependencies, and time allowances (and by doing so will engender interest in the program and willingness to contribute to group effort).[4]

Time allowances. The precedence network is a tool capable of planning first and last dates for commencement and completion of each activity, allowing a "float" of time to be established. The network is also capable of showing activities in relation to the period of development and key dates, the correlation of tasks, resource requirements, and progress. (See Fig. 7.12.) Certain dates become very important within the program and schedule, such as key dates for completion of certain tasks on which the commencement of many others depend. Other key dates are typically formal submission for approvals, last dates for receipt of approvals, the regular review of costs, and regular scrutiny of cash flow and program of payments.[4] (See Fig. 7.13.)

Work Packages

The division of the project into interrelated operations is based on professional advice and information obtained from technical drawings, specifications, bills of quantities, and manufacturers' specifications. Natural subdivisions are made by dividing the activities into clusters. Depending on the special needs of the project, any or all of the following divisions may typically be chosen as bases for activities:[2]

- Geographic division:

    Different infrastructure needs, recreational and service areas of the site under development

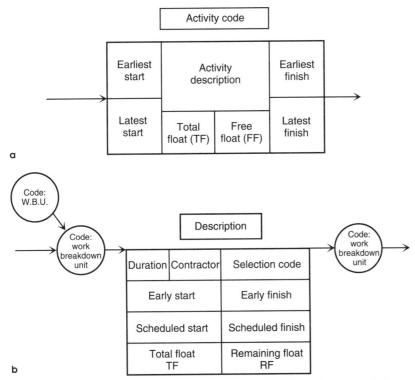

Figure 7.12 Precedence network activity box. (*a*) Simplified layout for an activity box. (*b*) Adapted for a network of a city hotel parking lot program. See Fig. 7.13. (*After Burman, 1972.*)

Different wings of the hotel complex

- Physical division:

  Structural elements, foundations, columns, floors, etc.

  Areas of responsibility, trades, crafts, skills

  Electrical, plumbing, air conditioning, kitchen, interior fit-out

- Equipment use:

  The hired use of large technical resources such as mobile cranes, which may be in limited supply (will influence the sequence of activities)

  End use, staged completion, opening dates, expediency (conservation of resources)

Staged completion of parts of the development will need separate subprograms which must be synchronized with construction and completion of other activities and cycles. Large hotel and resort projects will almost certainly have several correlated but separate subprograms during construction.

The preliminary listing is expanded from broad scale to detail, until the team is satisfied that all major activities are defined. The initial breakdown into activity components will vary in complexity according to the project type (resort or hotel); the market characteristics (mixed-use, recreation, business, convention, casino), the expected market

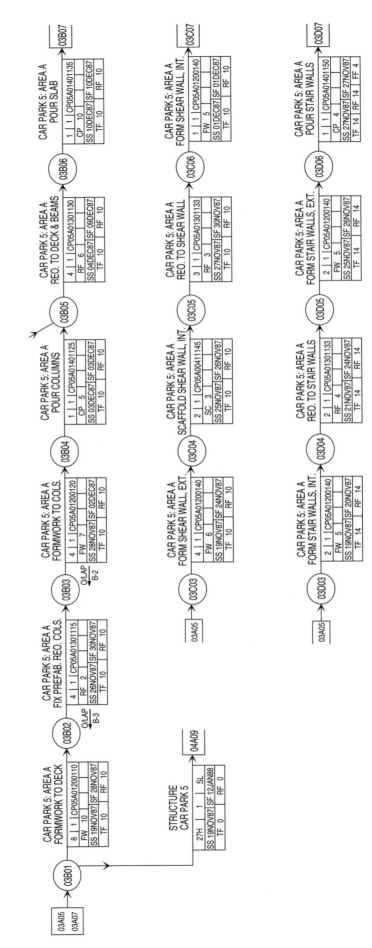

Figure 7.13 Precedence network, for lower level 5, parking lot of downtown hotel, Sydney.
This precedence network program develops the bar chart of Fig. 7.9, showing the duration of
time allotted for each task and trade, the total float, and remaining float allowances.
Descriptions of activities and task codes have been added to the boxes, and it can be seen
that the program is dependent on the completion of other tasks, (nodal point 83B85), while
Task 84A89 is dependent on the completion of an earlier task in the sequence (83B81).

level (luxury, five-, four-, three-star), and the size of the project.

The program for design and documentation verification and processing will contain three schedules of major importance: the drawing production schedule, the tender procurement schedule, and the schedule of key dates. Unlike the construction program which it resembles in overall format, the process of design deals with discrete activities containing technologies that are mutually influencing and interrelated. Building activities are, on the other hand, usually continuing processes that rely on the completion of a series of preceding tasks.[2]

Several questions should be asked about the activities to be programmed:

Is the activity continuous from start to finish, or must it depend on the completion of other tasks in the program?

Are the resources that are needed to undertake tasks constant, or must other resources be introduced at key times?

Is the activity small enough to make a reliable estimate of task duration? Should the activity be divided further into subactivities?

Cyclic activities. Some activities during construction are repeated several times and have a cyclic format occurring within the main program network (floor and/or room fit-out). These are programmed as subsidiary network loops and repeated whenever necessary.[4]

Chain activities. Chains are trade processes that remain practically the same for all construction work, varying only in accordance with differing characteristics of the overall design. The task sequences are therefore repetitive; an example is the installation of a sprinkler system by floor.

Establishing the Critical Path of Activities for Procurement

The initial event in the program (rather obviously called "start") commences the networking of all activities and progress through the system.

The timing of the commencement of construction, especially in the case of a resort in a remote location, is dependent on the time lag between the ordering of supplies and a confirmed (and verified) delivery date. It is therefore essential that ordering procedures be programmed to occur early enough to fit in with these schedules. For example, there may be a lapse of six months before a generator, necessary as the main source of power supply, is received on site, installed, and ready for use.

The network will present several paths of progress. A "critical" path emerges from these patterns and is the vital path into that other cycles are merged and on which progress depends. Events that influence the critical sequence relate to the special characteristics of the resort in combination with the owner-client's requirements for commissioning and opening, and also depend, for example, on the availability and condition of infrastructure—roads, water supply, sewerage, power supply, and perhaps an airstrip depending on transport and logistic requirements; logistics of materials and resources for construction and fit-out of service areas and kitchens; and progressive fit-out tasks leading to the commissioning by floor or units of guest rooms.

During development, the network should be carefully checked for task redundancies and loops that backtrack on progress and these should be eliminated from the program before the network is accepted as a basis for control.[4]

Plan to Finish

The commissioning phase is equally important to the design of the network program as the development and execution phases of the project. This phase contains the activities of final inspection, systems commissioning, the completion of the requirements of the contract, certification, acceptance, and handover to the client and operator. The client takes over the total asset and liability of the facility, including insurance policies which have previously been the contractor's responsibility.[2]

It is recommended that the project manager prepare a training schedule to suit the program of commissioning very early in the total program, for staff training program helps to ensure a smooth handover from contractor to client and operator groups. These programs should clarify technological features and functions provided for the facility so that they can immediately be incorporated into operational planning and, in addition, serve as the basis for long term management strategies.

The need to plan and implement training and commissioning procedures in good time is a priority for the support of client needs and requirements. Such plans are often overlooked with the result that the hotel management staff are unprepared to take over special technical features installed in the facility, and later these may cause many misunderstandings, problems, and disputes.

Progressive Occupancy and Staged Completion

Progressive occupancy of part of the total project provides several very desirable commercial advantages; for example, an income from the investment becomes available at a date prior to completion of the total project. Additionally, in this way dates desired and nominated for opening at precontract stage, and found to be unattainable, can be partially met and market opportunity captured at the critical time. It is clear that these advantages assist the initial financial feasibility of the project by showing an early return on investment.[5] Other advantages of staged completion and occupancy relate to the project manager's strategies of management and successful integration of program networks. A staged-completion program offers an opportunity for progressive staff training and progressive implementation of in-house management systems so that opening problems associated with total completion and a major deadline are minimized. Renovations and refurbishment plans can often be more easily adapted to the stage program.

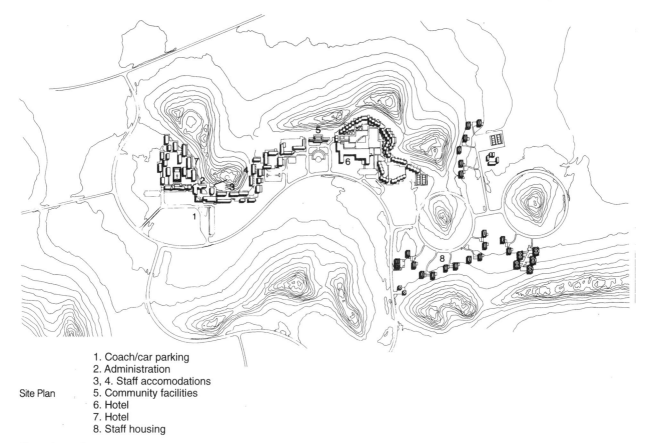

1. Coach/car parking
2. Administration
3, 4. Staff accomodations
5. Community facilities
6. Hotel
7. Hotel
8. Staff housing

Site Plan

Figure 7.14 Site plan, Ayers Rock Resort, Ayers Rock, Central Australia: staged completion.(Cox, Richardson, and Taylor, architects, Sydney, Australia.)

Staged completion is, therefore, dependent on good commissioning procedures to integrate the project management, construction, and opening program and schedules. (See Fig. 7.14.)

Some Disadvantages of Staged Completion

These may be considered under three headings: financial arrangements, planning staged handover, and programming construction.[2]

Financial arrangements. A strategy for staged completion implies a commitment to early purchase and construction starts of various systems, which may be a disadvantage relative to the client's financial arrangements. This commitment is typically connected with the need to install infrastructure and the early supply of power. An unexpected demand for an immediate lump-sum financial outlay can occur, if conditions vary during the process of development, or if redesign is required later during the construction process.

A cost-control program that includes contingency plans and alternatives must therefore be implemented at an early stage.[5]

Maximum and minimum limits should be set during the conceptual stage of the estimating process. The limits that are assayed for the work-breakdown structure, system by system, make it possible to compare and trade off costs flexibly over the whole budget.[5] This breakdown strategy has the advantage of nominally allocating a budget to the various work packages at precontract stage, when each cost can then be balanced with costs of other work-breakdown units in the system, and controls can be established for foreseeable deviations and alternatives. Cost-control tools which ensure accurate refinement of estimates and the detailing and integration of programs can be used to advantage in the recognition of areas of opportunities for cost savings and are reviewed if redesign becomes necessary for parts of the project.

Planning staged handover. As many activities in the staged-handover procedure will be out of sequence with the main program of construction, the interface between the operative hotel and construction activities becomes particularly difficult to manage. The problems are resolved by detailing design, programming, and orienting contract conditions and construction sequences to the peculiar demands for planning staged handover and occupancy.[6]

In the construction context, finishing activities fall out of sequence with the rest of the work on site. Often this signifies, for example, that service systems, such as power supply, must be temporarily installed. Guest transport and delivery of hotel supplies must consequently be commissioned in such a way as to avoid danger and conflict with the operation of construction. Problems caused by the juxtaposition of hotel operation and construction activities often limit guests' enjoyment, safety, and the hotel's capability of satisfying their demands and expectations. These problems are naturally of special concern to the operator of hotels and resorts under staged-occupancy circumstances.

A requirement for staged completion implies that the following will occur:

1. Early out-of-sequence need for the completion of infrastructure and services, sufficient to supply the hotel's operative areas until practical completion of the whole project is achieved

2. Separated access for operator, user, and construction activities, which will necessitate special and restricted movement for both hotel and construction operators

3. Safety—separation of the public from construction activity

4. Extra risk and insurance coverage in the head contract

5. Separate insurance policies so that the new buildings or areas to be occupied are insured by the owner on handover, while the contractor retains responsibility for the insurance covering the construction site and site works. These requirements make correlation of interfaces of insurance areas difficult

6. Extra approvals from relevant authorities for fire safety, health, and other amenities

7. Separately scheduled warranties and maintenance periods, as the periods will not run concurrently for the whole complex

8. Other specific limitations imposed on construction activities, such as the control of noise, in order to provide a "right of

quiet enjoyment" in finished sections

9. Redefinition of the total practical completion date

10. Adjustments of cost and budgetary estimates to allow for increases

11. Extra training and provisions for commissioning in order to correlate complete and incomplete guest and/or operator conditions and circumstances

12. A program for out-of-sequence landscaping completion for the provision of recreational facilities

It is clear that the owner and project manager must agree on and be prepared for many constraints and adjustments to be imposed on the overall design of the facility in order for early occupancy of parts of the development to be made possible.

Programming construction. The problems caused by a staged occupancy also affect the program of construction very basically. The contractual implications and constraints which affect the construction processes will be discussed in a later chapter.

Actions to Be Taken at This Time

- Project manager:

    Manage professional team members and supervise and control design and documentation

    Continually monitor budget requirements

    Scrutinize and control documentation output for content and to satisfy client's needs and requirements

    Monitor and supervise the development of all programs and schedules, and hold regular meetings for this purpose

    Schedule meetings, regular and when needed; set up format, attendances, and reporting procedures

    Monitor reporting procedures

    Obtain progressive client approvals of design documentation

    Develop time, cost, quality programs, and monitoring procedures

- Project team:

    Continue to define and develop technical criteria

    Prepare overall and subsidiary programs and schedules for development process

    Prepare documentation—design drawings and specifications

    Monitor quality of documentation

    Monitor budget requirements

    Contribute suggestions through discussion and participation at meetings

    Scrutinize documentation and program for risk and uncertainty

- Architect and engineers:

  Develop technical criteria according to site, geotechnical considerations, and market and client needs

  Develop design drawings and specifications

  Assist in the development of programs and schedules

References

1. **Principles of Hotel Design** (edited by the *Architects Journal* staff), 2d ed., The Architectural Press, London, 1974.

2. *Master of Project Management course notes,* University of Technology Sydney, Sydney, Australia, 1991.

3. Walter A. Rutes and R. H. Penner, *Hotel Planning and Design,* Watson Guptill Publications, New York, and Architectural Press, London, 1985.

4. P. J. Burman, *Precedence Networks for Project Planning and Control,* McGraw-Hill, London, 1972.

5. J. Mooney, *Cost Effective Building Design,* New South Wales University Press, Australia, 1983.

6. David M. Bennett, *Brooking on Building Contracts,* 2d ed., Butterworths Press, Pty. Ltd., Australia, 1980.

7. L. N. Duncan Wallace, *Hudson's Building and Engineering Contracts,* 10th ed., Sweet & Maxwell, London, 1970.

8

Bidding Procedures and Contract Formulation

Contracting for Procurement

Client and market needs influence both the content of the documentation and programs for project procurement, and the arrangements and forms of contract that are made with contractors and suppliers through a pattern of schedules and key dates, for example, staged-occupancy and fast-track contracts. Traditionally, the tender process is the means used for selection and appointment of a head contractor (or contractors) and subcontractors, and the acquisition of resources. The main contracts that are formed to generate the construction of the project are based on decisions derived from the results of this process.[1,2]

The Preparation of Documentation for Tendering

The project documentation is the most important communication tool used to transmit both information about and a description of project intent. It is essential for the preparation of all types of design-bid-construct combinations for contract formulation. If bids of quality and accuracy are to be submitted which truly reflect the project's worth, no quantity, instruction, or method must be left to chance and the documentation detail must be complete and comprehensive. Furthermore, if the documentation contains oversights and omissions, neither the needs of the owner nor the client or designer's wishes will be capable of interpretation. The resulting uncertainty becomes a major risk to the success of the process of development. It can be a source of budget increases, variations to time and quality, and later of disputes between the parties to the contracts.[3]

The document record. Hundreds of drawings, specifications, and reports are made to describe the work to be done for a large project. A method must be established (in parallel with production of the documentation), which records and coordinates all these documents, facilitates the management and control of the processes, and integrates the work packages of the different contractors. In this regard it is necessary to establish a flexible and strategic database that may be computerized when facilities are available. This register should include a record of documents received from the various professional designers and advisors and from trade sources, and incorporate separate lists for revisions, variations, and dates of issue. It is important that documents be easily recorded and revised.

The documents should be nearly complete by the commencement of the execution phase, although modifications are yet to be made, by means of shop drawings, which make details synchronize with available equipment and expertise.

The documentation data, therefore, is used both to assist the call for bids and as a basis on which to form the contracts between owner and construction companies, suppliers and trades. Once contracting companies are appointed, the information conveyed in the documentation enables the project management team and head contractor to assess the ramifications of the program and make final adjustments to the strategies for control of the process.

The selection of head and subcontractors. It is usual for the project manager to undertake the responsibility of managing and supervising the production of documentation, the initiation and supervision of bidding and negotiation procedures, and recommend the final selection of companies to the owner-client.

One of the main construction companies tendering for a major project work package is generally appointed as head contractor. This company becomes responsible for the management and control of the site, and supervision and execution of all the work associated with construction of the hotel buildings. Subcontracts, in turn, are made by the head contractor for trade work, usually by negotiation with one of the firms with whom they have worked before.

In the case when the owner-developer is the major construction company, this company controls all the works, including the design, civil and building works, trades, suppliers, and resources.

Invitations to Tender

Prices for the work of procurement are obtained in one of three main ways: the public or open tender, tender by invitation, or negotiation.

Public or open tender. The major disadvantage of this method for the client and project manager is the huge increase in the project team's workload because of the number of companies wishing to participate in the tender process. The workload increases not only in the initial preparation and issue of tender documents for bidding but also in the time involved in analysis and comparison between factors such as the various companies' prior experience and financial standing imposed by the large numbers of submissions.

An open, public tender, with strong competition will certainly produce low bids, but these are often unrealistically undercut, for a low bid, which is attractive at first sight, has a number of disadvantages. One problem in particular is attended by real risks to project completion and achievement of time and budget targets. For example, if an unrealistically low bidder in open tender is accepted, the company may exceed the tender price sometime during the construction process, and either fail to complete the contract or demand more money in order to finish the work. The company will have the owner and team "over a financial barrel" in spite of explicit contractual terms, especially in remote locations, where the difficulties and costs of substitution of another contractor would be prohibitive. Project managers, beware of assuming responsibility for this situation!

Tender by invitation. In this form, an invitation is offered to several chosen companies to submit tenders for the work, usually not more than four.

These companies are typically chosen on the following basis. The project manager is asked by the client to compile a list of companies with a good reputation and financial standing and with experience in similar works. Several contractors may be selected by the project manager for investigation through recommendation by others, such as financiers, developers, hotel management groups, or project controllers who have knowledge of the contractor's prior experience and standing. A limited set of tender documents are issued, and a short list—of perhaps two companies—is selected from the submissions, for the more concentrated effort of pricing the total work.

The work of preparing prices for the tender documentation is, of course, undertaken by each bidding company. This is expensive to the company and requires an extensive commitment, which is subsequently reflected in higher prices in the general costs of construction. The costs of tendering for limited or negotiated contracts are usually borne by the companies involved, although it has become far more common in recent years for the owner-client to offer a sum to (partially) cover overheads.

If only a few select companies are invited to tender for the work, a more realistic price can be obtained and more reliance can be placed on the standard and quality of work which is offered.

Negotiated contracts. An alternative procedure for the procurement of an acceptable price and the appointment of a head contractor to perform the work is by negotiation.

The project manager may be required to administer a negotiated contract, typically in one of the following ways:

1. A company, considered for nomination as head contractor, is known to the owner for their experience in international hotel and resort development.

2. The project manager, or other senior members of the professional team, may propose a known contractor's name for consideration and negotiation.

The negotiated contract may include the provision of design as well as construction work (package deal or design-construct form of contract), while the nominated company may subcontract to a local company for the supply of labor.

It is quite usual for the project management team, professional architects, engineers, or a construction company well known to the owner or client to be appointed by negotiation to a supervisory position for work in remote locations; most managers are seconded from among the company's permanent staff members for the period of construction.

The owner may always exercise the right to nominate subcontracting companies. Instructions must, however, be included in the contract between the owner, head contractor, and nominated subcontractors to secure formal assurance that cooperation between the companies takes place and their activities are correlated with the head contractor's program for the management and control of site operations.

The Tender Documents

A complete set of documents describing all the work required for inclusion in the tender is assembled and issued to the companies who have been selected or have registered interest in bidding for the work. These tender documents must also include a summary of data relevant to the global development. This enables the contracting companies to orient to the total concept and to plan and coordinate with site works that may be outside the range of their management and control, accordingly.

The project team's responsibility to coordinate the documentation of work-breakdown units becomes especially important if, in the case of a resort, there is more than one major contractor involved in development, for example, different contractors for hotel building construction, golf course construction, civil works, or airstrip construction.

Content. The documents that are prepared for bidding purposes usually consist of the following:

Notice to bidders

Conditions of submission

Form of submission desired

General conditions of the contract that will be offered to the successful bidder

Specifications describing the content of the work

Drawings

Bills of quantities[2]

Often the conditions of tender may also give an opportunity to the bidder to submit both a conforming bid and an alternative. Alternatives give a chance to the bidding company to depart in some way from the methods of production shown in the documentation; indeed, the project manager may issue tender documents with the explicit intention of inviting the bidding companies to include shop details, construction methods, equipment, or materials in the bid that are especially suited to the bidder, in order to obtain a competitive price and receive the benefit of their expertise. Cost savings and improvements in quality can be made in this way, and in-house expertise can be utilized.[1,2]

The Analysis and Evaluation of Bids

The project manager and the team are responsible for the evaluation of the offers and the assessment of the comparative merits of each tender. It is essential under tender conditions, that comparisons be impartially made.

In this regard, important project conditions must always be examined, and the project team will usually discover anomalies between the bids of different companies, caused by differing expertise and technology of one kind or another. Control of the quality and accuracy of the bids is, therefore, primarily assured through the degree of definition and detail of the documentation.

Thus, the work of evaluation is time consuming, and allowances of time must be anticipated in program planning.

The Lowest Bid

The lowest bid of the tender may present problems that prohibit immediate acceptance, but may be open to modification through negotiation between the parties. These problems are often of the following kind:

1. The lowest bid exceeds the budget. In this case, acceptable alternatives may be found by discussion between the project manager, project team, and winning contractor which bring the design and specifications in line with budget and scheduled limits.

2. The lowest bid offered may not be the most attractive bid, as other criteria, such as quality and conditions of contract offered by the bidder, may not be acceptable to the client.

3. An obviously wide discrepancy in price between the highest and lowest bids may be brought about by variations in quality, deviations from the design and product required, misunderstanding of the documents, underestimation of quantities, or omissions.

Scheduling

Delivery dates and availability of resources are of major importance to international hotel work, and the acceptance of a bid may very well depend on the contractor's ability to meet the scheduled deadlines and planned opening dates. If schedules do not coincide with the client's needs, savings on the costs of construction may well be lost several times over because opening dates are delayed.

The opportunity should be taken, as soon as contractors are appointed, to discuss the project documentation and obtain the team's evaluation of quality systems and design alternatives in order to take advantage of available technologies and expertise. It is not too late in the process to achieve savings on costs and time.

Conditions

All bidders are expected to conform with the dates set for submission, or lose the right to be considered for the contracted works. However, if an extension becomes necessary for some compelling reason, all bidders must be notified and offered the same opportunity. Questions and answers about project conditions that are received from bidders during the tendering process must be circulated to all participants.

The submissions must be opened in front of witnesses.

Contracts

Although contract agreement can be a simple procedure in its basic form, involving an offer and acceptance for a consideration, building contracts are usually very complex and lengthy. The costs of construction for an international standard hotel, for example, are usually in millions of dollars, and the investment of time, skill, and money must be protected against risks of all kinds. The final form that the construction contract takes, therefore, has many clauses aimed to protect all parties to the agreement.

Owners, clients, and contractors. The bidding process takes place for the explicit purpose of appointing a company who will be capable of providing the clients with such services of acceptable standard and quality, as are necessary for procurement of the project at a price that comes within the clients' budget. The contract must also include provisions to protect the investment against the contractor's default, for acceptable trade warranties, for formal commitments to implement commissioning, and to meet the owner-client's required opening date.

Contractors have similar objectives. These are typically to protect against risk, change of contract conditions, and variations in contract; to secure the company's investment (which is in the form of provision of technologies and services); to protect the company against unreasonable liability; to ensure regular payment for progress; and to secure the company against the client's default on conditions of acceptance and bankruptcy.

All parties require assurance that methods are available to monitor production and quality and provide an acceptable procedure for handling disputes.

Standard national forms of contract. Standard forms of building contracts are available in all developed nations and are designed to accommodate the requirements of a wide range of different types of commercial building. They are, therefore, general in format.[1,2]

In this author's experience, standard building contracts based on American or British legal systems provide a good foundation for international work. They can be tailored to meet special conditions of the project: the needs of owner-financier or client; professional advisors; the contractor(s); local social, political, and cultural requirements; and environmental characteristics of the hotel or resort project. It is usually the project manager's duty to supervise and make recommendations for the provisions of special clauses. The project manager must be prepared to advise international lawyers regarding the required content and the type of protection needed; however, contractual provisions may be very difficult to enforce in nations with less sophisticated legal systems.

Contracts for professional services. The contracts made to secure the services of professional companies, such as architects, landscape architects, engineers, and interior designers, set out the general conditions of employment appropriate to the task and technologies required, duties and liabilities, the structure of authority proposed for the project, and the duration of employment, and also stipulate the clients' budget and proposed professional remuneration.

Contract Documents

"Contract documents" in construction refer to the written instructions and agreements that form part of the legal content and on which the contract is based. These are typically

1. Articles of agreement—a short description of the works

2. Conditions—both general and special requirements of the project

3. The drawings, reports, programs, schedules, bill of quantities, and specifications that describe the work to be performed

4. Schedules of rates—may be combined in the contract to cover "PC" items, which are work packages that have been omitted from the tender quotations

5. Miscellaneous documents—often include the contractor's tender (all inclusions should be stated, and may be used later to clarify potential areas of dispute and ambiguity).[2]

The standard contracts include well-understood clauses which incorporate methods of dealing with such typically controversial issues as

Retention sums

Risk sharing

Competence

Cost

Completion time

Negligence

Liquidated damages

Suspension of works and determination of contract

Statutory regulations

Handling of disputes, arbitration

Methods of reconciling local social and cultural factors[2]

Variations

Defects and liability

Experience

Tax

Resource procurement

Delay

Performance guarantees are always included in the terms of the contract made with the successful bidder.

Appointment of contractors and subcontractors. The selection of contractors, traditionally made through the process of invited bidding procedures or negotiation, may take one of the design-bid-build (Fig. 8.1), or the design-build (or design-construct) contract forms. The latter form has recently become much more common.

Designs are prepared for the design-bid-build contract form of project delivery by an architectural-engineering team prior to commencement of the tendering procedure. Since most hotels are of very large and complex construction, prior design preparation by this

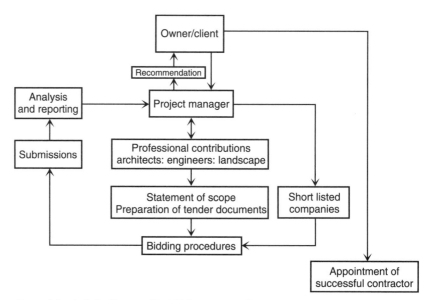

Figure 8.1 Activity diagram: the bidding process. The preparation, submission, and analysis of tender documents and appointment of a head contractor form major objectives in the design-bid-build program during the development phase of the project process. These activities occur as soon as the owner-client's concept has been defined and translated into sufficiently detailed architectural and technical documentation to ensure that a realistic price for the work is received.

method tends to be inefficient because there is an inadequate database, and a considerable amount of the detailed documentation and shop drawings production must necessarily be left for the chosen contracting company after appointment. A combination of the design-bid and design-construct contracts, or the design-construct contract alone (Fig. 8.2) is likely to be more appropriate for project delivery of the large, modern hotel. There may therefore be two different teams of architects and engineers preparing the total documentation package.

Contracts Based on Cost Structure

The English legal system has some well-known types of building contracts that are based on different types of cost structure. Some of these forms, which can be used for either the design-bid-build or design-construct formats, are the lump-sum or fixed- or firm-price contract, the schedule of rates contract, and the cost-plus contract.[1]

The lump-sum contract. The builder offering a lump-sum or firm-price contract agrees to complete the work for a price that cannot be varied if the work is completed exactly in accord with the tender documents. There are, however, two types of lump-sum contract: (1) the contract that contains no provisions for possible variations of price and extension of time and (2) a contract that provides for variations in price, referred to as a "rise and fall" provision. The rise-and-fall contract,

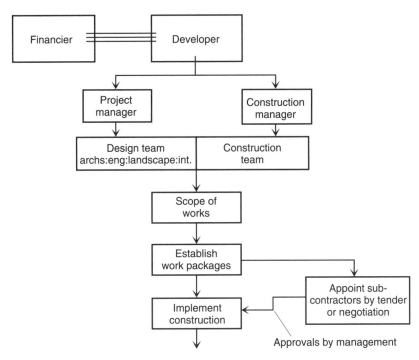

Figure 8.2 The design-construct contract for building works. During the early activities of design, technical documentation, programming, scheduling, and the establishment of work packages, the design and construction teams are closely coordinated. Technology that is appropriate to the company's expertise can therefore be immediately incorporated into the design, with associated cost savings. Negotiation and tendering for the appointment of subcontractors occur only when documentation and work packages are fully defined and so differ in level of effort from the design-bid-build contract process.

for example, may take into account increases in cost due to such causes as inflation and increases in costs of resources during production. The rise-and-fall provision is a very common form of contract, and for the large project, is easier than most to administer and control.[1,2]

Schedule of rates. This form of contract has a schedule of rates for each trade, which is set out prior to confirmation of the contractual agreement and applies to the work that will be performed. All work is measured, and rates are applied according to the schedule. It is a useful form of contract where the extent of the work is unknown, such as in the case of excavation, drainage, piling, and tasks requiring extensive earthworks. It may be combined with one of the other types of contract to advantage. However, administration of the contract requires constant scrutiny, measurement, inspections and approval of work as it is completed.[1,2]

Cost-plus contract. The cost-plus contract provides for payment of the actual cost of the works at an agreed-on rate. The contractor is then paid either an agreed-on percentage commission or a fixed fee. If the fee is fixed, the basis for determination will vary according to variations in the current price of construction.[1,2]

Contracts Based on Management Strategies

New construction management strategies also form a basis for contract formulation, while incorporating one or another of the accepted cost structures, and have a significant impact on the course of the delivery process. In particular, they have altered the traditional proportion of representation in design decision-making procedures, purchasing strategies, and control of total activity on site.

For example, two nontraditional management- and control-oriented contracts are the design-construct contract and the fast-track contract.

Design-construct contract. A design-construct form of contract is offered by a large contractor who employs different professional expertise in house and has the capability of providing project management, architectural and engineering design, as well as construction services. There is an identical requirement in this form of contract for accuracy in the process of surveying quantities and of estimating the cost of the work involved. For example, the balancing of prices across trades and work packages and the responsibility for revenues and returns rest with the company's project management team, who usually include quantity surveyors.

Fast-track contract. The appointment of a head contractor for a fast-track contract takes place early in the project process. Although fast-track construction may begin at any time in the process, it is quite common for various work packages to commence concurrently with the production of design drawings, specifications, and the tendering process for resources and trades. For example, site preliminaries such as rough excavation works and the connection of services to mains may well occur in parallel with architectural and structural engineering design.

The appointment of a contractor in the fast-track situation is often made by recommendation and negotiation. The contractor's prior experience and similar completed works are taken into account and play a major part in the project manager's recommendation to the owner and client.

Confirmation of Intent to Make a Contract

Several tasks must be undertaken once a decision has been made and a contractor selected. These are typically (1) immediate confirmation of client intent letter of appointment, (2) commitment reviews, (3) preparation for exchange of contracts, and (4) engagement of subcontractors and of separate contractors.[3]

It is essential that a written proof of intent be obtained from the owner and/or client for each appointment as a preliminary, for the preparation of the contract and exchange of contracts, especially the head contract for a large project, is time-consuming even if preparatory work has been carried out prior to submission of tenders.

Commitment Reviews

Commitment reviews are held with the extended project team, to communicate, discuss, and confirm contractual requirements and such issues as the details of documentation, the owner-client and operator needs, special obligations related to the project, the process, program, and schedules. The detailed shop drawings must now be completed and the tasks that prepare for early construction activities commenced.[3]

Engagement of subcontractors. The appointment of subcontractors will depend on market circumstances, and must be synchronized by the head or major contractors with the main program. Subcontracting companies who have been chosen for engagement may be occupied with other contracts at the critical times required by the program.

Separate contractors. The client may wish to appoint special contractors who are known or recommended, on a basis separate from that for the main contracts, for example, for hotel fit-out. The project manager and project team must decide on the most appropriate policy to incorporate these separate contractors into the site works and coordinate them with the activities of main contractors. Requirements for strategies that ensure cooperation and coordination must be written into the contract in order to establish control centers and nominate approval hierarchies.[2]

Interface between the Development and Execution Phases

The interface between the development phase of the process and commencement of the execution phase requires a major input and commitment of owner and client, and project manager and project team; for it is here that the main program of site management and control is to commence.

Key factors in the interface stage are the assessment and completion of detailed documentation and the consolidation of the main program paths of activity, including the cost-control programs and expenditure restraints.[4]

Risk Sharing

Under the issue of conditions of contract, the owner-client will usually include special conditions that aim to spread areas of risk, especially those which are unique to the project. Negotiations may take place to spread these risks which are common to all contracts, during contract formulation, although it is a difficult and complex task to make alterations to traditional legal clauses, which have become standardized through experience over a considerable period. Risk sharing can also be negotiable for special conditions and a contract designed accordingly.[3]

The companies tendering for the contract (of whatever type) will also wish to include conditions that protect their interests and spread the financial responsibilities for risk, although some responsibility for risk may eventuality be offered as part of their bidding strategy.

The problems of risk hedging demand creative lateral thinking, and suggestions such as changes to the program and the critical path of activities, and alternative source logistics, are worthy of joint consideration and offer opportunity for improvement in accord with the unique characteristics of the project.

A contractor bidding for work on a worldwide market includes strategies that have special reference to risks connected with international work and the characteristics of suppliers working under subcontract (who may be in another country). However, the negotiations should still take into account the advantages to be achieved from a shared savings on costs that may arise from jointly originated solutions to contingency and perceived opportunities.

The types of risk that may be shared by negotiation and agreement between the owner-client and contractor(s) in international resort work are typically delays caused through social and political conditions, changes to program and schedule caused by delayed imports of materials and supplies that affect key dates in the construction schedule, problems of climate and weather, and changes to plan design and program caused by geotechnical conditions unknown prior to arrival on site.

Contract Administration

Several very large contracts may be awarded for a single resort project, for example, site preparation and infrastructure, landscaping, building construction, and interior fit-out. A separate site construction manager may be appointed, and/or one of the main contractors may take responsibility for the administration of a major contract. However, the project manager must take the responsibility for the overall coordination of the participating companies on the client's behalf. (See Fig. 8.3.) Control of a large project is dependent on good communication and information processing to ensure coordination and compliance with key dates and sequences of activities in the program and schedule.

Construction procurement. The project manager and project team's activities so far have all been oriented toward the preparation for implementation and execution of construction. The project manager, at this point in the process, should have established sufficiently broad authority over the various elements of the project, to set in motion activities that are required to complete the project successfully, and should have authority, in design and technical decisions, over the development of the process by working in close alliance with the construction managers and teams.

During the execution and finalization phases of the process the extended teams are responsible for the satisfactory completion of program tasks; however, it is essential that the owner, client, and operator's approvals and signature be obtained progressively for all major stages in the project process.

Decision making for project management depends on agreement and the synthesis of data, requiring input from many different professional and trade sources, and the flexible characteristic of the project management system is now utilized to correlate the diverse and unique needs of the project and procurement processes.

The wide-based hierarchical structure is very adaptable to fluctuating conditions and environmental needs and has the capability to react quickly to multidisciplinary project demands for decision making. This attribute helps the project manager delegate management and control responsibilities across a much wider section of the team, and rely on project team members for up-to-date progress reports, information, and advice. The project manager must rely on the recommendations of the project team members to a much greater degree during the later phases of the project process.

The project manager's role becomes the focal point to integrate and implement responsibilities and activities, with the following typical results:

The project manager assumes increased accountability for team members' actions.

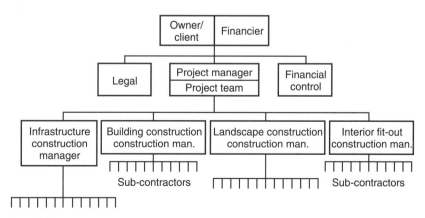

Figure 8.3   A simple structure for contract management and administration. The chart illustrates a very simple structure that could serve as a basis for contract administration of a resort.

Strong control and coordination are necessary.

The interfaces of project tasks must be planned, managed, and controlled precisely.

All planning and control strategies must be thoroughly integrated.

Implementing activities. Activities of the project management team and the construction management team that are undertaken during the implementation phase are summarized at the end of this chapter.

The project team is responsible for supervision and ensuring that the tasks and programs have been satisfactorily implemented. The team should approve all the main procedures taken, during the preliminary work, by the main contractors. (See Fig. 8.4.) These actions typically include the following points:

Check that insurance policies are in place to cover construction activity: project, public liability, and workers' compensation.

Insurance policies are the contractor's responsibility.

Commence induction programs: schedule and implement lectures and discussion.

Monitor safety programs for site work, and ensure that these conform with the requirements of government authorities.

Arrange for site and progress reports.

Establish notification procedures for delays and variations.

Production control. Many separate major work packages may occur simultaneously, especially on a large development. Project management has the task of coordinating the effort of the different major contractors on the site, which take place both simultaneously and in sequence. Sequences must be checked, found correct, and approved.

At commencement of the execution phase, therefore, the tasks involved in implementation assume a management hierarchy; the head contractor's project team take over construction management responsibilities from the project manager, and the project management team's tasks change in character to those of control, coordination, monitoring, and supervision of the project's global activities.

Programming for construction. The project management team's early definition of work packages now engenders the discrete construction programs. However, the construction teams need to redefine the content of the work packages to match the capabilities of their company and the sequences of an attainable construction program.[4] It is essential that all the teams reach agreement for programs and strategies of site presence, procurement, and detailed construction planning which can be correlated to suit their particular capabilities. Cost and quality control programs are also interconnected through meeting and discussion with the main project management programs.

Trade specialists refine design drawings and produce shop draw-

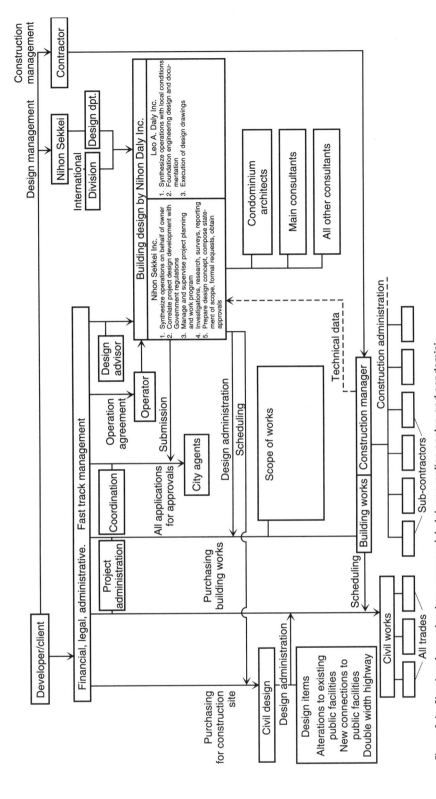

Figure 8.4 Structure for contract management, hotel, convention center, and condominiums: Nihon Sekkei, Project Managers, Design and Technology by Nihon Daly, Inc. The chart illustrates the allocation of responsibilities between three types of project management: design, construction, and administrative (including legal and financial). The various activities and responsibilities are coordinated at different levels and closely integrated throughout the structure.

ings according to the capability of their subcontractors, and recheck the availability and confirmation of delivery times of resources, according to their determination of the program and schedules. Subprograms and loops are built according to sequences, and special attention is given to key dates for completion of work-breakdown units and the interdependencies of trades, showing float and task dependencies. The main construction program acquires great accuracy and definition.

Meetings. Meetings form an important part of these activities for reasons of control, coordination, reporting, and spread of information. It is most important to nominate the personnel who are expected to attend, and send a reminder and program for discussion in ample time so that prior consideration can be given to topics on the agenda. Plans should be made to accommodate subsidiary meetings, whenever required.

Actions to Be Taken at This Time

The activities of project manager, project team, and construction manager and team occur simultaneously and overlap. The project manager must correlate these activities and build team commitment.

The following activities assume that a construction management contract has been agreed on. Actions included are also necessary for design-construct contracts, but strategies for management and administration will differ as many of the tasks listed for action by the project manager will be administered in house by the contracting firm.

- Project manager:

    Organize and implement tender procurement

    Review costs, compare with budget, and obtain agreements

    Recheck environmental constraints and requirements

    Analyze and compare tender submissions; advise client, recommend acceptances

    Confirm that all design requirements are complete: supervise the completion, submission, and approval of shop drawings

    Supervise finalization of contract negotiations and appointment of construction teams

    Confirm that bank guarantees are in place (these are for security and retention purposes and are required from the main contractors; however, on some occasions, the owner, too, may be required to arrange financial guarantees)

    Check that insurance policies are in place: project, public liability, workers' compensation, professional indemnity

    Supervise submission of other items to be provided by the contractor, such as confirmation of cash flow, a detailed program, quality manual, safety plan, and environmental protection plan

    Confirm and coordinate activities of main program

Initiate intercompany and personnel relations programs in order to overcome the "them/us" attitude among different contractors (this task should also be carried out by the main contractors in order to create team identification among subcontractors)

Prepare induction programs as required

Confirm communications network and program meetings: reporting format and hierarchies

Establish notification procedures and approval hierarchies: completions, approvals, delays, and variations

Confirm sequences of activities on site

Coordinate activities of all main contractors and their ingress on site

Supervise the establishment of safety measures

Prepare commissioning programs: plan to finish

Plan and initiate strategies and procedures for handling variations and other critical issues

Coordinate contractor's project managers with the project team

- Contractors:

  Implement program for submission of tender

  Confirm the feasibility of project schedules, design, and construction program

  Confirm dates for vacant possession of site

  Prepare costs, balance with budget

  Confirm logistics and schedules

  Negotiate and sign construction contract

  Commit personnel and resources

  Plan and initiate program for construction management

  Arrange for bank guarantees

  Arrange for insurance policies

  Negotiate, appoint, and confirm contracts with subcontractors

  Correlate subcontractor activities with the main construction program and schedules

  Arrange for detailed geologic examinations as required

  Complete detailed design documentation: shop drawings, programs, and schedules (about 50 percent are usually completed for bidding purposes)

  Arrange for site meetings, reporting hierarchy

  Hold preconstruction meetings

  Arrange for induction meetings

Plan and program site establishment; set funds aside for this purpose

Implement site safety program

Plan vehicular movement, materials access, and delivery to site

Plan people movement on site, and interface with access routes and sphere of activity of large-scale equipment

References

1. David M. Bennett, *Brooking on Building Contracts,* 2d ed., Butterworths Press Pty., Ltd. Australia, 1980.
2. L. N. Duncan Wallace, *Hudson's Building and Engineering Contracts,* 10th ed., Sweet & Maxwell, London, 1970.
3. J. Frost and H. McLennan, *Various Papers for the Master of Project Management Program,* University of Technology Sydney, Sydney, Australia, 1992.
4. Jim Mooney, *Cost Effective Building Design,* New South Wales University Press, Australia, 1983.

Bibliography

Harold Kerzner, *Project Management: A Systems Approach to Planning, Scheduling and Controlling,* 3d ed., Van Nostrand Reinhold, New York, 1989.

9

Execution Phase: Project Construction

It is perhaps most common for clients to appoint a separate supervisory project manager and project team to represent their interests. This team manages and controls the project from conception to completion and, in the course of project delivery, correlates and integrates the activities of several large construction companies.

Project Management Responsibilities: Execution Phase

The Project Manager

The project manager has responsibility for global management and control and, in particular, the implementation and supervision of the total program of work in progress; the management of communications between the owner, the users, and construction companies; client approvals; and monitoring. (See Fig. 9.1.)

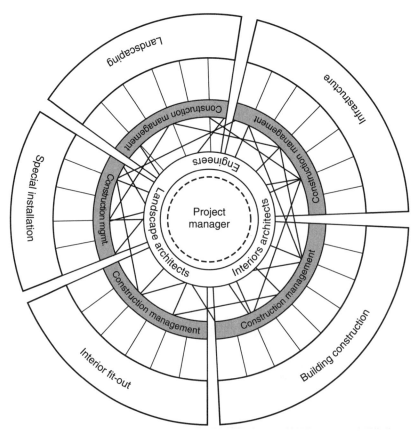

Figure 9.1 Implementation and commissioning phases: project management responsibilities. A different head contractor may be appointed to manage and control one major activity, for example, building construction, the installation of roads, or the construction of a golf course. The project manager has the duty to coordinate all these areas of responsibility into a global system, and to control progress. This simplified chart, suitable for resort development, illustrates the centralized duties of the project team, showing interconnections and lines of communication between the major areas of production and major areas of responsibility under the control of the construction managers.

At the commencement of this phase, the main work of managing the procurement of the project is concerned with the detailed planning of construction. This is primarily the concern of the construction manager and construction team. While the construction managers report to the project manager, they are responsible for the management and control of their own area of construction and the works of all trades subcontracting to their contract.

If a design-build, design-construct contract is agreed on, a project manager is often (but not always) appointed from this company. In this case, the company's personnel are allocated to the positions of both project manager and construction project manager and have total responsibility and control of the production of design documentation, the programming and scheduling of site works, and all construction activities.

During the execution phase, therefore, more than one type of project manager has duties and responsibilities to the project and client. In this chapter the terms *project manager* and *construction project manager* or *construction manager* are used to distinguish between their various fields of activity.

Preliminaries. The project manager and project team must first establish a strategy to correlate and integrate the work of all the major contractors. This strategy must incorporate a procedure to analyze and approve all the programs, schedules, and plans submitted for preliminary works on site. Each construction program relates to the whole scope and schedule of activities, and it is essential that sequences and physical activities on site do not conflict. Analysis of the construction programs includes, for example, a study of the use of site entrances and exits, schedules for the use of large equipment, site delivery times, security, and safety programs. To achieve the objectives of overall coordination, a detailed global program of control is prepared by the project manager and project team. Induction meetings should also be planned to include all project and construction management team members in order that they become familiar with their part in the total program.

Early Construction Management Activities

The successful contractor usually starts planning the basic and real-time (project under construction) management strategies and production control programs, before contract negotiations are complete. The construction management team must now examine the documentation prepared by the project design teams in detail and match requirements with resources, such as labor, equipment, supplies, and materials. The objectives of basic planning for construction are to allocate resources and establish a program and schedule that are capable of achieving completion of the project.[1,2] (See Fig. 9.2)

Comparing Alternative Programs

There are often several alternative ways to program construction. At first, alternatives are compared by running trials of costs and schedules, with the objective of matching work packages to the resources and methods available to the contractor. Priorities include the planning of resource use (with alternatives), cash flow forecasting, and subdividing tasks into partial area networks or "work-breakdown units."[3]

The chart in Fig. 9.3 summarizes actions that contribute to the detailed program planning for construction.

Resorts and high-rise hotels

Resorts. Although horizontal planning offers a good opportunity for partial or staged completion of various sections of the total resort project, the coordination of a construction program for resort development, which incorporates the expedient installation and adequate supply of utilities and resources, usually demands complex scheduling. Problems arise because a pattern of unrelated but simultaneous activities, spread over a large area, must be correlated. The need for utility services for both completed sections and continuing use in the construction processes are often, in fact, very difficult to plan and coordinate successfully and demand a control strategy capable of absorbing

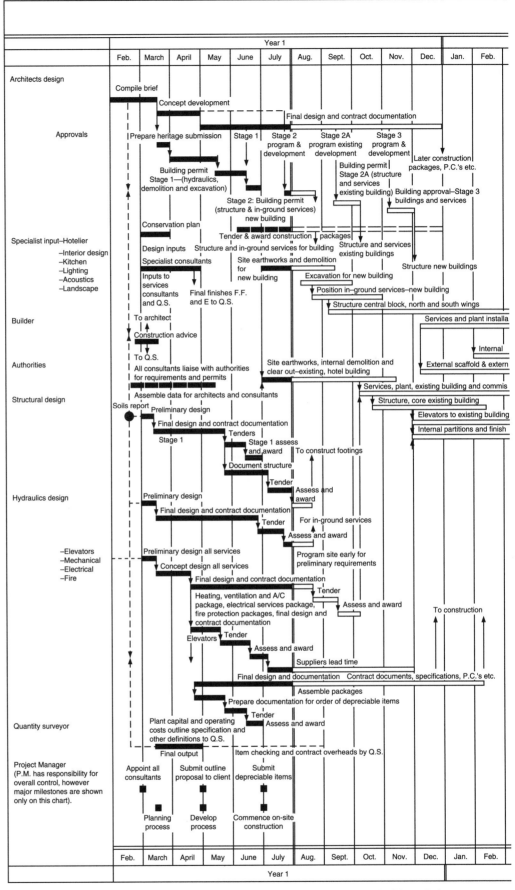

Figure 9.2 (*a*) Overall control program for the development of a hotel. This bar chart is made to assist the overall control of the redevelopment and extension of a hotel, which combines the renovation of an existing building (listed locally for preservation under the "Heritage" Act) with extensive new additions to the structure. The architects', engineers', and specialists' design input is correlated

THE HOTEL

	Year 2										Year 3						
March	April	May	June	July	Aug.	Sept.	Oct.	Nov.	Dec.	Jan.	Feb.	March	April	May	June	July

Complete 17 calender month
construction period
▽

Hotel
operational
▽

tion & commissioning

Elevator installation & building commissioning

walls & finishes

al brick walls

Provisions for delays

sioning

and commissioning

Hotel operator
fit–out and occupation

es

Prepared for:

Title:
Overall project
program

March	April	May	June	July	Aug.	Sept.	Oct.	Nov.	Dec.

Year 2

with the construction schedule. While supervising and controlling the total program, the project
manager has the duty to ensure that certain important milestones, such as authority approvals,
are achieved on time. These milestones are noted at the bottom of the chart. The chart might
also be used as a basic model for the preparation of programs for other projects, provided it
were adapted to specific requirements.

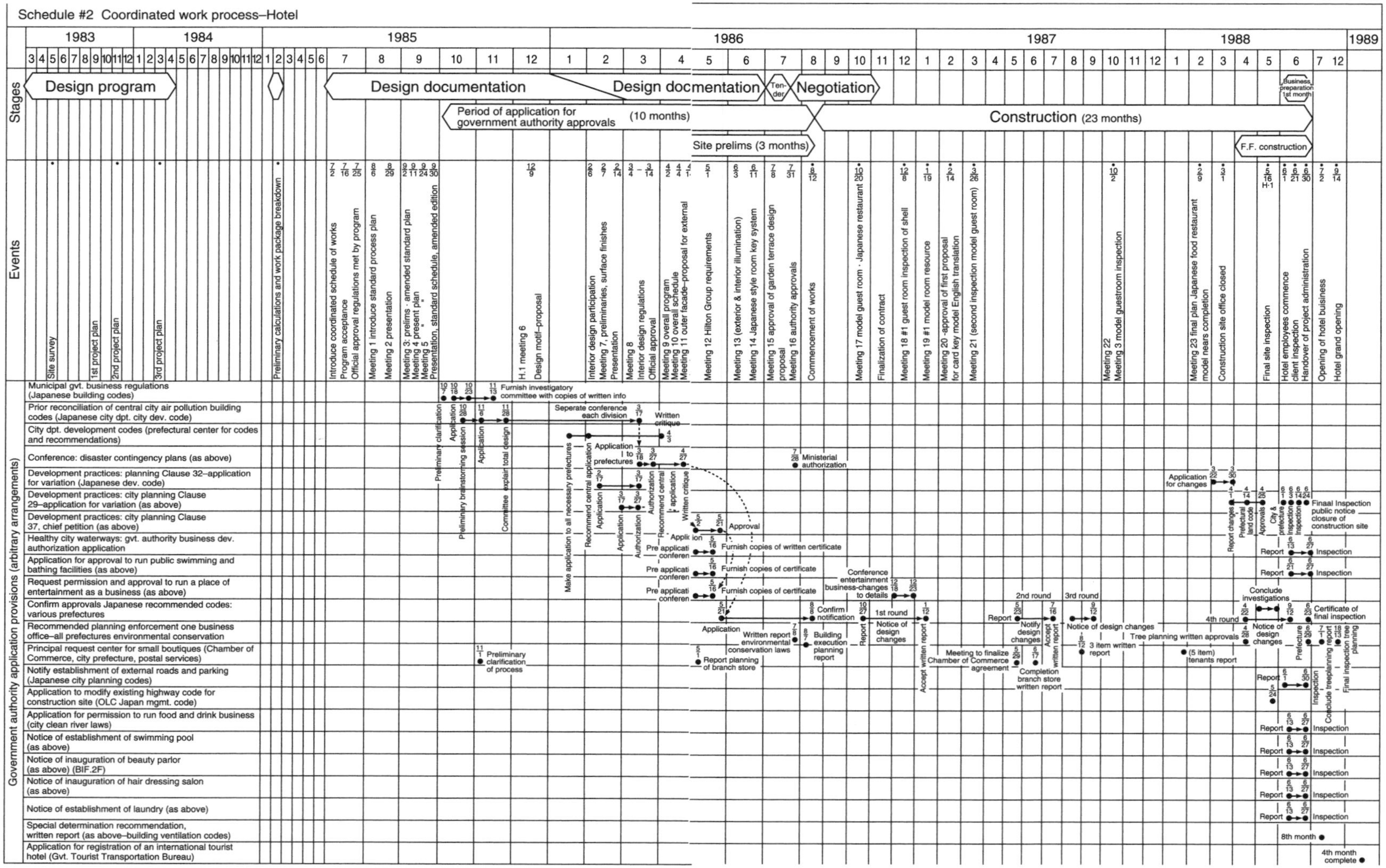

Figure 9.2 *(b)*The coordination of government authority permissions and approvals to the procurement of a hotel. The necessary schedule for securing government authority permissions, forms a sub-schedule to the design and construction program for the procurement of a hotel. Commencing with the development of the initial design concept, this chart relates the progress of approval acquisition to the process of procurement. It illustrates very well the complexity of the approval system in an advanced nation (Japan) and the importance and project team's obligation to acquire permissions and approvals within a tightly controlled schedule so that the design and construction processes can proceed without delays being incurred. Investigations, reports, and conferences are held well in advance of the date when approval is required. (Nihon Sekkei, Architects, Engineers, Project Managers, Tokyo.)

Schedule #2   Coordinated work process—Hotel

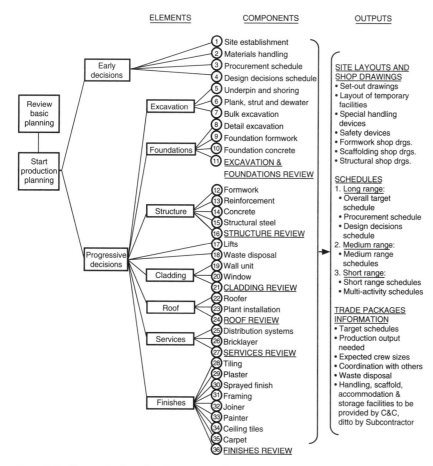

ELEMENTS COMPONENTS OUTPUTS

Figure 9.3 The production planning process. The chart summarizes the preparation and basic planning, decisions, elements, and components which culminate in production. Output includes detailed shop drawings, schedules, programs, and trade package information. *(Frost and Mechennan, University of Technology Sydney, 1991–1992.)*

many varied programming requirements. Extra cost outlay for out-of-sequence technological installation becomes necessary. The spacious site, however, offers a planning advantage in respect of the interfaces between construction activities and areas of safe public access, although control and supervision is essential.

High-rise hotels. The high-rise "footprint," on the other hand, concentrates such issues as delivery to site, utility services, equipment use, and building activity into a limited area. Therefore, danger zones between construction and public use, although clearly defined, are a greater potential hazard and demand careful planning and constant control and supervision. Commissioning procedures for the high-rise hotel usually follow the progress of construction—upward. However, like other types of high-rise building that are considered for staged completion, the difficulties imposed by vertical division, such as noise from construction processes and the programming and allocation of vertical transportation between construction activities and public use, may easily preclude progressive opening.[3]

Production Control

Networks and construction planning. Bar charts and precedence network programs are in common use to monitor and control the construction process. The construction team checks the key dates and deadlines of the final program on the critical path for feasibility, and target schedules are set for construction crews. Floats are analyzed, the earliest start dates are identified, and the whole program is finely adjusted to the technologies available to the contractor. Many subprograms which clarify the main network and control subsidiary work packages are necessary.

Methods that measure progress, quantities, resources, quality, and cash flow during the process of construction allow for comparison of progressive feedback with the original project objectives and recognition of variances as they occur in the head contract, budget, program, and schedule. Corrective action and replanning can then be carried out quickly to follow up contingency decisions based on this data.[4]

There are, however, some disadvantages associated with the use of network technology on the construction site of a large project. For example, bar charts and precedence networks are complex, and many tradespeople find them difficult or impossible to read. Time relationships are seldom visually portrayed and clear, although some charts do show interconnections. (Precedence networks are much better in this regard.) Key dates and milestones may also be unclear. Mooveover, it is difficult to alter the program, and the changes often take a considerable time even with the use of a computer.

A programmed introduction of training classes during the induction period helps solve some of these problems.

Recording and circulating data: meetings. All data that originates in the construction process must be recorded and circulated to the project and construction teams regularly on a need-to-know basis. Preconstruction meetings should be held to plan and confirm the format of project meetings and agendas, which are usually arranged at maximum monthly intervals.[3]

Preconstruction Task Analysis and Planning

Essential planning that takes place in the preconstruction interface following design development must include the following factors:

1. Programs of induction meetings for construction teams

2. Delays and special conditions

3. Conditions of appointment of head contractor and subcontractors

4. The status of design and documentation

5. Purchasing strategies

6. Detailed cost estimates

7. Construction preliminaries

8. Finance and insurance policies

9. Social and environmental issues and impacts[3]

Topics for Induction Meetings

Induction meetings should include a description of the project and site, programs and schedules (especially staged occupancy), safety measures, site restraints, environmental issues, and contract times and conditions.

Delays and special conditions. During development of the construction program, allowances must be made for delays occasioned by weather conditions, problems caused by long lead times, procurement of resources, industrial or social problems, and receipt of approvals. During preconstruction stage, programmed allowances of time (or float) are redefined and refined.[5]

Conditions of appointment of the head contractor and subcontractors. The extent of support at management and trade levels that is provided by the construction company depends on the terms of their contract agreement with the owner-client. For example, the company may contract to provide a project manager, construction manager, or both officers, and agree to allocate certain senior members of staff for positions on the team. Alternatively, nominations for senior positions may depend entirely on the composition and availability of company staff at the time the contract agreement is made and the project commences.

The management structure of the construction team is based in the matrix project management system, with members recruited from the permanent structure of the company. The construction manager, once appointed, assumes the duty of appointing other members of the construction team according to availability, experience and ability, and the extent of resources and technical support needed to deliver the project. A choice may be made between the use of permanent company staff, or the commissioning of a subcontractor. These decisions are influenced by current workload, and cost factors. The project manager must be advised of the contracting company's nominations for senior positions on the team and the client's formal approval of nominations will usually be necessary.

The status of design documentation. The status of the design documentation depends on the form of contractual agreement made with the owner-client.[6] For example, when contracts are exchanged, there may be no statement of scope or documentation available for the design-construct contract; on the other hand, a varying percentage of the whole will be completed for the traditional design-bid-build form, with some technical documentation remaining to be done. At commencement of a mixed design-build, design-bid-build type of contract, usually very little detailed technical design work is accomplished and the head contractor acting as project manager becomes responsible for programming the production of detailed design by staff architects and engineers and/or outside professional companies.

The contractor therefore first analyzes the status of the development of the design documentation and establishes the extent of work that remains to be completed for construction purposes. For example, the range of documentation that may still need to be examined includes the establishment and initiation of quality assurance requirements and programs; the status of authority approvals, constraints and conditions; the initiation and confirmation of programs for cost control; opportunities for cost saving; areas of opportunity, and methods to monitor, assess, and optimize work strategies and processes; risk areas.

Purchasing. This topic covers both the appointment of subcontractors (resource procurement) and the ordering and delivery of supplies. Programs and schedules must be checked and confirmed, if, for example, it is found that a schedule cannot be met, it is essential that alternative sources be located. Other factors that influence the purchasing strategies and schedules are the limits to the head contractor's responsibility, confirmation of subcontractors contracts, integration of nominated subcontractors into the construction program, allocation of responsibilities for scheduling orders and the delivery of imported supplies and materials, method of obtaining approvals, and allocation of responsibilities for off-site schedules for purchasing (Fig. 8.4 showed that purchasing duties were undertaken in a particular system by a financial-administrative project team), and the exclusions of materials and resources from the contract price (these are classified as "PC" items, and a lump sum is set aside to cover estimated total costs).

The limit of the building contractors responsibility for purchasing is also defined by the type of contract made between the head contractor and the owner-client.[6] The contract for interior fit-out, for example, of hotels and resorts is commonly awarded to a different company specializing in interior work, and the head contractor may control their site activities only insofar as construction must have reached a certain stage before interior work can begin. Purchasing of interior technical equipment, fixtures, and fittings is undertaken by the interior specialist.

Figure 9.4   Nikko Hotel: facade under construction. This view was taken across the freeway from Darling Harbor as precast panels were being installed. Safety hoardings of highest rating protect the freeway, which runs under part of the hotel.

Estimating. The team quantity surveyors are responsible for the estimation of quantities and costs of materials and resources. Quantity estimates are based on design documentation and specifications, if they are available; otherwise similar construction details from other work are used as a guide. Programs and schedules are made for work packages, work units are defined and detailed, and the budget is balanced and allocated across the process.

In a design-bid-build contract, the contractor's estimating work commences with the preparation of tender documents. Only about 50 to 60 percent of detail is likely to be completed for bidding purposes. Detailed estimating by contractors, therefore, continues after the award of the contract into the commencement of the execution phase.[3]

Once the contract is agreed on, the price is fixed, subject to various contingency clauses in the contract. Some prices are purposely left out of the budget, and allowances are made for them in the form of PC items. The reasons for this action, especially in international work, are in general

Detailed budgets for various materials and finishes cannot yet be made. For example, interior designers and contractors may not have been appointed; it is therefore more appropriate to set aside an agreed-on percentage of the budget for this purpose.

A supplier has not been appointed, so it is early enough in the process to research suppliers of a quality product locally and decide later whether an imported product must be purchased

Information on prices is unreliable.

It is difficult to obtain confirmation of delivery dates, so orders have not been placed; this is a risky situation that may affect scheduled opening dates and must be rectified as soon as possible.

Construction preliminaries. Work packages are naturally developed to suit the special requirements of the project's construction process, and nontypical parts of the program are studied and incorporated into the network during detailed development.

The installation of building services, the repetitive fit-out of guest rooms, and other interior fit-out procedures will always occur on the critical path of hotel construction. Special consideration needs to be given to the correlation of repetitive tasks into the program, for savings of time and cost can often be made with careful planning. The work of construction of the main fabric of the building is programmed to support these requirements.

Other factors that are studied at preconstruction stage are typically programming, scheduling, and integration of construction, building services, and interior fit-out activities; programming project planning workshops in order to discuss the coordination of the various work packages, programs, and schedules; establishing a method for the issue of drawings (formal signatures and approvals are essential); planning and implementing the issue of programs and day/date calenders to team members; establishing programs for regular and key future meetings, with attendances, including project management, design, and construction personnel; initiating public relations programs and activities; implementing safety programs and procedures and, in the case of a large resort, for example, coordinating these with other major site activities; and reviewing programs for commissioning and completion. (Plan to finish!)

Finance and insurance policies.   It is essential that several contractual obligations be fulfilled and business arrangements completed before site preliminaries commence. The project manager has the duty to request formal evidence that these actions have in fact been completed, as they play a vital part in protecting both the contractor's and owner-client's interests:[3]

Security deposits are in place

Insurance policies are in place

Progress claims and cash flow procedures are established

Other important financial arrangements to be established are supporting in-house accounting procedures, an auditing system, and a method of recording variation advice and variations to budget.

Social and environmental issues and impacts.   Both social and environmental changes cause concern to the community, even though the hotel or resort is expected to provide employment for many local people. The project team must plan and implement a strategy to promote acceptance, community approval, and a sense of identification with the project, for the hotel or resort depends on the surrounding district for at least some of its supplies as well as labor. The project and construction managers should evaluate factors which are likely to cause conflict, develop a program for information exchange, and investigate local opinions and suggestions with the goal of establishing good permanent public relations. Local residents should be invited to attend exhibitions of the project models and perspectives, discussions of the concept and explanations of the construction schedule, and other functions which seem appropriate.

Development concepts are generally exhibited to the district at sketch plan stage, because in many locations, authority approvals cannot be obtained without exposure of the proposal to the local community for comment. Questions and problems that are of concern to the local community, for example, the duration of noisy activities such as piling and the inconveniences caused by interference with local traffic flow, are discussed, and if possible adaptations made for local needs and opinions. Noise-generating activities are commonly restricted between certain hours, and it is recommended that this limitation should be observed even in locations were there are no regulations.

Variations to (and deviations from) the contract.   Variations to the contract are legally described as additions or alterations to the works. These may typically be caused by extras, enlargements, alterations, additions, deviations, changes, omissions, substitutions, and modifications.

Variations are a very fertile source of dispute between owner, client, and contractor, and for this reason, clauses are nearly always written into the formal contract[6] for protection and to give guidance for the handling of disputes. The contractor with a lump-sum agreement is especially vulnerable to any major changes in design and price, for repercussions will immediately affect the final contracted price and schedule (and therefore profits) for the project.

Variation quotations. During the construction of a large development, it is very important that the contractor give a "variation quotation" or "variation price" before proceeding to implement the variation, and essential that this price be recommended by the project manager and formally approved by the owner-client, before any action is initiated. The contract usually provides a format for written variation orders (the costs to be confirmed by the contractor in writing), and indeed this procedure is necessary for the proper control of cost and budget. In the case when a client desires a variation or change or addition to the design, the project manager must draw attention to the probable delays that will affect the schedule while the additional documentation and allocation of resources and supplies are provided.

Administering the Contract: 1

The Production Program

The process of project delivery is composed of a constellation of activities that are managed, coordinated, integrated, and controlled by the project and construction managers. The work packages may occur simultaneously or sequentially and are procured by the use of interdependent or separate contracts of varying formats. Management plans differ according to the needs and philosophies of the client, characteristics and location of site (downtown or a remote location), market type (resort or high-rise hotel), and environmental conditions.[2]

Contract clauses.[6] The contract for construction has a significant influence on the final form and quality of the hotel and resort, by means of clauses and options which the client can choose to include in order to define the strategies for control. For example, these options may set down conditions in detail for the designation of authority, the checking and approval of completed work, a purchasing policy, the acquisition of resources, site agreements and restraints, and other matters relating to the real-time construction process. The project manager is responsible first for reviewing and reconciling the contractor's offer with both the tender documentation and the conditions of contract and subsequently for making detailed recommendations to the client during the final negotiations prior to signing of the contract agreement.

Clauses in the contract, which are, in general, negotiated between the client and contractor, control such conditions as the contractor's legal obligation to adhere to the design drawings and specifications (the documentation forms part of the contract), the amount of retention sums to be held and conditions of release, defects liability, the allotment of liabilities for stoppage and delays, conditions for progress payments and overtime payments, requirements for coordination among contractors, and requirements for maintenance and warranties. There will also be special clauses and conditions that relate to unique characteristics of the project written into the contract documents. Unless all these issues are defined and specified in the contract in detail, they may later lead to dispute between the parties to the contract during the periods of real-time construction and postcompletion.

The project manager's responsibilities to the client are especially important with regard to the negotiations and agreements that affect quality assurance and control, the management of construction costs, acceptance of completed works and approval of progress payments, and variations to the documentation and contracted works. The following list summarizes some other factors that also influence procurement options:

Clauses relating to location; social, political, and environmental conditions

Methods of selection of subcontractors

The capability of the contracting company to provide the contracted work

Provision for industrial and labor relations

Safety precautions

Scheduled availability of contractor's resources

Communication skills

Budgetary requirements

Management and Control of Postcontract Costs and Budget

Objectives. The objectives of cost planning, management, and control during the development phase are to obtain value for money, to positively influence design decisions toward efficiency, to assess the economics of the project development, and to use the results in preparation for tendering. Estimating activities during this phase are concerned with investigation, monitoring, and the balancing of costs against an agreed-on budget. The design of any work unit can still be amended to produce a reduction in costs, or even abandoned if costs are too high; indeed, the price continues to be negotiable through to the submission of bids. The signing of the contract for the work is a milestone of considerable importance in the achievement of an accurate estimate of the total budget.[7]

Contingency. It is unusual, however, if after the process has been completed, the final agreed-on costs of development are exactly the same as the original tender price. For this reason, a nominated sum for contingencies is usually built into the contract price. The allowance for contingency must be based on a realistic estimate, and include inflationary or deflationary tendencies. Contingency sums may sometimes be resorted to by the contractor as a security cover (in a high estimate), or a competitive tool for bidding purposes (low estimate). This position must be avoided at all costs as it will surely lead to dispute.[7]

As postcontract construction or "real time" work progresses, options and opportunities for change and amendment become increasingly limited and, depending on the type of contract that has been negotiated, have a bias toward considerations of program and schedule. It is in the owners', users', project manager's, and contractors' major interests, for example, to rigorously monitor and control these factors, especially in fast-track production when change would cause delays and cost overruns.

Control Strategies

An efficient cost-control system is dependent on the generation of a definitive statement of the clients' budgetary allowances and commitment, cash flow requirements, proposed future expenditure patterns, a good communication system, and regular reporting at established intervals. The program controls that are established during the early development phase by the project manager are delegated to the charge of a team member who plans the cost-control program and researches all official orders, drawings, and letters as they are issued. The contractors' detailed construction estimates are incorporated as soon as they become available. Negotiated contracts are excellent vehicles by which to initiate these controls.[6] It is in the interest of both parties to achieve a sound working basis for design and real-time cost control while discussing contract objectives and conditions in collaboration, and the establishment of good team commitment and relationships between the project and construction teams contribute to the success of the program.

Data, which is current to the stage reached in the process, must be recorded continuously and communicated to team members in order to enable them to monitor expenditure and forecast possible areas where increases in cost may occur, record and forecast cash flow and schedules for progress payments, and report ongoing expenditure to the client for approval. The records are used to evaluate the cost-effectiveness (or otherwise) of any major changes, additions, or variations as work proceeds.

Cost-control strategies in context. The detailed actions that must take place to manage and control costs are influenced by each type of contract. For example, the contractor with a lump-sum agreement estimates the cost of the work included in the contract documentation, by assessing the material quantities and labor involved in each work unit and adding a percentage for overheads and profit. The method of assessing payment (or reductions) and adjustments for the nominated subcontractor's work and for omissions and variations must also be agreed on by client, project manager, and contractor.[8]

Evaluation of construction quality systems. The word "quality" used out of context has very little meaning. Quality is defined by the extent and degree of satisfaction produced in meeting the designs and specifications required by the owner, and the measure of compliance with standards set by the industry, which include rigorous safety and protection measures whenever appropriate.[9]

Extra expense is incurred if there are deviations, and this is often considerable, for not only are there initial costs of production, but in addition, future costs for rectification or replacement must be incorporated in the total price. Problems of substandard materials, equipment, and finishes are particularly burdensome to hotel management, especially housekeeping staff, when building services break down or malfunction, and interiors require constant maintenance or even early renovation.

Two different developments in "quality assurance" have arisen in recent years. The Total Quality Control (TQC) technology, which developed in Japan, is based on strategies to increase employee responsibility, self-monitoring and commitment, and general improvement of group dynamic practices.[10] An alternative technology, developed in the United States, analyzes the costs associated with the production of quality products that meet set standards, and the effect on profits when there are deviations.[4,10] Estimates are made for the total budget based on market surveys and experience of maintenance and replacement costs. Both methods are important contributors to the technology for quality assurance and agree in principle that (1) quality performance must be controlled by a delegated manager, who is appointed well before production commences; and (2) it is costly and ineffective to monitor and react to poor quality in the traditional way, that is, by initiating further tests and increasing inspections.

Quality assurance.[4]   Quality assurance programs are often difficult and expensive to introduce in the functional management context, because the technology demands major changes to the system. However, the flexibility of the project management system offers the project manager an excellent opportunity to introduce training for quality assurance programs on the lines of TQC, particularly in the early phases of the process when the encouragement and creation of team commitment is in progress.[4] Later analyses of the cost-effectiveness of the installation are based on feedback from the production process and take account of all maintenance problems that have occurred.

Example: the Nikko (Corn Exchange) Hotel, Sydney.   A program for quality assurance was undertaken for the supply, tender, and erection of repetitive precast panels for the facade of the Nikko Hotel (Figs. 9.4 and 9.5), Sussex Street, Sydney, built by Civil and Civic Constructions Pty. Ltd. Assessments of the capability of suppliers were carried out prior to finalization of the contract, and the successful manufacturer's quality plan was reviewed.[3]

The supply of the panels required a long lead time, and had to be imported into Sydney, when there was possibility of damage to the panels. Seven hundred facade panels were required for 14 floors, and the design varied slightly at the corners of the building and other locations on the facade, so that five different molds had to be made for casting. The panels were given an epoxy undercoat prior to ship-

Figure 9.5   Precast panels: facade, Nikko Hotel, Sydney, Australia. (Civil and Civic Constructions Pty. Ltd., Sydney.)

ment, and storage and final surface treatment were also to be arranged in Sydney.

A program and schedule, with a critical path of activities and key dates, were made for the supply, quality control procedures such as testing and inspection, and the erection of the precast panels. The program was planned to take into account likely problems of manufacture, delivery, storage, and finish, so that a quality panel met the set standards was achieved and made available for erection. Each panel was tracked through the manufacturing sequences, through shipment and delivery to final installation. It was essential that the program correlated with the critical path of activities and key dates of the main program of construction, because the fit-out of guest rooms was scheduled to begin as soon as the work of erection was completed on each floor.

Detailed site planning and the procurement of resources and technologies depend on the type and characteristics of the building's design and the cultural and geographic location of the project. For example, the characteristics of the location and geological conditions will modify the type of plan and building structure, impose constraints on construction activities (access and egress, hours of work, availability of plant and other resources, authority regulations), and influence the schedule and budget.

Preliminaries: Site Establishment

Site establishment is necessarily the first real-time activity in the construction process. Preparatory work is generally commenced on site as soon as formal arrangements between owner-client and contractor allow, and while other planning connected with the detailed administration of construction is still proceeding, for the work of foundation construction cannot begin until the major components of the preliminary work are completed. Preliminary work typically includes installation of roads, safety and protective measures, sewerage lines, water supply, connection to electric mains, shoring of adjacent buildings (if required), and rough excavation work.

Planning procedures. The preliminary planning of site establishment usually follows a typical pattern of procedures in order to coordinate with the schedule of the main construction program:

1. Confirm first activities on the main construction program and schedule.

2. Confirm that all authority approvals necessary for commencement have been received.

3. Confirm that all necessary geotechnical surveys and reports are completed, check with design documentation.

4. Confirm availability of resources.

5. Plan the site layout, use, circulation and sequences, safety, delivery, and accommodation for management, professional staff, and tradespeople.

6. Complete contract agreements with subcontractors responsible for early site works.

7. Plan the installation of temporary services.

8. Set up materials handling system.[3]

Implementation of preparatory tasks. The practical steps that are taken to prepare the site for construction, are first divided into work-breakdown units, and correlated by a subprogram and schedule. The type, standard, and quality of many of the essential technologies are laid down by codes and regulations. These must be adapted to the characteristics and constraints of the particular site and environment. For example, safety hoardings are essential for public protection around a city site and are controlled by regulation. These structures are manufactured in several standards and grades, selected according to the degree of hazard expected from construction processes on the particular site and location. Alternatively, a construction site in a remote area may be secured against public entry by chain-link fencing only. (See Fig. 9.6.)

Tasks may be completed in stages or may be implemented simultaneously provided there is no sequential dependence on completion:

Erect hoardings and protective fences.

Prepare all weather access to site, sidewalk crossings, ramps, and gates.

Install environmental protection measures.

Install safety measures, fire hydrants, hand rails, screens, penetration protection, lighting, and signs.

Provide safety gear for construction workers.

Install communication systems.

Plan and implement delivery of large material handling and other equipment, such as cranes, bulldozers, hoists, concrete lines, and pumps.

Erect worker accommodation.

Establish accommodation for managerial staff.

Prepare unloading and storage areas.

Plan rubbish-disposal procedures.

Protect adjacent properties, underpinning and shoring.

Figure 9.6 Public safety control: Huis Ten Bosch Resort, site under construction; Nagasaki, Japan. The large resort site is separated from the public road by fencing; a guard house, situated behind the photographer, enables the security guard(s) to monitor and closely control any unauthorized access that is attempted. Nihon Sekkei, Inc., architects, engineers, and project managers.

Bulk and detailed excavation and foundation review. (See Fig. 9.7)

Work-breakdown units. Infrastructure construction is scheduled in accordance with the demands of the construction program and development type. Tasks such as contouring, and the provision of roads, sewage disposal, water and powerlines may be required in only one area of the total resort site in the beginning, to allow the first structures in a staged occupancy program to commence. Site preparation will nearly always continue throughout most of the process, especially if the site is a large resort area intended to provide recreational facilities, such as a golf course, marina, tennis courts, or ski-run.

In summary, details of the work of site establishment discussed above are very dependent on the special characteristics of the project design and construction type, site characteristics, environmental conservation, and market needs. The program and schedule of implementation are designed in accordance with the main construction program and schedule. (See example in Figs. 9.8 and 9.9.)

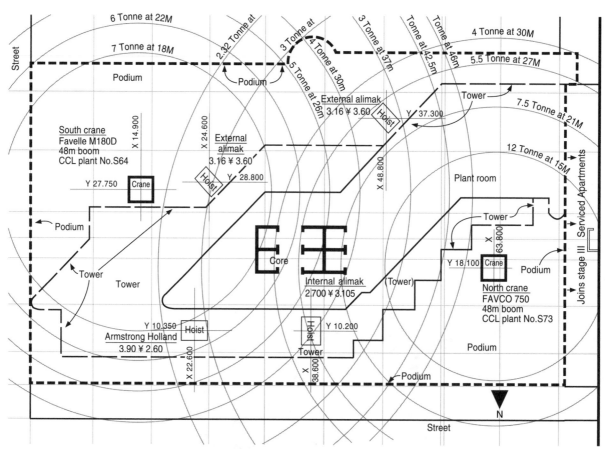

Figure 9.7 Preparing a site for construction: location plan, cranes and hoists. Hotel construction, Sydney, Australia. One of the many preliminary planning tasks necessary to prepare for construction; this plan shows crane range, position with respect to the proposed building, and surrounding roads. Cranes were installed following the construction of the two-story podium. Access for site delivery is from the east.

Actions to Be Taken at This Time

The project manager and project team participate during the execution phase as main project controller, integrating the work of various contributors and establishing team commitment to the project. Cooperative relationships must be encouraged between the various major contractors. This objective is typically accomplished by means of induction programs, and the implementation of information processing and communication network systems.[3]

- Project manager:

  Supervise analysis of tender submissions

  Recommend awards of contract to client for approval

  Make recommendations for contract content and coverage to the client and the formation of clauses

  Advise and assist client with contract negotiations

  Synthesize and coordinate work programs and schedules of all major contractors

  Monitor the establishment of main programs and schedules of construction

  Supervise and coordinate site schedules

  Obtain approvals: owner, user, authorities

  Establish variation handling and auditing procedures and reporting

  Implement cost control and quality assurance programs

  Supervise postcontract costs and budget

  Supervise quality assurance programs

  Schedule, supervise, and record main project meetings

  Program and schedule induction courses for all project personnel

  Program and implement training programs

  Organize reporting format and hierarchies

  Supervise communication networks and flow of data

- Construction managers:

  Negotiate contract

  Prepare detailed costs of construction

  Prepare all shop drawings and detailed specifications

  Delegate personnel to construction project team

  Prepare construction programs and schedules; confirm key dates for approvals, milestones, date for practical completion

  Confirm availability; prepare and implement procurement program for materials and resources, obtain approvals

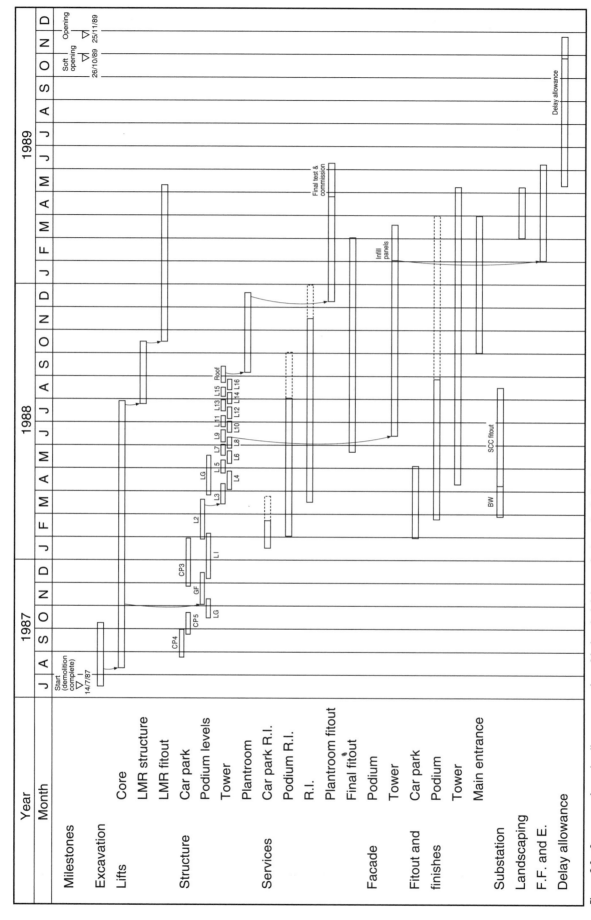

Figure 9.8 Summary of construction program for a 16-story hotel tower, Sydney, Australia. Bar chart.

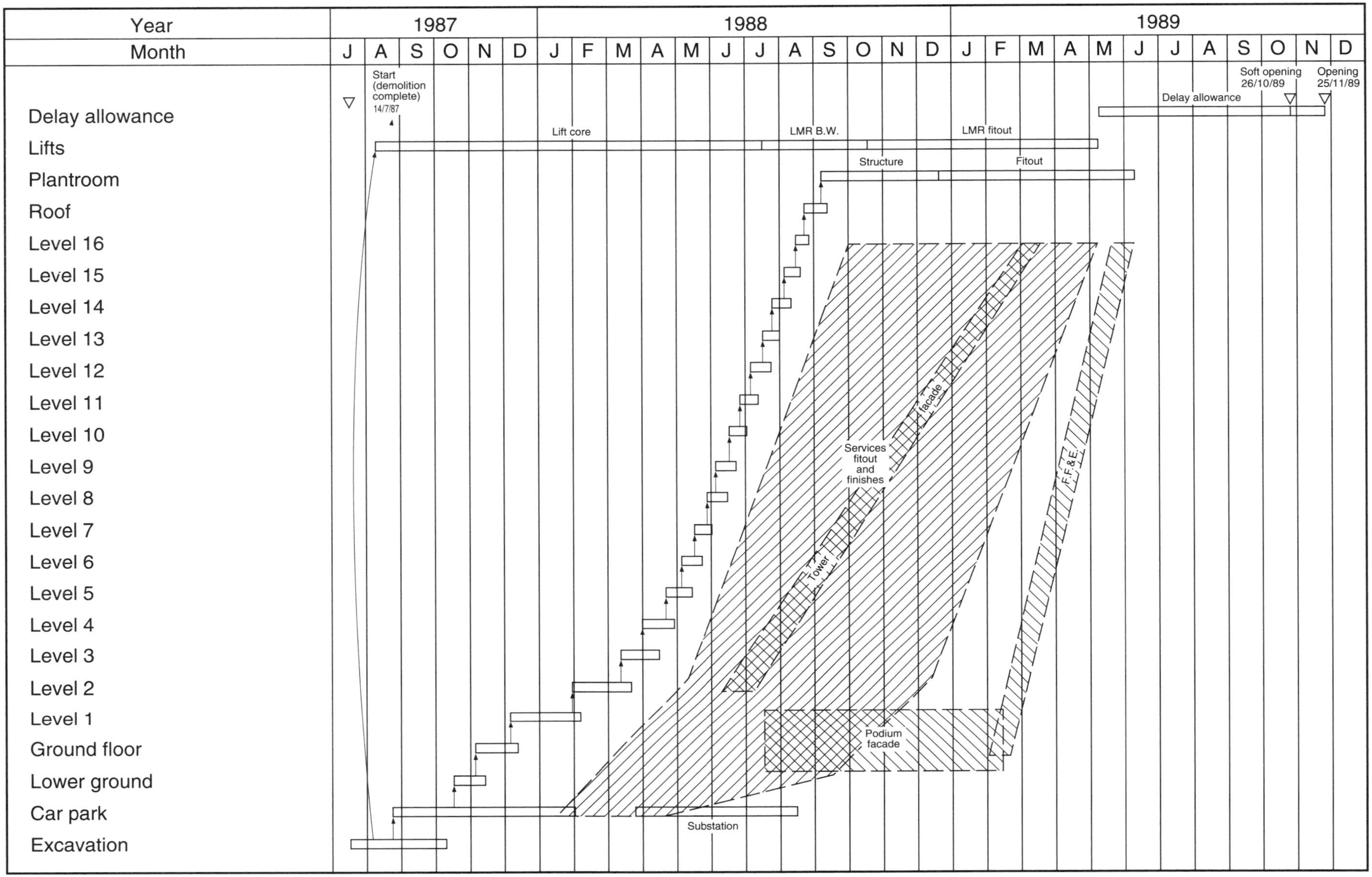

Year	1987						1988												1989						
Month	J	A	S	O	N	D	J	F	M	A	M	J	J	A	S	O	N	D	J	F	M	A	M	J	J A S O N D

Row labels:

- Delay allowance
- Lifts
- Plantroom
- Roof
- Level 16
- Level 15
- Level 14
- Level 13
- Level 12
- Level 11
- Level 10
- Level 9
- Level 8
- Level 7
- Level 6
- Level 5
- Level 4
- Level 3
- Level 2
- Level 1
- Ground floor
- Lower ground
- Car park
- Excavation

Chart annotations:

- Start (demolition complete) 14/7/87
- Soft opening 26/10/89
- Opening 25/11/89
- Delay allowance
- LMR fitout
- Fitout
- Structure
- LMR B.W.
- Lift core
- Services fitout and finishes
- facade
- Tower
- T.T. & E.T.
- Podium facade
- Substation

Figure 9.9 Summary of construction program for a 16-story hotel tower, Sydney. The bar chart also illustrates the "climb" of the tower in relation to weeks of construction effort.

Program and schedule project meetings and reporting format

Program, schedule, and implement induction and training programs for both management and tradespeople

Prepare and implement program and schedule for site establishment and site works

Implement quality assurance strategies

Prepare and implement methods of inspection to obtain formal approvals of works and progress payments

■ Architects, engineers, landscape architects, and interior designers:

Assist analysis of tender submissions

Recommend awards of contract to project manager and client for approval

Monitor and complete design documentation and shop drawings

Assist and advise client in contract negotiations with contractors

Advise and assist implementation of formal agreements for variations to contract

Assist implementation of cost-control procedures

Assist implementation of quality control procedures

Assist the preparation and monitor the procurement program

Prepare and implement programs to monitor and supervise site works

Recommend work for approval to project manager and client

Schedule site inspections, establish approvals format, and make recommendation for progress payments

References

1. W. B. Foxhall, *Professional Construction Management and Project Administration,* 2d ed., American Institute of Architects, McGraw-Hill, New York, 1976.

2. Frank Harris and Ronald McCaffer, *Modern Construction Management,* Granada Publishing, London, 1979.

3. J. Frost and H. McLennan, Master of Project Management Course Notes, University of Technology Sydney, Sydney, Australia, 1991–1992.

4. Allan Marshall (Manager, Q. A. Consultancy Services, Sydney, Australia), "**Quality Standards and Requirements,**" *Project Management Course Notes,* University of Technology Sydney, Sydney, Australia, 1992.

5. P. J. Burman, *Precedence Networks for Project Planning and Control,* McGraw-Hill, London, 1972.

6. David M. Bennett, *Brooking on Building Contracts,* 2d ed., Butterworths Press, Australia, 1980.

7. D. J. Ferry and P. S. Brandon, *Cost Planning of Buildings,* 4th ed.,

Granada Press, London, 1980.

8. J. Mooney, *Cost Effective Building Design,* New South Wales University Press, Australia, 1983.

9. W. B. Leadbetter and J. A. Burati, "How Can Quality Be Properly Managed on Major Projects?" *Building Economics & Construction Management,* Vol. 4: *Managing Projects,* University of Technology Sydney, Sydney, Australia, March 1990.

10. Masao Nemoto, *Total Quality Control for Management, Strategies and Techniques from Toyota and Toyada Gosei,* Prentice-Hall, Englewood Cliffs, N.J., 1987.

Bibliography

Rush, R. D. Ed., (The American Institute of Architects), *The Building Systems Integration Handbook,* Wiley, New York, 1986.

"Fragmented Dreams, Flexible Practices and New Directives in Project Delivery," *Architecture Magazine, Technology & Practice,* pp. 80, 87 (publ. Robert G. Kliesch), May 1992.

Project Administration, 2d ed., American Institute of Architects, McGraw-Hill, New York, 1976.

10

Project
Commissioning
and Handover

Planning to Complete the Process: Commissioning

The task of controlling a major project can be undertaken only as a collection of subsidiary projects divided into work-breakdown structures (WBSs) and managed by delegation.[1] The operations involved in "planning to finish" are defined as the detailed study and integration of construction methods occasioned by the need to complete, and form a stage when additional gains and a reduction of construction time can be achieved.[2] The need to "plan to finish" involves reviews and reconciliation of construction methods, timing of the process, and control, made by comparing trade-offs of time, cost, and quality within the pattern of conflicting needs of work packages and program constraints.

Thus, contingencies and floats are reconciled to allow for a grouping of tasks that are critical to the commissioning or completion process. The achievement of the goals and objectives of completion, which are usually uniquely influenced by project location, market,

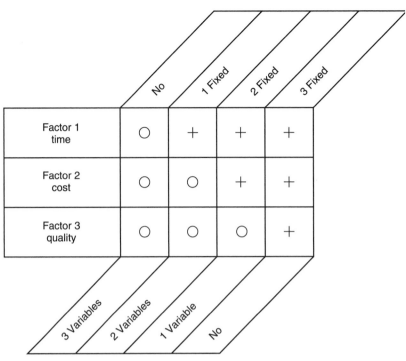

Figure 10.1 Trade-off matrix. Managers are continually concerned with factors of time, cost, and quality. It is difficult in the context of the construction process to achieve a perfect balance of these factors; therefore, the relative merit to the program of each is judged and compared by holding the factors fixed or variable alternatively.

owner, and operator requirements, must always be monitored throughout the construction program.

Trade-Off Analysis

Managers are continuously concerned with the balance between time, cost, and quality, which form a triangle of performance criteria. Unfortunately, it is not always possible to find a perfect balance for these three factors, and a desirable solution to one must be sacrificed in favor of another which is of critical importance to the context of the project. In this regard, the possible variations or trade-off between the factors may be considered as a matrix based on assignment: (1) one factor fixed, others variable; (2) two factors fixed, one variable; or (3) all factors variable.[3] (See Fig. 10.1.)

The solutions to conflicting demands must always, of course, fall within the constraints of the project. It is also important to remember that the changes to one factor will affect all others in some way and alternatives must be approved and decisions taken accordingly; for example, the sacrifice of time will generally affect quality of performance. Some authorities recommend a systems approach to balance these conflicting factors (Fig. 10.2), which include recognition of the causes of conflict, a continuous recollection of goals and objectives, analysis of the project environment and external constraints, identification of alternative courses of action, selection of the best alternatives with client approval, and correlation and integration of the changes into the program.[3]

With these considerations in mind, a further analysis of the detailed effects of the changes on capital expenditure, cash flow, time to completion, resource procurement, profits, user satisfaction, capability of operation, and the total construction program must be made; for the trade-off analysis affects global interrelationships between the main construction program and schedules and the required dates for commissioning, project handover, and opening. This is especially true for staged completion.[4]

Influence of the Client's Original Concept Intent and Decisions on the Commissioning and Completion Stages

Client decisions.   The client's decisions for the project are, of course, fundamental to the establishment of the project brief, and so influence the course of commissioning and completion, principally by means of budget and financial management influences; opening schedules, marketing expectations, and the requirement for staged completion; contractual clauses affecting the coordination of the project: the appointment of separate contractors (normal for hotel work) and work that is to be undertaken by the client's own company.

During the first definition of the project brief, detailed design, allotment of work packages, and division into work-breakdown units, the strategies and methods that must be used for commissioning and finalization become clear-cut, and in turn, influence the critical path of construction.[1] The potential to carry out efficient commissioning procedures, to successfully complete the project, and therefore to satisfy the owner-client's expectations is generated by the quality of the planning work achieved during the definition and development phases.

Design.   All major design changes that occur in the postdevelopment phase are likely to have very important and costly effects on the progress of development. These may typically be caused by a client who requires late additions or changes to the design and program intent during the process. The incorporation of such additions and changes into the program will necessitate alterations to documentation,

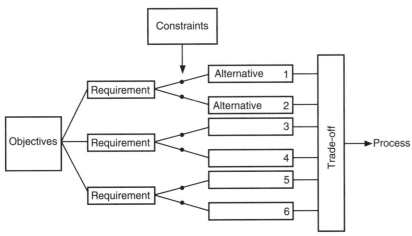

Figure 10.2   The analysis of trade-off factors. Design or construction requirements are studied and proposals for alternatives optimized by comparing each against a background of project constraints, time, cost, and quality. *(After Kerzner, 1989.)*

will delay programs and schedules, and may require further approvals to be obtained from authorities. Major changes of this kind are likely to cause a budget blowout, and most certainly will delay the completion date.

Decisions for procurement. Other decisions that influence the course of the completion and finalization process are the strategies taken to approve and implement purchasing and resource procurement. These are developed by both the head contractor and by interior designers and subcontractors before submission for approval to the client. Last-minute rushes are caused by the unexpected unavailability of resources and delayed deliveries and force deviations from schedule and program and delay completion.

Methods of construction. The method and materials that are selected for construction of the project are appropriate for site conditions and budget. Additionally, the contractor's policy decisions, management strategies, planning, and control of the construction program generate the type of commissioning and completion procedures necessary. Some important detrimental factors may be financial difficulties sustained by head or subcontractors and changes to key personnel.

Implications for Commissioning a Program of Progressive Completion

Among the several contractual advantages to be gained by both clients and contractors from progressive completion of some sections of the contract are the availability for partial release of bank guarantees and retention sums and the reduction of the total sum held for contingency. The funds then become available for use elsewhere within the development process, for progress and other payments.

Major effects of staged or progressive occupancy are found in the implications for design and construction planning, and can be most easily illustrated by the example of a large resort. In order to satisfy the requirement for a sufficiently marketable number of guest units, for example, infrastructure in certain areas must be phased in to support hotel functions and guest activities. Guest units are grouped for the purposes of supply of power, water, and other building services, such as air conditioning and security systems, and proximity to front-of-house, restaurant, and entertainment facilities. Housekeeping services, staff accommodation, and temporary operational facilities are, of course, essential. The whole program of development must be reconciled with the program, and decisions in favor of either temporary or a partial installation of permanent facilities must be made.

Successful programs for out-of-sequence construction planning and control require a basic understanding of building systems and methods of hotel management and operation.[5] Plant locations must be considered in relation to both hotel function and use and ongoing construction activities on the remaining areas of the site. Planning and provision for safety of access, egress, and fire; preservation of the environment; and implementation of precautionary measures to separate and protect the public from the operation of large technological equipment in use for construction purposes are of particular concern to the construction managers and teams. An experienced hotel operator will contribute valuable advice and assistance toward the task of planning the sequence of requirements for the staged program and occupancy.

Other important considerations that affect the planning of the staged construction program and schedule are typically out-of-sequence construction work affecting the main construction program and critical path of activities; out-of-sequence purchasing; the location of the major plant rooms, and the necessity to install multiple groupings of plant facilities; separation of users, workers, people, cars, and hotel services; and security of the completed hotel goods and furnishings. (Fig. 10.3.)

Contractual implications. Many design criteria for staged completion are controlled by conditions of contract and authority regulations. Such requirements are often complex and difficult to incorporate in the program. Chief among these are the need to progressively change the responsibilities for building operation and insurance from the contractors to the owner-operator and the need to define the interface between the two responsibilities.

The transfer of responsibility for control and operation of a part of the structure demands the issue of authority approvals, certification, and insurance policies which may be made provisionally dependent on many factors, typically those of security and safety. The provisions always include some restrictions on construction programs and schedules such as "rights of quiet enjoyment" of hotel-resort operation, public access, the issue of warranties, and the commencement of maintenance periods.

Owner and Operator Requirements for Nominated and Separate Contractors

It is very likely that the owner-client and operator will nominate and wish to reengage certain separate contractors on the basis of their experience of previous projects and knowledge of the quality of their work and expertise. In this writer's experience, hotel and resort procurement is undertaken by separate contractual arrangement far more often than other types of commercial building. This is particularly true of interior work packages, which may be included under the head contractor's responsibility on site, but which are nearly always awarded to a nominated interior design firm and specialized interior fit-out contractors. The client will therefore instruct the project manager to negotiate for their services.

The reasons for the use of separate contractors are as follow:

1. The companies are highly specialized and experienced, and understand and relate easily to operator requirements and expertise.

2. There is increased confidentiality and security. This is particularly important to interior fit-out in locations where skilled trades are difficult to procure and the main construction has been achieved by utilizing many semiskilled or unskilled workers.

3. In the event that there is a high capital outlay and low site cost for labor, it is preferable if quality furniture and furnishings are imported onto the site. The separate appointment of specialized contractor-suppliers avoids the payment of an unnecessary commission to the head contractor.

4. Conflicts of timing and interests often exist between the arrangements required for the supply of resources and services and the head contractor's ability to fulfill demand. If separate specialized contractors are appointed early in the contract, the provision of their special supplies and services can be opportunely integrated with the main program and schedule. See Fig. 10.4.

5. The owner's and operator's requirement to process their own work. This is again a typical procedure for fit-out contracts for a hotel.

It is essential that all prerequisites of appointment which are recommended by the project manager, and/or required by the client for nominated and separate contractors, together with the conditions for the coordination and integration of the presence of their trades on site, be defined in detail at precontract stage and written into the main contract agreement between the head contractor, contracts with the separate and nominated contractors, and client.[2]

Achieving Completion and Commissioning

Several major tasks must be undertaken during the commissioning processes. These include arranging operator training, inspection and testing of completed work packages, the production of maintenance manuals and warranties, and obtaining final approvals from the client and authorities.

Operator Training and the Commissioning Process

Commissioning, the task of bringing the total hotel or resort to operational status, forms a critical stage in the program. At this time, induction programs must be arranged for hotel staff, and the inspection and testing period prior to completion provides an appropriate opportunity for them to become conversant with the technical aspects of the project's specialized equipment and resources. Data derived from induction and training forms a basis for planning detailed management and operational strategies.

It is important that the project manager's global program for the control of commissioning integrate with the more detailed programs of interior and building construction. Therefore, a commissioning program and schedule should be planned at an early stage in the process and the tasks of program management, implementation, and control delegated to a member of the project team.

It is recommended that this officer produce a schedule of meetings with attendance requirements and comprehensive checklists for discussion of each separate work package. Commissioning procedures

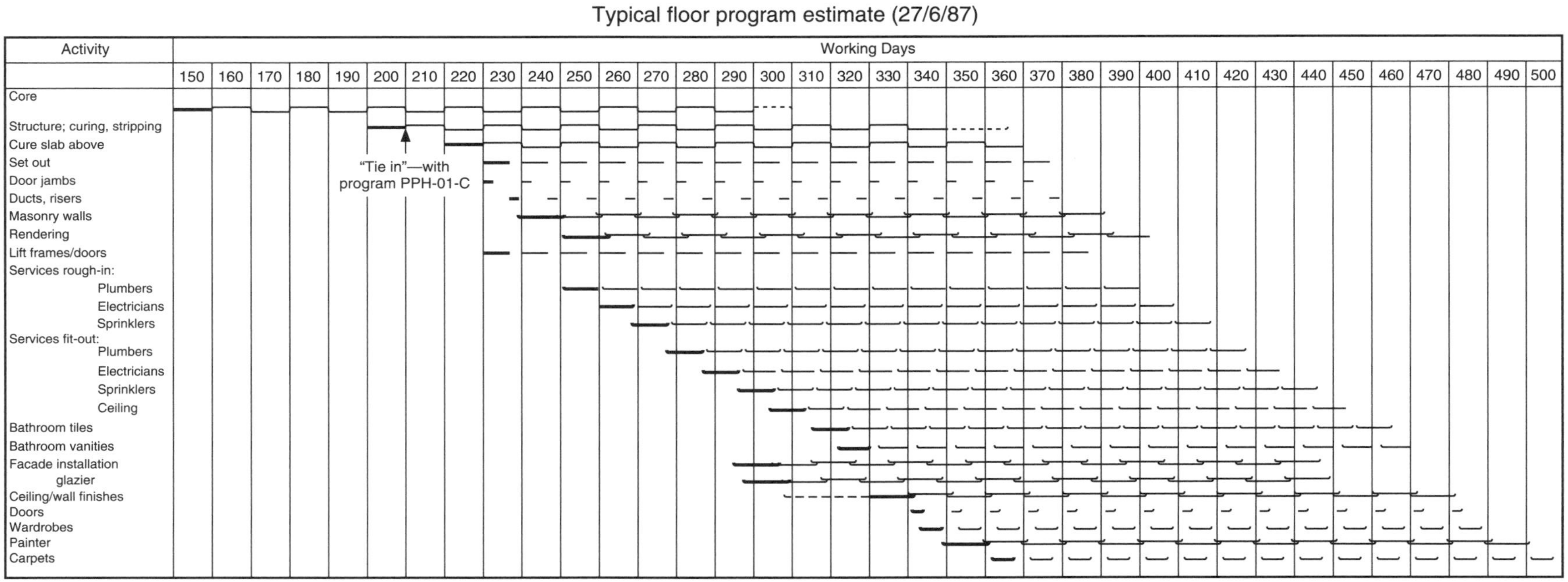

Typical floor program estimate (27/6/87)

Working Days

Activity	150	160	170	180	190	200	210	220	230	240	250	260	270	280	290	300	310	320	330	340	350	360	370	380	390	400	410	420	430	440	450	460	470	480	490	500

Core
Structure; curing, stripping
Cure slab above
Set out
Door jambs
Ducts, risers
Masonry walls
Rendering
Lift frames/doors
Services rough-in:
  Plumbers
  Electricians
  Sprinklers
Services fit-out:
  Plumbers
  Electricians
  Sprinklers
  Ceiling
Bathroom tiles
Bathroom vanities
Facade installation
  glazier
Ceiling/wall finishes
Doors
Wardrobes
Painter
Carpets

"Tie in"—with
program PPH-01-C

Figure 10.3   A typical fit-out program, by floor. The bar chart lists construction sequences and testing procedures with respect to later fit-out activities.

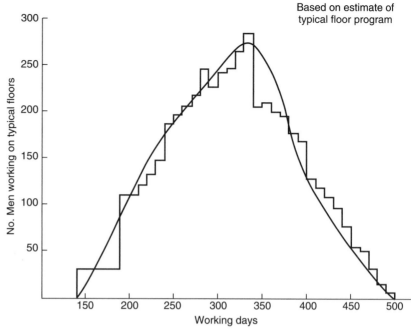

Figure 10.4 A manpower histogram for fit-out construction. The manpower demand histogram for the fit-out of typical guest room floors for a 16-story hotel tower shows a normal curve which peaks at a loading of 300 persons, (including many trade skills). The peak, in the middle of a 350-work day period, has a duration of approximately 100 days. The head contractor may experience difficulty in fulfilling this demand, especially on international location. (*Harrison, 1985.*)

require a contribution from many specialist team members, including architects, building services engineers, interior designers, construction teams, specialized technical experts, and the hotel management groups, themselves. Training in the use of technical equipment, methods, and sequences is most effective if it is offered in both oral and written form; however, for the long term, the production of a manual is perhaps of greater importance.[3]

In summary, as the hotel staff plan an implementation program for the following functional operations, training programs should be executed to assist their assumption of management and administrative duties and to familiarize them with technological equipment:

Planning and preparation of housekeeping arrangements

Provisioning of storage and guest rooms

Commissioning of kitchens, bars, and restaurants (food and beverage)

Preparation and implementation of front-of-house and back-of-house administrative functions and on-line computerized programs—reception, accounting, and purchasing

Training for the maintenance of internal and external materials and equipment

Testing of safety technologies and the implementation of security procedures

Therefore, throughout the commissioning stage, the project team, as in other processes in the project delivery system, play an essential role of interpretation, integration, and supervision of the total commissioning process.

Problems of control.   If the activities involved in final completion are left unplanned or are planned ineffectively, many important tasks such as final accounting; completion of as-built documentation; inspections and rectification of defects; site cleaning; and removal of working materials, tools, and rubbish can cause extra expense and delay to the client and operator until well after the official opening dates, as well as considerable annoyance. For example, technological equipment may be left on site and incur the unnecessary and unwelcome payments for interest on hire charges.

Thus, marketing opportunities may be missed.

Testing of Services

The work-breakdown units of the construction process and fit-out work are inspected for standard, quality, and compliance with contractual specification and conditions, and systems are subjected to a series of tests as each reaches completion. It is usual practice for inspections to be made by project team representatives accompanied by the construction manager, and defect lists should be compiled and reports made well in advance of dates for completion. The defects are then made good on a progressive basis as the deadline for completion approaches.

Approvals.   The head contractor must ensure that work has been completed to a standard demanded by the contract agreement, and certificates are issued by the appropriate specialist team member. A certificate is granted when a list of outstanding defects has been compiled, for by contractual agreement, these must be rectified before final completion is achieved. Certificates are presented to the project manager for examination and then to the owner-client by the project manager for approval.

In summary, the administrative procedures relating to arrangements for inspections and the rectification of defects are as follows:

Notifications of test dates are sent to the client, authorities, and technical consultants.

Testing times are scheduled with extended hours if necessary.

Inventories are made of details to be checked and other factors needing confirmation.

A group is nominated to attend the inspection, including the construction manager, project manager, and specialist team member responsible for design.

A record of times, dates, and attendance of the inspection must be kept by a delegated member of the project team.

All defects must be officially recorded by the construction and project teams and a date set for rectification.

The appropriate trades must be notified.

A discussion of solutions should take place, and the project and construction managers should agree on a program and schedule for the rectification of the defects.

Final certification. When final inspections, testing, and certification of all systems, materials, and services has occurred, the project is handed over to the hotel or resort for operation. Legal arrangements begin to change the responsibility for the facility over from the contractor to the hotel or resort owner and operator. Responsibilities include those for insurance and the management and control of plant, building fabric, and grounds. At the same time, final approvals are obtained from the client and authorities, local landowners, and owners of adjacent properties.

Detailed Commissioning Manuals

The commissioning manual is used as a basis for (1) testing, recording results, and certification; (2) operator training; and (3) to assist future operational and maintenance procedures. These three functions serve as a checklist for commissioning measures, as a format to record test results, and to clarify operational programs in detail, including procedures to be taken in case of breakdown or emergency. A list of spare parts must also be compiled for maintenance purposes.

Carrying out tests to meet detailed manual requirements. The procedures commence with a notification, submitted by subcontractors to the construction and project managers, that an installation is sufficiently far advanced to commence testing and commissioning.

The detailed tasks that are implemented during the testing procedures are in accordance with instructions in the manufacturers' manuals. The type of instruction varies and typically includes manufacturer's recommendations and basic instructions for operation and maintenance. More detailed instruction may be issued separately and form another agreement.

Test results. On-site tests and measurements of the conditions, duration, and quality of materials and equipment are carried out in series during commissioning, until all responses are found to be satisfactory and the interface with other systems is approved and certified. The member(s) of the project management team allocated to the detailed commissioning control program should work in close cooperation with the hotel operator and head contractor in order to integrate the results of the test programs for the various work packages which may include infrastructure, landscaping, building works, plant, and interior fit-out, with the implementation of the hotel operation. Checks are made, for example, of the availability and capacity of the mains power supply and emergency supplies. (Generators and other services are tested for winter and summer loading.)

It is simpler to test various groups of technologies in sequence, and in this respect progressive completion has an advantage. When, for example, fit-out procedures are carried out in parallel, the team are obliged to carry out many commissioning tasks at the same time, and problems of shortages in staffing and resources arise.

Tests Relating to the Fit-out Program

Many testing activities for a hotel must be planned to relate to the fit-out program and schedules. Testing activities may be in conflict with sealed and completed areas, certainly "wet work" such as the testing of plumbing and fire sprinklers must be programmed for completion before interior finishing trades commence.[2]

Checks of capacity, placement, and emergency functions (in accordance with contract specifications) are made for sprinkler and power outlets and will require access to ceiling space and other controls. The electrical control systems for bedside consoles, computers, security alarms, and other technical installations are checked for flexibility and spare capacity and cross-referenced to correlate with other systems such as lighting and air conditioning.

The coordination of programs and schedules plays a vital part in the successful commissioning of these serial activities.

Operator training. It is, of course, especially important for the operator to understand maintenance procedures and the interfaces between different systems.[5] Explanations and instructions should be included to clarify the interrelations of technologies, established procedures, and necessary intervals for testing and maintenance. The operator will be assisted in the future by the receipt of maintenance manuals, warranties, and maintenance agreements, and on completion, the receipt of "work as executed (as-built)" drawings and specifications. As the submission of these documents to the owner and operator is sometimes overlooked, or left for a considerable time after completion, it should be borne in mind that manuals and as-built documents form an important source of data for the understanding of the building function and maintenance requirements.

Warranties

The period of time, usually between 6 and 12 months following final completion, is allocated by contractual agreement to the "defects liability" period when the rectification of defects and deviations from contractual requirements and maintenance takes place. Warranties are made to cover and clarify problems and conditions of maintenance during this period, and sometimes take the form of a contract for continuing maintenance, especially for elevators and air conditioning. Warranty documents are usually issued by the head and subcontractors on a progressive basis up to final completion as work is approved.

The degree of contractor responsibility is dependent on the conditions of the contract agreement; therefore, conditions of warranty and preventive maintenance should be set while the project team prepare and negotiate conditions for the main contract agreements between the client and head contractors and subcontractors and be made a condition of acceptance. Such agreements are sometimes overlooked during contract negotiation and executed only later in the project process when provisions, which are in the client's favor, are more difficult to negotiate.[2]

Rectification orders apply to defects that cannot reasonably be expected to be disclosed while the work is being carried out, during inspection, or before a certificate of final completion is issued. Such defects, for example, include water leakage caused by storm and other conditions that are specified in the contract. Warranty provisions usually cover errors or omissions in computation of accounts and under warranty the owner-client may have the right to recover damages if the condition is due to faults in design.

Agreements for future maintenance inspections can also be negotiated to take place on a regular basis after the termination of the warranty period.

Completion

Management strategies and controls that allow work packages to be completed, inspected, and certified progressively as other work continues through the implementation of project commissioning and completion are vital. Owner-clients and contractors in construction work have traditionally utilized a contract that divides the process into the two-phase operation of practical completion and final completion: (1) practical completion and (2) certificate of final completion, preceded by the defects liability stage.

Practical Completion

Practical completion is said to occur when tests have been satisfactorily completed to establish standards, statutory requirements are met and the construction are capable of statutory requirements, and the construction is capable of being properly used for the intended purpose. It is defined, for the construction of real estate, as "the stage when the building is reasonably fit for use and/or occupancy." On the date set for practical completion, responsibilities or "ownership" for the project are transferred by the contractor to the owner and operator for "soft opening" and occupancy of the premises, the assumption of responsibility for insurance policies, the safety of occupants, and the management and maintenance of the hotel buildings and grounds.

The complex network of activities relating to implementation, such as checking, testing, commissioning of separate tasks, and the integration and certification of all systems, are basic activities that must be completed to meet the deadline set for practical completion. However, the period between practical and final completion that is set aside for the rectification of defects, gives an additional opportunity for last-minute tasks of commissioning to be undertaken; nevertheless, if detailed planning and programming procedures for commissioning and handover have been carried through successfully, one finalization date and handover should be achievable.

Tasks are typically classified into building works acceptance, service works acceptance, interior works acceptance, landscaping, and acceptance of related constructions, and final accounting. An example of the other changes in legal and contractual status mentioned above, it is usual to return to the contractor one-half of the money which has been retained as a bank or other retention sum guarantee for possible damages or default during construction, according to the contract agreement.

Tasks that lead to completion of contract: accounting procedures. Many of the work packages and trades are closely interdependent and must be processed simultaneously. The basic work-breakdown structures (WBSs), together with the programs of continuous cost control, which are developed as systemic tools to plan and control the construction processes, contribute to the simplification of the final accounting procedures, and provide a current database from which to monitor costs and link account finalization to the issue of "certification of releases."

The importance of account processing on a progressive basis cannot be overemphasized.

Payments are correlated with key dates on the construction program, and schedule and claims are certified for payment as work packages are progressively completed. In this way, accounting and contract finalization is managed with a sequential completion of a series of small projects, which simplify the activities of monitoring, control, and certification for approval.

In summary, some important project management strategies are established in the development phase, which help simplify accounting procedures in the final stages of completion of the project; for example, (1) the schematic cost-control program that is made for the work packages of the main development programs; (2) the detailed cost accounting system that relates to work-breakdown units; and (3) on the basis of the work-breakdown unit, a detailed network program developed to link the critical path of construction to cash flow and budget. This program coordinates the budgets for all materials and resources. Final accounting must operate in two ways: a generalized statement based on the progressive completion of the main project work packages and a summary incorporating the contribution of detailed organizational (subcontractor) breakdown structures.

Thus, it is essential to summarize and record progress payments as they are made. Additionally, there are several other formal procedures to be attended together with the accounting activities and the process of certification of work:

Progressive agreements must be achieved in detail as each work unit is completed.

Payments to subcontractors are controlled by the head contractor and are not made directly by the owner.

Claim times for progress payments are defined by the contract agreement.

Claims must be administered fairly.

Certificates of release are issued promptly.

Work packages of long duration must be subdivided for progressive payment claims.

Work-breakdown units must be remeasured and inspected progressively, area by area.

Variations and claims for payment must be systematically recorded and processed.

Agreement to variations. Written agreement and approval must be obtained for all medium and major variations to work at the time they are requested and a detailed record made of instructions received, including their source and approvals, and the details of such transactions. Variations generally alter budget conditions and may easily become a source of dispute between the owners, the professional consultants, and the contractors if they are not systematically recorded and approved in detail.

Surprise claims often cause major argument, this can be averted if an investigation is made and details are reported fully. The project managers must request a submission supported by evidence, together with any arguments refuting the claim. The project manager is advised to obtain independent advice if no solution is reached quickly.

Use of standard documents. The experienced project manager will usually have a selection of standard documents of approved format suitable for utilization to record and summarize all the information that is required during the finalization of contract. Construction companies also supply their own procedural documents which are made to suit the needs of general administrative and recording procedures for inspections, report writing, acceptance of work packages, and issuance of certificates.

The Preparation of Final Accounts

Supplies. Final accounting for materials and supplies is completed progressively, when these orders are delivered to the site, and after they have been inspected and approved. Checks and inspections must be thorough before delivery is accepted, for the standard and quality of the materials, if inferior, may have both serious ramifications for the general success of the project, and financial implications for the project manager, design consultants, head contractor, and subcontractors. These may include the delay of final certification of a work-breakdown unit, delayed practical completion, delayed dates set for release of retention sums, and the release of bank guarantees, and, in the worst-case scenario, may result in legal action.

The head contractor's final accounting. The head contractor's final claims (see Fig. 10.5) are made with regard to, and in consultation with, the work of the subcontractors and in accordance with contract requirements. The head contractors are, at this time, concerned with expediting release dates for their own company's bank guarantees and retention sums. For this reason, the supply of detailed information received from the subcontractor must be monitored for content and accuracy with particular attention given to delayed claims: liquidated damages, time and financial settlements, and particularly to the processing and evidence for claims for variation.

Cost management summary no. Costsum						($000)				Month ending:		
Cost category	Budget				Forecast cost at completion							Variance
	Appr.budget Aug. 86	Approved adjustmt.	Allowance for inflation	Total	Unlet. wk. current est.	Contract let	Variations		Escalation		Total	
							App.	Ant.	App.	Ant.		
Building costs												
Asbestos removal												
Demolition												
Structure												
Mechanical												
Electrical												
Hydraulic												
Fire												
Lifts												
External works												
Landscaped courtyard												
Car park												
Preliminaries												
Escalation												
Contingencies												
Site allowance												
FF & E												
FF & E–Escalation												
Total building costs												
Construction costs												
Project controllers contingency												
Professional fees												
Developers insurance												
DA and BA Fees												
Other abortive costs												
Total construction costs												
Construction margins/fees												
Construction finance												
Establishment costs												
Developers fees												
Establishment fees												
Land acquisition & holding costs												
Site acquisition												
Land holding costs												
Property finance												
Other development costs												
Pre-opening expenses												
Promotion												
Operating supplies												
Development finance												
Total cost												

Figure 10.5   This cost management summary sheet was made for control of construction costs for a downtown hotel in Sydney, Australia.

A checklist of items requiring attention is prepared in detail for each WBS. This varies, of course, for each hotel or resort project according to its design, environmental, and locational influences; however, standard lists serve as a good basic format and reminder of general items that must be considered.

Subcontractors prepare their reference lists of all items that need to be inspected and certified, for attention and action by the project manager, the project team (which must include professional consultants appropriate to the work-breakdown unit), and the head contractor for the work packages whether: buildings, infrastructure, and landscape works, so that approvals can be obtained for final settlement of payments. This preparation includes the following conditions:

Defects that have been rectified or repairs that have been completed (or are to be completed) must be listed.

Quality assurances are supplied in association with warranties and maintenance agreements (responsibilities for warranties are accepted and issued by subcontractors).

Maintenance manuals must be issued to the client and operators.

Preventive maintenance measures and testing are completed, certified, and accepted by project management and client.

Work-as-executed drawings are completed and made available for the client's future use.

All clearances and authority certifications previously have been received.

Operator training programs are completed.

All spares previously have been received and made available for client use.[2]

At this time, when the transfer of insurance policies to the owner and client are correlated with the administration of accounting procedures, it is the project manager's and head contractor's responsibility to reevaluate the basis of the previous insurance policies and adjust the new policy to suit the clients' requirements and cover the hotel or resort in operation. Inflationary factors should be included for the computation.

Postcontract Analysis

The owner, operator, and project manager usually require general postcontract analyses and appraisals of the project delivery achievement. These are a project management performance responsibility, and include an analysis of the degree of success achieved in meeting the global objectives of the client's original project concept, such as accordance with market demands, budget, quality, environmental constraints, target dates, and technical requirements.

Business results are measured by profits and return on investment; managerial performance is measured by overall effectiveness, leadership, and team performance. Construction companies contribute their own analyses of performance to the study, covering cost-effectiveness, programming, and target achievement.

Such analyses not only assist the project finalization procedures but also form a source of information and criteria for use in planning future strategies. The sources of performance data offer opportunities to make improvements in the conduct of future commissions.

Project manager's review.   The project management review covers the project manager's effectiveness in developing overall direction and leadership during the phases of the project process, for example, development of project team commitment, program control and coordination, and development of flexibility and response to risk among team members, by the recognition and proposal of alternatives and opportunities to support the program. The following topics and questions form part of the review content for discussion:

To what degree is the design in accordance with original objectives and customer requirements?

What is the future operational capability of the hotel or resort to meet market and performance criteria?

Have cost-effective budgets been met?

Were programs and schedules on target?

Were management policies appropriate for delivery of the unique project? (Additional issues for review include the difficulties imposed by special conditions and constraints of the project.)

Have quality assurance standards been achieved?

Were the cost-control programs effective?

Have the reporting and review systems been effective?

A series of project completion workshops are probably the best way to achieve a worthwhile review of the main components of each project contribution. The project manager should nominate a team member for the responsibilities of presentation and review of each work-breakdown unit and encourage free discussion.

A list of attenders for a construction management workshop would typically include the project and construction managers and representatives from the project team, the construction team, the hotel operator's team, key designers, subcontractors, and site-supervisors for the work-breakdown unit under discussion.

The workshop findings and recommendations must be reported to the owner and clients in order that they may gain an understanding of the purposes of the review; however, it is probably better, in general, that team members alone participate in the workshops in order to encourage free discussion, with optional client participation as desired.

Actions to Be Taken at This Time

The project manager's responsibilities continue to be of an integrative and supervisory nature, while project team members, delegated to the monitoring and control of various management functions, bring the established plans and programs of cost, quality control, and commissioning to a conclusion. Many small items remain to be completed, requiring continuous attention and supervision. The project manager and project team depend on the realization of well-detailed commissioning programs for control at this time.

Many of the tasks listed for the project manager and for the architects, engineers, landscape architects, and interior designers are integral with the duties of the construction manager. At the same time, construction crews will be concerned in the completion of works on site, testing and inspections. They will prepare reports and applications for approvals and certification.

- Project manager:

  Monitoring and supervision of progressive and staged-completion programs

  Monitoring and supervision of induction programs, liaison with operator teams

  Supervising inspections, testing, reporting, approvals acquisition, and issuance of certificates of release

  End-of-contract personnel coordination, and management

  Ensuring correct handover procedures, including changeover of insurance policies

  Monitoring and supervising the production of manuals, as-built documentation

  Supervising the agreement and issuance of warranties

  Supervising and controlling general small "end of project" tasks (which tend to be overlooked)

  Supervision of final accounting

  Preparation of programs and schedules for postproject analysis, including the coordination of input from consultants and contractors

- Architects, engineers, landscape architects, and interior designers:

  Responsibilities for the control and supervision of final completion of work packages appropriate to their speciality

  Supervising completion of final contract requirements

  Attending inspections

  Scrutinizing test data

  Preparing reports, recommendations for approval, and certificates of release

  Supervising the rectification of defects; inspections

Monitoring and supervision of as-built documentation, production of manuals and warranties

Preparing programs for induction and commissioning related to speciality for hotel staff

Providing information and supervising preparation of final accounts, including the supply of all details regarding variation agreements

Contributing to postcontract analysis

- Construction manager:

Preparing training programs for operator use of technological systems

Testing of services

Carrying out inspection for quality assurance

Preparation of maintenance manuals and warranty agreements

Defects rectification

Last-minute tasks related to relinquishing the site and ;handover to the owner and operator: removal of materials and equipment

Proper cleaning of site, rubbish removal

Head contractor's final accounts

Approving subcontractors' final accounts

References

1. F. L. Harrison, *Advanced Project Management,* 2d ed., Gower Publishing Company, Ltd. Aldershot, Hants, 1985.

2. J. Frost, *Master of Project Management Course Notes,* University of Technology Sydney, Sydney, Australia, 1992.

3. H. Kerzner, *Project Management, a Systems Approach to Planning, Scheduling and Controlling,* 3d ed., Van Nostrand Reinhold, New York, 1989.

4. W. B. Foxhall, *Professional Construction Management and Project Administration,* 2d ed., McGraw-Hill, New York, 1976.

5. Chuck Y. Gee, *Resort Development and Management,* 2d ed., The Educational Institute of the American Hotel and Motel Association, East Lansing, Michigan, 1988.

11

Huis Ten Bosch Resort-Town, Nagasaki, Kyushu, Japan *

Introduction

Huis Ten Bosch Resort is located on the southern Japanese Island of Kyushu, on the Bay of Omura, close to the city of Nagasaki. (See Fig. 11.1.) This city holds a unique place in the history of Japan and therefore provided an obvious source for inspiration and a motif to the owner and the designers during the definition (project brief) phase and design development of the concept for the new town.

History of the Region

From the seventeenth to the nineteenth centuries, Japan adopted an almost totally isolationist policy and closed all her ports to foreign trade and diplomatic representation, with the exception of Dejima Island, Port of Nagasaki. During this period, the port remained accessible only to Dutch traders from Europe and local traders from China.

---

* Project Managers and Design Consultants: Nihon Sekkei Inc., Tokyo.

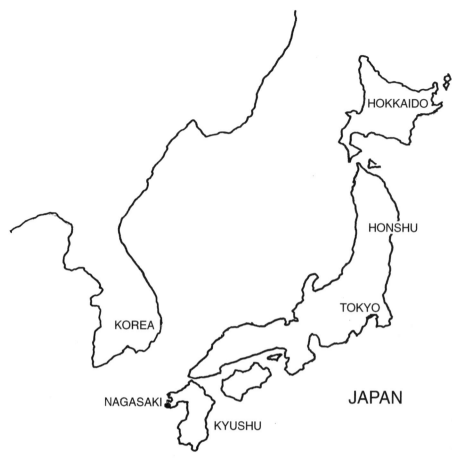

Figure 11.1   Location map: Nagasaki, Japan.

The Dutch received permission from the Japanese government of the time to establish a small settlement overlooking the town and docks. Nagasaki then became Japan's center for trade with, and the only source of information about, Europe and much of the outside world at that time.

The knowledge acquired through trade ultimately spread to other cultural and business centers in Japan. Thus the city became the source of foreign technological and cultural information, and subsequently exercised an important influence on national development, providing the basis for modernization in the 1860s.

Nagasaki City and region are therefore of great historical and educational interest for modern Japanese people.

In Nagasaki City itself, an interesting mixture of traditional Japanese and imported cultures is still to be encountered. European influence can be seen in many buildings, such as centuries-old churches, Dutch-style residences, and European artifacts. The design of the City's palanquins (made to carry the local gods on their annual visit to the City during the famous Okumchi Festival in October) are based on the shape and pattern of old Dutch sailing ships. The influence of the neighboring Chinese culture continues in a cuisine that is unique to Nagasaki.

Concept

The concept for the Huis Ten Bosch project grew out of the success of the previous development in the same area, which also incorporated the history of Nagasaki as a motif for design development. This earlier project is the now well-known "Nagasaki Holland Village," in the Nishi Sonogi region. The village was planned around a harbor, marina, museums, and restaurants. It was designed by Nihon Sekkei Inc., and completed in 1983.

Nagasaki Holland Village quickly proved to be an exceptionally popular location for day tours (the number of visitors to the center exceeded 600,000 in the first year), providing a cultural and educational experience, combined with Dutch ethnic entertainment. Buildings in the village are designed to resemble a traditional historic townscape in the Dutch style.

Following this initial success, Huis Ten Bosch Resort (see aerial view in Fig. 11.2) was conceived as a self-contained town, occupying a 375.44-acre (152-ha) site of reclaimed marshland on Omura Bay. The town is planned to specialize in tourism with educational and recreational themes, and offers mixed-use accommodation, for example, hotels and serviced apartments, restaurants, a retail center, marina, museums, boutiques, and apartments for long-term residence. In this respect the project differs from Nagasaki Holland Village, which has no provision for overnight accommodation.

The Owner

The owner and initiator (also the owner-developer of Nagasaki Holland Village) is a private investor who combined with government

Figure 11.2   Aerial view, Huis Ten Bosch resort-town. Nihon Sekkei Inc., architects, engineers, and project managers. (Photograph: Suikosha.)

agencies and the private sector, to form a joint-venture corporation for the development of the Huis Ten Bosch Resort project. The major proportion of financial backing for the development came from the private investors, who have had, therefore, considerable influence on the form and character of the project. The outcome of the development incorporates their original ideas.

The corporation proceeded to appoint a committee of 15 members (the "Committee of Fifteen") to assist in the establishment of a policy and general guidelines for design development. This policy was to include the continuation and expansion of the historical and educational themes and a requirement for an awareness and sensitivity to the needs for preservation and restoration of the natural environment. The development of a resort-town was proposed, that would accord with the natural surroundings of the area and where the interaction between the water and the built environment would play an important role in establishing character.

Many of these original objectives were successfully achieved by the official opening date in 1992, a difficult feat in consideration of the complexity of the project management and control tasks for a resort as large as Huis Ten Bosch.

The Project Management Structure

The project manager and the project team were appointed by the matrix system from Nihon Sekkei's staff, and the strategy for management took the form of a simple "flat" structure. Nihon Sekkei's project and design teams worked in close collaboration with the owner during the procurement of the project, and Nihon Sekkei's president became the chairman of the Committee of Fifteen.

Within this basic management structure (Fig. 11.3), the project management team controlled, supervised, and correlated the design documentation and unique technological contributions such as urban planning and development, water science and technology, communications, sociology, and architectural details. The team members were responsible for the coordination of the global programming, scheduling, and control of the procurement processes. No head contractor was appointed; however, in some instances, the contracting companies themselves were the sources of the special conceptual designs and technical documentation for the development.

Special technological design requirements. The special technical knowledge that was required for the design of details unique to the project was provided by Dutch architects and other experts, such as specialists from the engineering disciplines, culture and the arts, history, and medicine who had been appointed as advisory members of the committee. These specialists proceeded to act as consultants to the project during the planning and implementation phases.

Division of the project process into work packages. The project process of a very large development such as Huis Ten Bosch demands

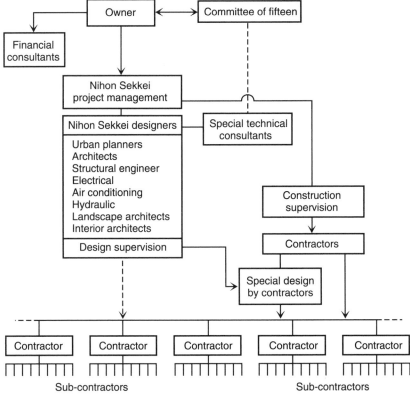

Figure 11.3   Project management structure: Huis Ten Bosch. The chart shows the close connection between the owner, the Committee of Fifteen, project management, and the design teams. Project management coordinated and supervised the global program of activities of the various major contractors on site, as a head contractor was not appointed.

that the main procurement program be divided into subsidiary work packages, which are managed as subproject programs within the total process. This procedure was observed by the Huis Ten Bosch project management team.

Major contractors.   The major contractors were as follows:

Building construction

Civil works

Environmental construction, including utility services

Area heating and cooling

Landscape construction

Bridge construction

Elevators

Residential building construction

Interior construction

Swimming pool construction

Special heavy machinery: hire and operation

Telephones and Fax, computer installation, etc.

Defining the Project Brief

The experience and success of Nagasaki Holland Village indicated that a similar achievement could be expected for the Huis Ten Bosch enterprise. However, the addition of overnight accommodation facilities made it essential to carry out market research in order to forecast areas of likely risk and to analyze the financial potential of the additional proposals for hotel, serviced apartments, and long-term residential accommodation.

Influences

Factors that influenced the characteristics of the project typically arose from the following sources:

1. The clients (the owner and Committee of Fifteen) and the market

2. The guests

3. The environment and ecology

4. Cultural influences

5. Geotechnical conditions existing in Omura Bay

The clients and market demand. Unlike America and Europe, Japanese vacations have been of only very short duration for there is no tradition of extended holiday periods among the Japanese population. Day trips for relaxation are very popular. This phenomenon is gradually changing to a pattern of longer vacation periods more akin to Western custom.

In support of the proposal to include several types of facility for overnight or extended stay, it was assumed that the length of the customary period for Japanese vacations is changing, and in addition, it would remain difficult for many people in Japan to travel overseas and experience a culture as different as Holland's for some time to come.

The owner therefore requested preliminary research to determine, as far as possible, current and future business trends and cultural changes in vacation patterns, followed by feasibility studies to assist the evaluation of financial risk and return on investment for the development of a resort-town which would include both hotels and apartment accommodations, in this region.

The guests. Guests are expected from all cities and regions of Japan, and from other countries. In particular, it is anticipated that the local history, size, and quality of the resort-town and the beauty of the region will attract not only local guests and guests from neighboring countries such as Hong Kong and visitors from Southeast Asia but also Dutch and other European travelers.

The ecology and the environment. The climate is the mildest of the major islands of Japan, and Kyushu currently supplies much of the fruit produce for the Tokyo markets. The island has a magnificent landscape, and the mountainous chain, known in Honshu as the "Japanese Alps," continues south from the larger island down through a central ridge.

The site location lies on a belt of flatland on Omura Bay, surrounded by hills. The site itself, formerly marshland, presented a fragile marine ecosystem, and the river and marsh once provided an important breeding ground for fish and wildfowl. Small traditional villages grew up over the centuries in support of a local fishing industry. Unfortunately, this ecology was damaged by reclamation work after World War II.

Cultural influences: water. Holland is well known for its system of canals and for the successful reclamation of land and control of sea encroachment. It is perhaps less well known that some traditional Japanese towns were also built around a system of waterways which were central to business and social life. Tokyo is typical of this urban pattern. The city center is still focused on the castle and moat, which used to form a hub for a radiating system of canals and waterways.

Japan's waterways served several important purposes, for example, as a source of fresh water, a location for festivals, transportation, a cool place to gather in summer, and a general center for the community life of the city. Local people understood the necessity of maintaining clean water and preventing pollution for the sake of the health of the township's population. Technical expertise grew from this need, and the river cleaning process was controlled and implemented by swiftly running currents directed through a system of stone dikes.

Geotechnical factors. A major factor influencing the design of the project was the need to restore and enhance the natural environment of Omura Bay. A structural system was needed that would protect the bay and resort site from storm (as the coast of Japan is subject to recurring typhoons) and be capable of encouraging the revitalization of the natural local ecosystem.

Development of the Concept

Urban Planning and Architectural Design

The creation of waterways and the design and treatment of the interface between the resort site and the sea played a very important role in the development of Huis Ten Bosch. A major design objective was established whereby beauty would be created by the use of reflected light in a combination of townscape and water. The waterways would serve as a means for transportation and outdoor meeting areas, and restaurants could be built on the banks as an attraction for social activities.

This concept formed an appropriate motif for design implementation by Japanese and Dutch designers who were able to draw on their extensive traditional expertise to assist the technical design required for the installation of canals and improvement of the reclaimed land and saltmarsh. Nihon Sekkei's urban planners, therefore, commenced design work with an in-depth study of the environ-

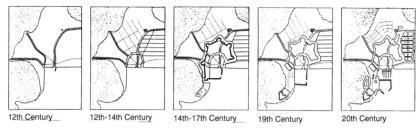

| 12th Century | 12th-14th Century | 14th-17th Century | 19th Century | 20th Century |

Figure 11.4   The historical development of the urban plan. The sketches illustrate a pattern derived from the studies of the development of a typical European medieval township. The urban design of Huis Ten Bosch was evolved from this model, and the influence of typical town fortifications and the encircling wall can be clearly seen in the nucleus of the plan.

ment and assessment of problems associated with existing site conditions.

Traditional styles in Dutch architecture.   The design methodology for the development of the urban plan was based on studies of the premodern growth and maturation of a traditional Dutch town. The designers conceived the objective of combining some of the richness and quality which would naturally be achieved by regular historical development, to the environment of the resort. The growth of a Dutch town was consequently traced from the twelfth to the twentieth centuries, and the results of the study were used as a planning guide. (See Fig. 11.4.) Several famous elevations of Dutch buildings are also designed into the urban scene.

From the re-creation of a typical central square (see Fig. 11.5.), the town is planned to extend outward to meet the modern hotels and shopping centers which form the total of the integrated resort development. The town is divided into five "city" zones: the Royal Harbor Front, Binnen Stad, the Urban Villa, Forest Park, and Moen Dijk. These offer guest accommodations of various types and star ratings, a multipurpose sports dome with swimming pools, a health club, and parks. In this respect the development adheres more nearly to the standard expectation of an international resort than the owner's first project (Nagasaki Holland Village) and is an innovation for both the tourist industry in Japan and for the clients.

The construction of Huis Ten Bosch, Stage 1, which included hotels; city gates, squares, canals, and locks; shopping centers; a market; museums; and a marina, was completed and opened in March 1992. (See Fig. 11.6.) The long-term vacation apartments and permanent residential section are planned for completion in successive stages.

Design Constraints

As is so often the case, constraints arose from the following sources:

1. The client

2. The market: exposure to risk

3. The environment

4. The guests

5. Local government (Prefecture), codes and regulations

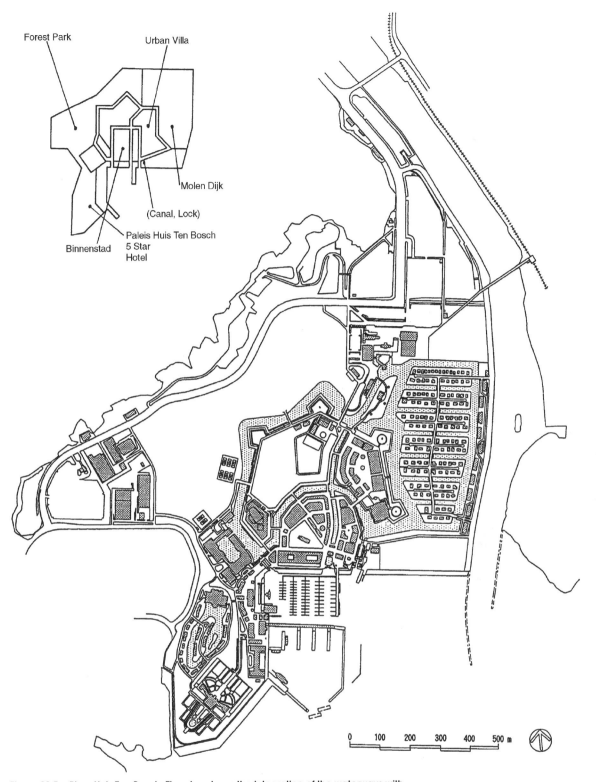

Forest Park

Urban Villa

Molen Dijk

(Canal, Lock)

Paleis Huis Ten Bosch
5 Star
Hotel

Binnenstad

0 100 200 300 400 500 m

Figure 11.5   Plan: Huis Ten Bosch. The plan shows the integration of the waterways with
the urban townscape. The resort is divided into five sections: Binnen Stad (Central Square
and nucleus of the development), Paleis Huis Ten Bosch Hotel, Molen Dijk, The Urban
Villa, and Forest Park (sports activities). The canal is connected to the bay by an
entrance lock which accommodates international craft.

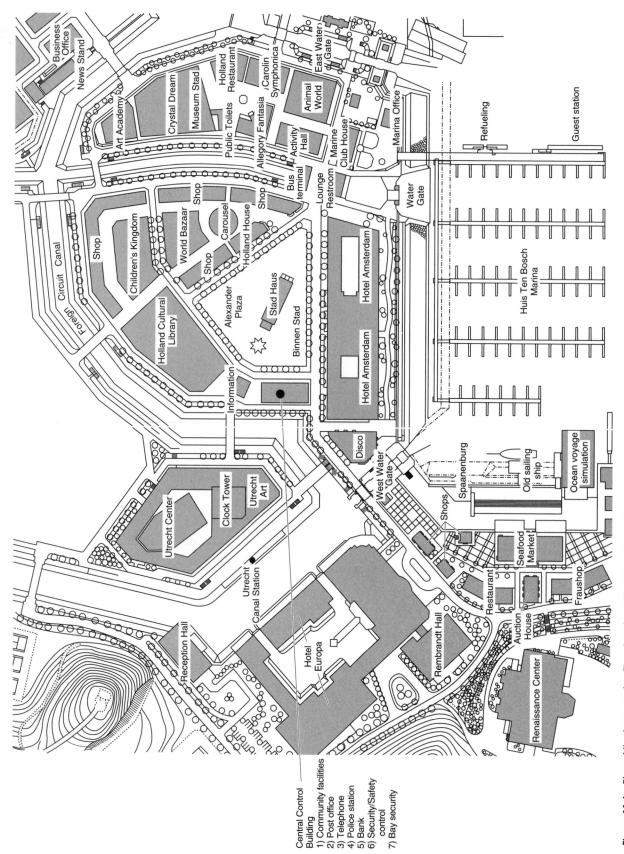

Central Control
Building
1) Community facilities
2) Post office
3) Telephone
4) Police station
5) Bank
6) Security/Safety
   control
7) Bay security

Figure 11.6 Plan of the town center. The plan shows the integration of the waterways with the hotels, shops, museums, and other functional buildings of the "downtown" area.

The client. The success of Nagasaki Holland Village served as both an influence and a constraint on the creative process. The motif of historic Dutch character was a charge on the designers, particularly for the central "downtown" area of the project, yet the facilities which are implicit to the modern luxury hotel, that include the modern technologies for the control of technical services and communication, were absolutely essential to the development. (See Fig. 11.7.) These two facets of the procurement process and the requirements of each distinct building within had to be correlated by the design team.

The market: exposure to risk. The owner had no prior experience of a large resort of similar type with hotel accommodation, on which to base go/no-go decisions. The potential for financial success and return on investment was uncertain, and introduced a factor of risk into the analysis of the outcome. A market analysis and a preliminary study of feasibility were essential.

The environment. Preparation of the area for industrial use in the 1950s had denigrated the quality of the land, and because of water shortages, the site was later abandoned and had become sterile.

Soil restoration. The area that the site now occupies was reclaimed from the original natural saltwater marshland, leaving the soil with a high content of salts. Concrete structures had been installed to protect the shoreline; unfortunately, breakwaters made from this material have been found to destroy the flora and fauna of the seashore. Similarly, concrete slabs that had been laid in preparation for industrial building construction after World War II had prevented the penetration of rainwater and nutrients to the soil below, the chemical composition had deteriorated, and temperatures unsuitable for growth were generated.

The deterioration of the existing soil composition imposed constraints with respect to the design of structure and infrastructure, soil chemistry for planting, and drainage. The project team had to implement an appropriate restorative program for the soil chemistry once concrete surfaces had been removed. (See Fig. 11.8.)

Control of pollution in Omura Bay. Omura Bay is linked to the Pacific Ocean by two narrow channels. This factor causes poor tidal action and a weak circulatory system in the bay, producing a naturally delicate type and quality in the local ecosystem.

The goal of restoring the natural environment and reclaiming the land and shoreline to a standard and quality true to the original system imposed constraints and limits to planning, the areas to be selected and utilized for the construction of buildings, and the type and spatial composition of the design, and made it necessary to install high-grade sewage-treatment plants, requiring special planning and design technologies. No sewage is released into the bay.

The guests. It is estimated that a maximum of 80,000 visitors will arrive in Huis Ten Bosch during any one day, or a total of 4.2 million visitors a year. These large numbers will obviously place considerable stress on the environment and local natural ecology.

Figure 11.7   Clock tower and terraced houses, completed 1992.

Figure 11.8   The site under construction: 1990. The clock tower and Stad Haus are in the middle distance.

It was essential to plan the interfaces between the resort's guests and the outdoor environment, in detail, whether artificial gardens or natural afforestation, and the volume of demand anticipated for utilities such as the provision of potable water and waste-disposal systems. Special areas were therefore designated for construction and circulation which could be maintained and controlled, and hard-wearing materials installed to protect external surfaces. (See Fig. 11.8.)

Authority codes and regulation. Development projects in any country must comply with local codes and regulations, and receive authority approval. Japan is no exception, and legislation relevant to real estate development is issued and controlled by the Japanese Prefectures. The codes and regulations are very detailed, typically in relation to fire security regulations and earthquake and environmental impact. There are often several overlapping prefectural requirements that are applicable to the same development (see Fig. 9.2b, Chap. 9). Design development and the program of construction must therefore be carefully scheduled so that approvals are obtained when required.

Some codes were of particular relevance to the development of Huis Ten Bosch. These concerned the construction of waterways and canals and the effect of such proposed installations on the protection, development, and maintenance of a salutary environment. An English adaptation from the Japanese Code is illustrated in Fig. 11.9.

Japanese Prefectural codes and regulations. Laws for the establishment of canals and waterways for resort facilities (for owners inside the Gulf Ward).

Applicable laws and ordinances	Clause	Contents
Bay law	Section 3	In the case when an application is received to construct a canal in the bay area, which significantly changes the existing conditions of the bay and maintenance of the environment, then the plan must be adapted to suit authority requirements, or permission must be obtained for alteration to the code.
Bay law	Sections 37 and 38/2	Permission must be obtained from the authority in order to 1. Construct a canal in the bay area 2. Alter the shoreline 3. Utilize a canal for transport
Seashore law	Section 8	Permissions must be obtained from the authority, if the canal is to be constructed in a protected area.

Figure 11.9 **Japanese Prefectural building codes. Codes control the construction of canals and waterways in the Omura Bay area of Kyushu. They are a typical example of local codes and regulations which must be observed during the design development of an international resort in any advanced nation.**

Applicable laws and ordinances	Clause	Contents
Law concerning the proper use of government funds		In the case where a public seashore is developed by the construction of a canal, and the construction is subsidized by the government, the sub-sidy is in the form of a loan and must be refunded at a later date.
City planning law (forest law, farm law)	Section 29/33	In the case where a canal is built as part of a resort, in a city plan-ning area, this is regarded as a devel-opment, and permission must be obtained from the authority.
As above		In the case where the land is designated for forest or farm, forest or farm law is to be applied to the construction, and permission must be obtained from the authority.
Construction standard law and law regulating development of a residential area	Sections 8 and 88	In the case where a canal is built and is extended to a residential area, the builder must obtain permission from the authority under the law regulat-ng development of a residential area. If the canal extends to an area which is not regulated, it must be registered as a fabrication under construction standard law.
Real estate law	Section 81/8	King Tides: In the case where the land is covered by the sea at Equinox, it is regarded as lost land (i.e., ownership is lost). In the case where the land has economic value, it must be demonstrat-ed that the sea can be con trolled at any time by the use of lock gates, in order to retain ownership.
Canal law	Sections 1 and 2	In the case where a canal is built for the purpose of trans-port, then permission must be obtained from the minister. If the canal is built as part of a resort, then such permission will not be necessary.
(Translation has been adapted to suit English usage.)		

Figure 11.9 *(Continued)*

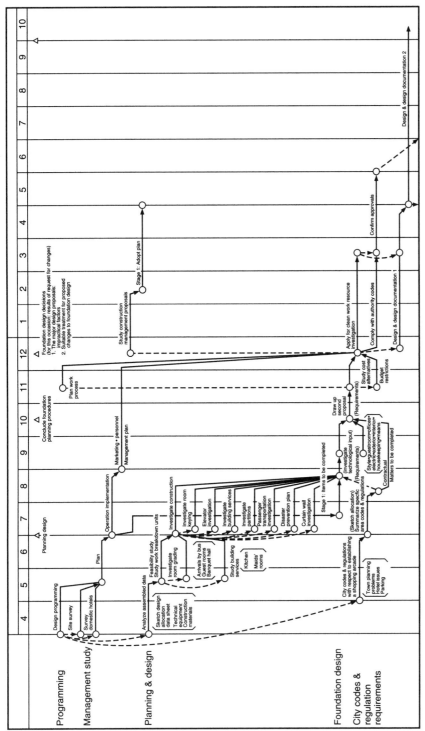

Figure 11.10 A basic hotel design program. This chart is a general format on which to base a hotel design program. It is utilized as a subprogram for the design development of a single work package in a resort.

Design Solutions

The design concept progresses by means of a hierarchy of solutions, which build one on another. Data fed back from the environmental impact study and geologic survey of site conditions formed the foundation for design decisions, and design production was controlled by a subprogram loop in the overall program and schedule. (See Fig. 11.10.)

Solutions that were implemented for some of the major issues are outlined below.

Protection of the shoreline. Natural rock was selected for the construction of breakwaters, for its ability to encourage the renewal of many different forms and colonies of marine life and promote regeneration of the microsystem. This was installed along the waterfront in Omura Bay.

Canals and the marina. A 6-km canal system was closely integrated with the urban plan for hotels; museums; and recreational, entertainment, and functional areas. The canals were designed for sailing and other marine pursuits, and, like the breakwaters, have natural stone banks. These are landscaped and incorporate areas designed for recreation (see Fig. 11.11.) The decision to construct the canals and locks demanded that the recycling system of the canal water was interrelated to the circulatory system of the bay. The natural tidal action between the two volumes of water was improved and controlled by the installation of canal sluice gates. Pumps, underwater fans, and movable sluice gates were added with the purpose of stimulating the natural water flows and circulation patterns. (See Fig. 11.12.) The growth of microorganisms were enriched by the use of natural materials and by the aid of water purification and aeration technologies.

Transportation. The quality of roads in the Omura Bay area are good; however, the direct and quicker route between the Resort and Nagasaki Airport is by sea (25 minutes as opposed to 45 minutes by road). (See Fig. 11.13.) This factor and the aesthetic appeal of water transportation initiated the alternative proposal to establish a ferry connection between the airport and the resort, which coincided with the main design theme. Guest transportation and circulation routes were planned within the resort by bus and canal transport, and a boat links the ferry terminal, hotels, and other major terminals. (See Fig. 11.14.)

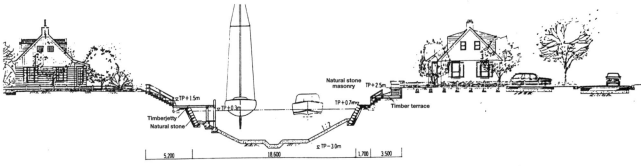

Figure 11.11   Cross section through the canal. This section indicates the use of natural stone and timber surfaces on the banks and areas surrounding the waterways.

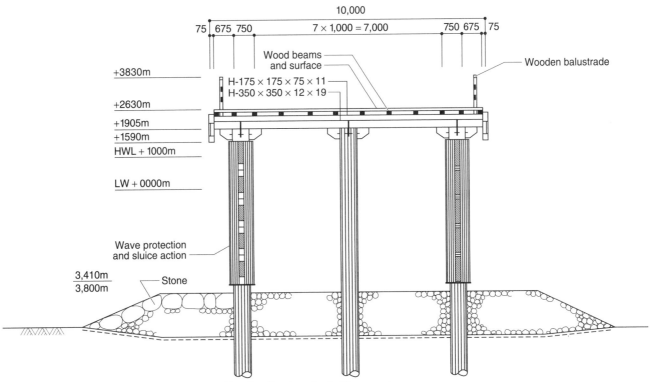

Figure 11.12　Section through an entrance road. The shoreline is protected from wave depredation, and the canals from the infiltration of weeds by underwater sluices and other mechanical techniques.

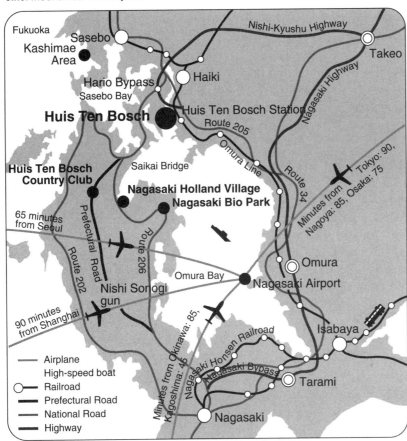

Figure 11.13　Plan of Omura Bay. Nagasaki Holland Village and Huis Ten Bosch face each other across the water, and a fast ferry of 25-minute duration connects the resort and Nagasaki Airport. It can be seen that the sea entrances between Omura Bay and the ocean are narrow and restrict circulatory action within the bay.

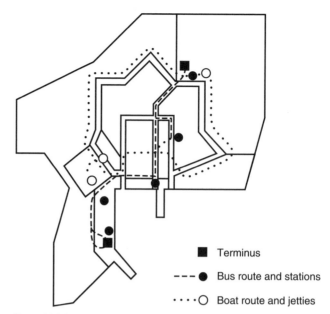

Terminus

--- ● Bus route and stations

···· ○ Boat route and jetties

Figure 11.14 Internal transportation. Boats circle the central area
and connect with a cross-town minibus service for guests.

The "Smart" Resort: Information Processing and Computerized Control

A central computerized system network has been installed, with particular emphasis on the capability to manage and integrate the following systems:

Financial control

Security and disaster prevention

Building automation

Utility services

The installation is a large local area network (LAN) computer system with mainframe and underground grid designed to centralize control and link the peripheral subcenters of the project. (See Fig. 11.15.) The system coordinates the various areas of the resort-town by establishing a monitoring and feedback system and enables information to flow between the different areas and facilities. It encompasses, for example, security monitoring procedures, the control of motorized equipment, lighting, and data handling, and is programmed to suit the needs of each facility.

Utilities

The long-term problems experienced with the supply of fresh water, the residual marshland tendencies, and poor condition of the soil made it imperative to design a sympathetic technological system for the supply of utility services to the township.

In resolution of this problem, an underground duct system has been installed that carries power, communications, water, steam (produced by a cogeneration system using gas turbines), and sewer con-

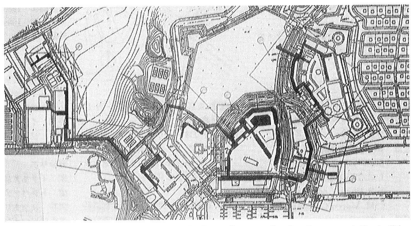

Figure 11.15 Underground utility network. An underground network connects the buildings of the five divisions of the resort. It allows global control of utility services, communication, and the like, to be exercised over the whole area.

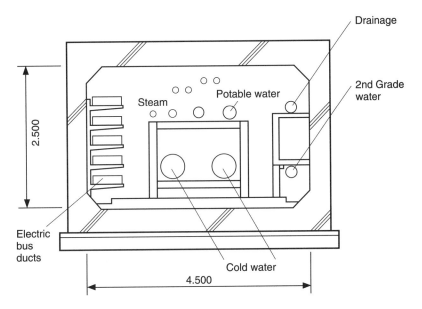

Figure 11.16 Cross section of utility duct. An underground duct transporting utilities such as steam heating, power, potable water, second-grade water, drainage, and communications.

nections between all parts of the resort. (See Fig. 11.16.) Each resort facility links into the supply from the grid.

Water. A water system of two-grade quality has been installed: potable water and second-grade water. The second grade now supplies 40 percent of demand, and is used, for example, for air conditioning, the flushing of W.C.s, and garden sprinklers. A purifying plant for sea water that produces 1000 m³ of water per day is in operation.

Sewerage and drainage. There is an advanced sewage treatment plant installed that reduced 2000 tons of common sewage water per day to a biological oxygen demand (BOD) of 5 parts per million (ppm). The major portion of the treated water is reused for second-grade water requirements. The remainder passes through soil-activated bacteria to be absorbed by the ground or displaced by evaporation.

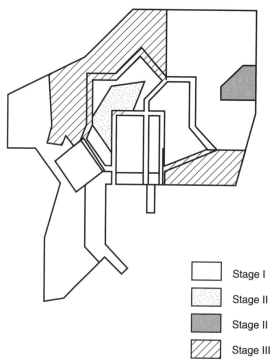

	Stage I
	Stage II
	Stage II
	Stage III

Figure 11.17 Progressive completion. The project was scheduled for completion in three stages. Stages 1 and 2 were completed in 1992. Long-term serviced holiday and residential accommodation are due for completion in Stage 3.

Implementation

The Huis Ten Bosch development was programmed to be completed on a progressive basis, from the central area of the town square, outward to the perimeter of the project. Long-stay apartments and permanent residences on the northern boundary of the site are programmed to be completed in the final Stage 3 period. (See Figs. 11.17 and 11.18.)

Contractual Arrangements

Rates and contracts were negotiated by the owner and project managers with contractors nominated by or on behalf of the owner. This is a typical method used for the appointment of consultants and contractors in Japan.

Agreements were made in several cases whereby a quotation was accepted for rates for costs of materials and labor plus a percentage for contractors' profit, resembling a cost-plus contract, which has been discussed earlier in this book.

Form of contract. In Japan, there is a standard form of building contract, made and in use by all the following institutions:

Architectural Institute of Japan

Architectural Association of Japan

Japan Institute of Architects

Associated General Contractors of Japan

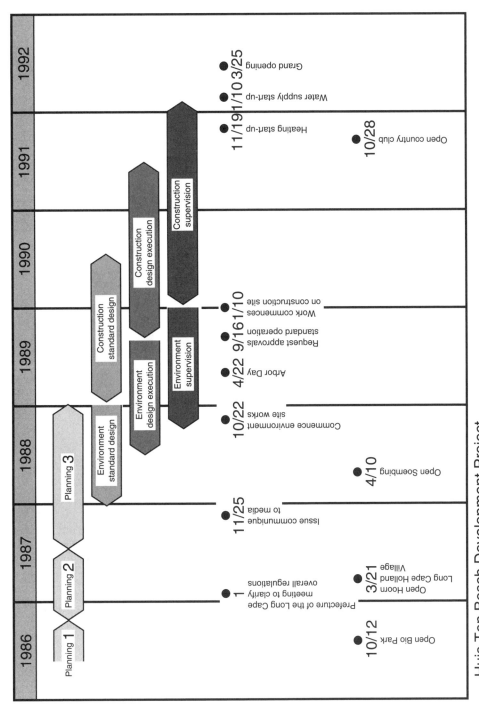

Huis Ten Bosch Development Project

Figure 11.18 Huis Ten Bosch resort development program.

Figure 11.19 The progress of real-time construction, 1990.

Figure 11.20 The Stad Huis, under construction, 1990.

Figure 11.21 Bennen Stad. The photograph is taken overlooking the Central Square (Bennen Stad and Alexander Plaza), following the grand opening ceremony in 1992. The Stad Huis occupies the middle of the photograph.

This contract is subject to minor adjustments according to the type of input required of the contractor.

Subcontractors. Subcontractors were appointed by each major contractor, except in cases where the owner desired to appoint special consultants or subcontracting firms. These companies were then integrated into the overall development program by the project management team.

Risk. The virtual absence of labor disputes and the cost-plus-type structure of the contract implies that the owner alone bears construction risk in Japan, unlike business conditions in other Western nations where risk may be shared between the parties of the contract, and is subject to negotiation.

In Japan, major risks during construction arise from natural disaster; in the Kyushu region these are, for example, typhoon and earthquake. Other factors that were considered to be a potential for future risk, if not anticipated beforehand, arose from the schedule of progressive completion. The most significant of these factors were

1. The need to acquire repetitive approvals from local Prefectural authorities, with the risk that requirements might change during the project life cycle.

2. The ability to procure standard and nonstandard materials and supplies to meet a staged schedule, and in accordance with earlier construction applications

3. An unexpected or unforeseen increase in costs over time associated with supplies, materials and labor.

The Construction Program

Land restoration, seawall fabrication, followed by a civil works program for installation of the lock and canals, the main utility grid, and foundations for urban construction, were the first work packages to be programmed. Each of these works was undertaken by an appropriate contracting company under the supervision of the project manager and extended project team's design and technical consultants. (See Figs. 11.19. and 11.20.)

Quality assurance. Management and quality control through group discussion is a traditional procedure in Japan; it enhances project management methodology, and the group potential to recognize risk and find alternatives contributes to quality assurance technologies. Close identification with the project was established for the Huis Ten Bosch project in this way, and personnel were encouraged by proximity in the workplace to form close team relationships.

Site accommodation. Prefabricated accommodation was erected for the use of the project management team, site architects, engineers, the construction management team, tradespeople, and construction workers. Daily transport for workers was arranged to and from the site.

Security. Construction preliminaries had to include the provision of site security. The project's extensive level site has several kilometers of boundary, which presented a problem for the maintenance of security and public safety. Security against unauthorized intrusion into the real-time construction site was solved by locating a series of guard stations so that the boundaries could be monitored at all times. In this way constant supervision was accomplished, which was assisted by a strategy for the issuance and inspection of permits at the main entrances. (See Fig. 11.21.)

Reference

All information used in Chapter 11 has been provided by kind permission of Nihon Sekkei Inc., Shinjuku-Mitsui Building, Shinjuku-ku, Tokyo, Japan.

Bibliography

AFR Survey; Indonesia, Australian Financial Review, Sydney, Australia, May 28, 1991.

American Hotel and Motel Association, *Lodging,* 1989–1992.

Balsdon, J. V. P., *Life and Leisure in Ancient Rome,* McGraw-Hill, New York, 1969.

Baud Bovy, Manuel, and F. Lawson, *Tourism and Recreational Planning,* Architectural Press, London, 1977.

Bennett, David M., *Brooking on Building Contracts,* 2d ed., Butterworths Press Pty. Ltd., Sydney, Australia, 1980.

Bosselman, F. P., *In the Wake of the Tourist,* The Conservation Foundation, Washington, D.C.

Burman, P. J., *Precedence Networks for Project Planning and Control,* McGraw-Hill International, London, 1972.

Cambridge, E., Senior Vice President, Leo A. Daly Architects and Engineers, *Discussions: Ko Olina Resort Development,* Honolulu, Hawaii, 1991.

Dessler, G., *Organizational Theory: Integrating Structure & Behavior,* Prentice Hall Inc., Englewood Cliffs, New Jersey, 1987.

Dilsaver, L. M., *Effects of International Tourism, A Bibliography,* Council of Planning Libraries, Monticello, Illinois, 1977.

Duncan Wallace, L. N., *Hudson's Building and Engineering Contracts,* 10th ed., Sweet & Maxwell, London, 1970.

Featherby, Alan, *Discussions,* Radisson Hotel Group, Australia, 1991.

Ferry, Douglas J., and Peter S. Brandon, *Cost Planning of Buildings,* 4th ed., Granada Press, London, 1981.

Foxhall, W. B., *Professional Construction Management and Project Administration,* 2d ed., American Institute of Architects, McGraw-Hill, New York, 1976.

"Fragmented Dreams, Flexible Practices and New Directives in Project Delivery," *Architectural Magazine, Technology & Practice* (publ. Robert G. Kliesch), May 1992, pp. 80, 87.

Frost, J., and H. McLennan, *Various Papers for the Master of Project Management Program,* University of Technology Sydney, Sydney, Australia, 1991–1992.

Frost, J., Project Director, Civil and Civic Constructions Pty. Ltd., *Discussions: Nikko Hotel, Sussex Street, Sydney, Australia,* Sydney, Australia, 1992.

Gee, Chuck Y., *Resort Development and Management,* 2d ed., Educational Institute of the American Hotel and Motel Association, 1988.

Gunn, Clare A., *Tourism Planning,* 2d ed., Taylor & Francis, New York, 1988.

Harris, Frank, and Ronald McCaffer, *Modern Construction Management,* Granada Publishing, London, 1979.

Japan Travel News, Japan Tourist Organization, Tokyo, February 1987.

Katz, R. J., Comm. LL.B., *Discussions Concerning Currency Exchange and Hedging Techniques,* T.N.T Pty. Ltd., Sydney, Australia, 1991.

Kerzner, H., *Project Management, A Systems Approach to Planning, Scheduling and Controlling,* 3d ed., Van Nostrand Reinhold, New York, 1989.

Lady Ochikubu, *Ochikubu Monigatari* (Translated by Wilfred Whitehouse and Eizo Yanagisawa), Hokuseido Press, Tokyo, 1968.

Leadbetter, W. B., and J. A. Burati, "How Can Quality Be Properly Managed on Major Projects?" *Building Economics and Construction Management,* Vol. 4: *Managing Projects,* University of Technology Sydney, Sydney, Australia, March 1990.

Levine, Harvey A., "Implementing Project Management: Commitment and Training Ensure Success," *Project Management Journal,* Vol. VI, No. 1, January 1992, pp. 35–37 (publ. Project Management Institute), Drexel Hill, Pennsylvania.

Marshall, Allan (Manager, Q. A. Construction Services, Sydney, Australia), "Quality Standards and Requirements," *Project Management course notes,* University of Technology Sydney, Sydney, Australia, 1992.

Marshall, Harold E., *Techniques for Treating Uncertainty and Risk in the Economic Evaluation of Buildings,* U.S. Department of Commerce, National Institute of Standards and Technology; NIST Special Publication, 757, Washington, D.C., 1988.

Master of Project Management course notes, University of Technology Sydney, Sydney, Australia, 1990.

Mooney, J., *Cost Effective Building Design,* New South Wales University Press, Sydney, Australia, 1983.

Morris, Ivan, *The World of the Shining Prince; Court Life in Ancient Japan,* Penguin Books, London, 1964.

Nakane, Chie, *Japanese Society,* University of California Press, Berkeley, 1972.

Nemoto, M., *Total Quality Control for Management: Strategies and Techniques from Toyota and Toyoda Gosei,* Prentice Hall, Englewood Cliffs, New Jersey, 1980.

Nihon Sekkei Inc. (Architects, Engineers, and Project Managers), *Data, Charts and Illustrations: Huis Ten Bosch Resort, Kyushu, Japan,* Nihon Sekkei Inc., 50th Floor, Shinjuku Mitsui Building, Shinjuku-ku Tokyo, Japan, 1992–1993.

Noonan, S., General Manager, Seven Spirits Bay Resort, *Discussions: Resort Development,* Seven Spirits Bay Wilderness Pty. Ltd., Cobourg Peninsular, Northern Territory, Australia, 1991.

Peirson, G., R. Bird, and R. Brown, *Business Finance,* 4th ed., McGraw-Hill, Sydney, Australia, 1989.

Principles of Hotel Design (edited by the *Architects Journal* staff), 2d ed., The Architectural Press, London, 1974.

Project Management Body of Knowledge (PMBOK), Project Management Institute of America, Drexel Hill, Pennsylvania, 1987.

Project Delivery System, Canadian Public Works Department, Ottawa, Canada, 1989.

Rossy, Gerard L., and Russell D. Archibald, "Building Commitment in Project Teams," *Project Management Journal,* Vol. XXIII, No. 2, June 1992 (publ. Project Management Institute), Drexel Hill, Pennsylvania, 1992.

Rush, R. D. (Editor), *The Building Systems Integrated Handbook,* The American Institute of Architects and John Wiley & Sons, New York, 1986.

Rutes, Walter A., and R. H. Penner, *Hotel Planning and Design,* Watson Guptill Publications, New York, and Architectural Press, London, 1985.

Shannon, C. E., and W. Weaver. *The Mathematical Theory of Communication,* University of Illinois Press, 1949.

Soseki Natsume, *Kokoro* (Translation by Edwin McClellan), Charles E. Tuttle Co., Tokyo, 1987.

Tourism in Japan 1986, Japan National Tourist Organization, Tokyo, 1986.

Turner, R. L., and J. Ash, *The Golden Hordes—International Tourism and the Pleasure Periphery,* St. Martin's Press, New York, 1976.

White, J., *A History of Tourism,* Leisure Art, London, 1967.

World Tourism Organization (various publications), Madrid, Spain, 1991.

Index

About the Author

Margaret Huffadine is a registered architect, directs her own company, and is senior architectural representative for the Japanese architectural and engineering firm of Nihon Sekkei, Inc., in Australia. She has served as lead project manager on several large international construction projects throughout Asia, Australia, and the United States.